W9-BVB-319

This book is dedicated to the people who gave us MP3, AAC, Apple Lossless Encoding, and the various iPods.

No iPods were harmed during the writing of this book.

Discard
NHCPL

How to Do Everything™

iPod® &
iTunes®

Sixth Edition

NEW HANOVER COUNTY
PUBLIC LIBRARY
201 CHESTNUT STREET
WILMINGTON, NC 28401

About the Author

Guy Hart-Davis is the author of more than 70 computer books, including *The Healthy PC, Second Edition, iPad & iPhone Administrator's Guide, Integrating Macs into Windows Networks, Mac OS X System Administration, PC QuickSteps, Second Edition, How to Do Everything with Microsoft Office Word 2007,* and *How to Do Everything with Microsoft Office Excel 2007.*

About the Technical Editor

Janet Cloninger spent years as a chemist and a computer programmer in the textile field before finding herself a stay-at-home mother and a writer at The Gadgeteer, a well-respected technology review site. Her innate love of gadgets came from her father, who never met anything he couldn't fix or improve.

PUBLIC LIBRARY
201 CHESTNUT STREET

How to Do
Everything™

iPod® &
iTunes®

Sixth Edition

Guy Hart-Davis

New York Chicago San Francisco Lisbon
London Madrid Mexico City Milan New Delhi
San Juan Seoul Singapore Sydney Toronto

The McGraw·Hill Companies

Cataloging-in-Publication Data is on file with the Library of Congress

McGraw-Hill books are available at special quantity discounts to use as premiums and sales promotions, or for use in corporate training programs. To contact a representative, please e-mail us at bulksales@mcgraw-hill.com.

How to Do Everything™: iPod® & iTunes®, Sixth Edition

Copyright © 2012 by The McGraw-Hill Companies. All rights reserved. Printed in the United States of America. Except as permitted under the Copyright Act of 1976, no part of this publication may be reproduced or distributed in any form or by any means, or stored in a database or retrieval system, without the prior written permission of publisher, with the exception that the program listings may be entered, stored, and executed in a computer system, but they may not be reproduced for publication.

McGraw-Hill, the McGraw-Hill Publishing logo, How to Do Everything™, and related trade dress are trademarks or registered trademarks of The McGraw-Hill Companies and/or its affiliates in the United States and other countries and may not be used without written permission. All other trademarks are the property of their respective owners. The McGraw-Hill Companies is not associated with any product or vendor mentioned in this book.

1 2 3 4 5 6 7 8 9 0   DOC DOC   1 0 9 8 7 6 5 4 3 2

ISBN   978-0-07-178674-4
MHID   0-07-178674-0

Sponsoring Editor Megg Morin	**Technical Editor** Janet Cloninger	**Composition** Cenveo Publisher Services
Editorial Supervisor Janet Walden	**Copy Editor** William McManus	**Illustration** Cenveo Publisher Services
Project Manager Harleen Chopra, Cenveo Publisher Services	**Proofreader** Claire Splan	**Art Director, Cover** Jeff Weeks
Acquisitions Coordinator Joya Anthony	**Indexer** Claire Splan	**Cover Designer** Jeff Weeks
	Production Supervisor Jean Bodeaux	

Images used Courtesy of Apple, Inc.
iPod® classic image used by permission and © 2011 Doug Rosa Photography.
Album cover artwork used by permission of Island Def Jam Music Group.
iPod nano® and iPod shuffle® images photographed by Frederick Lieberath for Apple, Inc.

Information has been obtained by McGraw-Hill from sources believed to be reliable. However, because of the possibility of human or mechanical error by our sources, McGraw-Hill, or others, McGraw-Hill does not guarantee the accuracy, adequacy, or completeness of any information and is not responsible for any errors or omissions or the results obtained from the use of such information.

Contents at a Glance

Contents

PART III   Learn Advanced Techniques and Tricks

Acknowledgments

I'd like to thank the following people for their help with this book:

- Megg Morin for developing the book—for the sixth time
- Joya Anthony for handling the acquisitions end of the book
- Janet Cloninger for reviewing the manuscript anew for technical accuracy and contributing many helpful suggestions
- Bill McManus for editing the manuscript with a light touch
- Harleen Chopra for coordinating the production of the book
- Janet Walden for assisting with the production of the book
- Cenveo Publisher Services for laying out the pages
- Claire Splan for creating the index

The publisher would like to add special thanks to Lori at Doug Rosa Photography, Emmanuel Tanner at Marek and Associates, Ami Brown and Russell Fink at Universal Music Group, and, as always, big thanks to Sue Carroll and the Permissions Group at Apple, Inc.

Introduction

iPods are the best portable music players available. Small enough to fit easily into a hand or a pocket, an iPod classic can hold the contents of your entire CD collection in compressed audio files, your entire photo collection, and enough hours of video to keep you entertained for a week or more. An iPod nano holds much less but is correspondingly smaller and cuter. And an iPod shuffle, the tiniest of the lot, not only holds enough music to keep you listening all day but also has enough battery life to play it all.

Whichever model of iPod you have, you can download a dozen CDs' worth of music from your computer to it in less than a minute, and you can recharge the iPod quickly either from your computer or from any handy power outlet. And whether you use Windows or Mac OS X, you can enjoy music on your computer with iTunes, the best all-round jukebox and music-management application available.

But you can also do more—much more.

This book shows you how to get the most out of your iPod.

What Does This Book Cover?

Chapter 1, "Choose the Right iPod for You," explains what the iPods are and what they do; how to distinguish the current models from each other; and how their capabilities differ. The chapter then suggests how to choose the model that's best for you.

Chapter 2, "Get Your Computer Ready to Work with Your iPod," shows you how to get your PC or Mac ready to work with your iPod. You learn first what the iPod needs—the operating system, connection hardware, and so on. Next, you learn what you may need to add to your PC to keep your iPod happy. Last, you learn what you may need to add to your Mac for the iPod.

Chapter 3, "Configure iTunes and Load Your iPod with Music, Video, and Data," runs you through the steps of installing iTunes on your PC or Mac and connecting your iPod for the first time. The chapter then shows you how to start creating your library and how to load your iPod with songs, videos, and data—and then disconnect it safely.

Chapter 4, "Enjoy Music and Video on Your iPod," shows you how to connect your speakers or headphones to your iPod, how to use its controls, and how to use its main features.

Chapter 5, "Get More Out of Your iPod with Hardware Accessories," discusses the various types of accessories available for the different iPod models, from cases and stands to speakers and radio transmitters.

Chapter 6, "Use an iPod as Your Home Stereo or Car Stereo," discusses how to connect your iPod to your home stereo or car stereo. You'll learn how to use your iPod as your main music machine instead of as a solitary pleasure.

Chapter 7, "Create Audio Files, Edit Them, and Tag Them," shows you how to use iTunes and other tools to build a library stuffed with high-quality, accurately tagged song files. You'll learn how to choose the best location to store your library, how to configure iTunes to get exactly the audio quality you need, and how to work with compressed audio in ways that iTunes itself can't manage. You'll also learn how to convert other audio file types to MP3, AAC, Apple Lossless Encoding, WAV, or AIFF so you can play them on your iPod, how to create audio files from cassettes or vinyl records, and how to save audio streams to disk so you can listen to them later.

Chapter 8, "Buy and Download Songs, Videos, and More Online," explains your options for buying song and video files online. The chapter starts by covering what digital rights management (DRM) is, what it means for computer users, and how Apple has now largely moved beyond it. It then discusses what the iTunes Store is, how to set up an account, how to find music and videos by browsing and searching, and how to buy and download music, videos, and other items. The chapter also discusses other online music stores that you may want to examine, points you to sites where you can find free (and legal) songs online, and tells you about other sites you are better off avoiding.

Chapter 9, "Create Video Files That Work with the iPod classic," shows you how to create video files for the iPod classic. You can buy video files from the iTunes Store or from other online stores, but unless you're as rich as Croesus, you'll also want to make suitable files from your own video content. You can do this easily enough—but it helps to understand the legalities involved, particularly before you rip your DVDs.

Chapter 10, "Make Your Music Sound Great and Customize the iTunes Window," shows you how to make the most of iTunes for playing back music—with or without the monstrous graphical visual effects the application can give. You'll learn how to use audio features such as the graphical equalizer, crossfading, and Sound Enhancer; and you'll find out how to control iTunes via keyboard shortcuts.

Chapter 11, "Manage Your Music and Video Library with iTunes," explains how to browse, mix, and import and export music and videos; how to share items with others and access the items that others are sharing; and how to tune into podcasts. You'll also learn how to move your library from one folder to another, remove duplicate items from your library, and even use multiple libraries on the same computer.

Chapter 12, "Use Multiple iPods, Multiple Computers, or Both," explains how to synchronize several iPods with the same computer and shows you how to load an iPod from multiple computers. The chapter walks you through the processes of moving an iPod from Mac OS X to Windows or the other direction and shows you how to change the computer to which your iPod is linked.

Chapter 13, "Use Your iPod for File Backup, Storage, and Transfer," shows you how to use your iPod as an external drive for backup and portable storage. You'll learn how to enable disk mode on an iPod and transfer files to or from an iPod.

Chapter 14, "Recover Your Songs and Videos from Your iPod," shows you how to transfer files from your iPod's library to your computer—for example, to recover songs and other items from your iPod after the hard disk on your computer fails.

Chapter 15, "Troubleshoot Your iPod and iTunes," discusses how to troubleshoot your iPod and iTunes when things go wrong. You'll learn how to avoid making your iPod unhappy, how to approach the troubleshooting process in the right way, and how to perform essential troubleshooting maneuvers. Plus, you'll find solutions for problems that occur frequently on the iPod and in iTunes.

Conventions Used in This Book

To make its meaning clear without using far more words than necessary, this book uses a number of conventions, four of which are worth mentioning here:

- Note, Tip, and Caution paragraphs highlight information to draw it to your notice.
- The pipe character or vertical bar denotes choosing an item from a menu. For example, "choose File | Open" means that you should click the File menu and select the Open item on it. Use the keyboard, mouse, or a combination of the two as you wish.
- The ⌘ symbol represents the COMMAND key on the Mac—the key that bears the Apple symbol and the quad-infinity mark on most Mac keyboards.
- Most check boxes have two states: *selected* (with a check mark in them) and *cleared* (without a check mark in them). This book tells you to *select* a check box or *clear* a check box rather than "click to place a check mark in the box" or "click to remove the check mark from the box." (Often, you'll be verifying the state of the check box, so it may already have the required setting—in which case, you don't need to click at all.) Some check boxes have a third state as well, in which they're selected but dimmed and unavailable. This state is usually used for options that apply to only part of the current situation.

PART I

Enjoy Audio with an iPod and iTunes

1

Choose the Right iPod for You

HOW TO...

- Understand what iPods are and what they do
- Distinguish the different types of current iPods
- Choose the right iPod for your needs

If you don't already have an iPod, you'll need to beg, borrow, or buy one before you can make the most of this book. This chapter tells you about the iPods available at this writing, and suggests how to choose the one that will best suit your needs.

If you're already the proud owner of an iPod, you may prefer to skip directly to Chapter 2, which shows you how to get your PC or Mac ready to work with the iPod.

What Are iPods?

iPod is the umbrella term for the wildly popular portable music and video players built by Apple Inc.

At this writing, there are four main families of iPod:

- **iPod classic** This is the full-sized iPod, with a control wheel on the front.
- **iPod nano** This is the small, square iPod with a touch-sensitive screen.
- **iPod shuffle** This is the tiny iPod that doesn't have a screen, just control buttons on the front.
- **iPod touch** This is the iPod with a large, touch-sensitive screen.

 This book covers the iPod classic, iPod nano, and iPod shuffle in depth, together with iTunes, the software for managing and syncing the iPods. For full coverage of the iPod touch and its capabilities, see *How to Do Everything: iPod touch*, also published by McGraw-Hill.

Apart from these current models, Apple has also produced—and discontinued—five earlier generations of regular iPod (like the iPod classic), five earlier generations of the

3

iPod nano, three earlier generations of the iPod shuffle, and one generation of the iPod mini, a medium-sized iPod built around a miniature hard disk called a Microdrive.

All current iPods connect to your PC or Mac via USB, enabling you to transfer files quickly to the iPod using a regular USB port on your computer. (Older models connected via FireWire, an alternative connection technology that Apple has now phased out of iPods.) The iPod classic and the iPod nano connect via a narrow, wide port called the Dock Connector port. The iPod shuffle recharges through an extra connector buried deep inside its headphone socket.

What the iPods Do

The main focus of the iPod classic, iPod nano, and iPod shuffle is music—but each has other capabilities too, as you'll see in this section.

Audio Playback

The main feature of the iPods is high-quality audio playback. Let's look at this briefly here so that we don't need to cover it for each individual iPod.

The iPods can play audio files in these formats:

- **Advanced Audio Coding (AAC)**   This is Apple's preferred format for getting high audio quality on small devices such as the iPods, iPhone, and iPad.
- **MP3**   This is the rest of the world's preferred format for getting high audio quality on small devices.
- **Audible**   This is the MP3-derived format used by Audible.com for its audiobook files.
- **Apple Lossless Encoding**   This is Apple's format for full-quality audio.
- **WAV**   This is an industry-standard format for full-quality, uncompressed audio.
- **AIFF**   This is an industry-standard but Mac-based format for full-quality, uncompressed audio.

The iPods don't support other formats, such as Microsoft's Windows Media Audio (WMA), RealNetworks' RealAudio, and the open-source audio formats Ogg Vorbis and FLAC. But you can convert audio files in those formats to AAC, MP3, or another supported format easily enough; see Chapter 7 for details.

Video Playback

The iPod classic can play several types of video files, including H.264 files and MPEG-4 files. If you have video files in other formats, you can convert them to one of these formats (see Chapter 9 for details).

Radio

The iPod nano has a built-in radio tuner that you can listen to through the earphones.

Carrying Your Contacts and Calendars

The iPod classic can also act as a contact database, calendar, and notebook, enabling you to carry around not only all your music but your vital information as well. You can also put other textual information on an iPod so you can carry that information with you and view it on the screen.

Carrying and Showing Your Photos

The iPod classic and iPod nano can also carry your photos and display them, which is great for taking them with you and sharing them with others. You can display the files either on the iPod's screen or on a TV to which you connect the iPod.

Carrying Your Vital Files

You can also use an iPod as an external disk for your PC or Mac. This provides an easy and convenient means of backing up your data, storing files, and transporting files from one computer to another. And because the iPods are ultra-portable, you can take those files with you wherever you go, which can be great for school, work, and even play.

Synchronizing with Your Computer and Buying Songs and Videos Online

The iPods are designed to communicate seamlessly with iTunes, which runs on both Windows and the Mac. If you prefer, you can use the iPods with other software as well on either operating system.

If you use an iPod with iTunes, you can buy songs from the iTunes Store, download them to your computer, and play them on either your computer or the iPod. You can also buy and download videos from the iTunes Store and play them on the iPod classic.

The iPod classic and What It Does

The iPod classic is the sixth generation of regular iPod. The iPod classic is a portable music and video player with a huge capacity, a rechargeable battery good for up to 36 hours of music playback (or up to 6 hours of video playback), and easy-to-use controls.

The iPod classic is built around the type of hard drive used in small laptop computers and comes at this writing only in a 160GB capacity. (The capacity is engraved on the back of the iPod.) Larger hard disks are available, but not yet in the slimline format that the iPod classic needs. So far, as hard-disk manufacturers have released higher-capacity hard disks, Apple has continued to release higher-capacity iPods, so the maximum capacity seems certain to rise. The more space on the iPod's hard disk, the more songs, video, or other data you can carry on it.

The iPod classic (see Figure 1-1) has a 2.5-inch color screen with a resolution of 320 × 240 pixels, which is called Quarter VGA resolution, or QVGA for short. (VGA resolution is 640 × 480 pixels—twice as much in each direction, so four times as much overall.) The screen can display videos, photos, and album covers as well as the iPod's

FIGURE 1-1   The iPod classic is the latest of the full-size iPods. (Image used courtesy of Apple Inc.)

menus, information about the song that's currently playing, and text-based items, such as your contacts, calendars, and notes.

Below the screen is a control device called the Click wheel. The Click wheel has four buttons built into it, which you click by pressing the wheel so that it tilts slightly in the required direction. You drag your finger around the surface of the Click wheel to scroll through items such as menus. You press the Select button or Center button, in the middle of the Click wheel, to access the item you've selected by scrolling.

At the top is a headphone socket and a Hold switch that you slide to put the iPod on hold (which locks all its controls) or to take it off hold again.

With extra hardware, you can extend an iPod's capabilities even further. For example, with a custom microphone, you can record audio directly onto it. With a custom media reader, you can transfer digital photos to the iPod's hard disk directly from a digital camera without using a computer. This capability can make an iPod a great travel companion for a digital camera—especially a camera that takes high-resolution photos.

Did You Know?

Why the iPod's Capacity Appears to Be Less Than Advertised

One hundred sixty gigabytes is a huge amount of music—around 40,000 four-minute songs at an acceptable 128 Kbps quality, or enough for about 80 days' solid listening. It's also a decent amount of video: about 700 hours at the compression rate the iTunes Store uses. But unfortunately, you don't actually get the amount of hard disk space that's written on the iPod.

There are two reasons for this. First, you lose some hard-disk space to the iPod's operating system (OS—the software that enables it to function) and the file allocation table that records which file is stored where on the disk. This happens on all hard disks and solid-state devices that contain operating systems, and costs you anywhere from a few megabytes on the iPod shuffle to a few dozen megabytes on the iPod classic.

Second, the capacities of the iPods are measured in "marketing gigabytes" rather than in real gigabytes. A real gigabyte is 1,024 megabytes, a megabyte is 1,024 kilobytes, and a kilobyte is 1,024 bytes. That makes 1,073,741,824 bytes (1,024 × 1,024 × 1,024 bytes) in a real gigabyte. By contrast, a marketing gigabyte has a flat billion bytes (1,000 × 1,000 × 1,000 bytes)—a difference of 7.4 percent.

So an iPod will actually hold 7.4 percent less data than its listed size suggests (and minus more for the OS and file allocation table). You can see why marketing folks choose to use marketing megabytes and gigabytes rather than real megabytes and gigabytes—the numbers are more impressive. But customers tend to be disappointed when they discover that the real capacity of a device is substantially less than the device's packaging and literature promised.

The iPod nano and What It Does

The iPod nano (see Figure 1-2) is the smallest iPod that has a screen. At this writing, the iPod nano comes in 8GB and 16GB models and in various colors.

The iPod nano has a touch-screen on the front, three control buttons on the top, and the Dock Connector port and headphone socket on the bottom. The back of the iPod nano is a clip that you use to attach the iPod to your clothing (or your ear, if you like to mix pain with your listening pleasure).

The iPod nano can also display photos and album art on its screen or on a TV.

The iPod shuffle and What It Does

The iPod shuffle is the smallest and least expensive iPod. At this writing, the model Apple is selling is the fourth-generation iPod shuffle. This iPod (shown in Figure 1-3) has a rectangular metal case with controls on the front and a clip on the back for attaching the iPod to your clothing. It contains 2GB of flash memory.

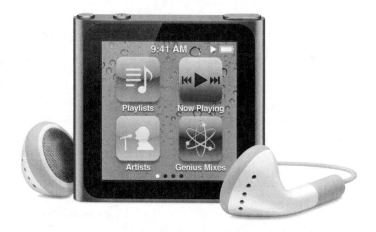

FIGURE 1-2 The iPod nano is very small and contains flash memory rather than a hard disk. It has three control buttons on the top, a touch-screen on the front, and the Dock Connector port and headphone socket on the bottom. (Image used courtesy of Apple Inc.)

 The second-generation iPod shuffle looks similar to the fourth-generation iPod shuffle, but with smaller controls. The third-generation iPod shuffle is very different: a sleek metal slab with a clip on the back, a single switch on the top, and its remaining controls integrated into the headset cord.

The iPod shuffle has no screen and two play modes, either playing back an existing playlist in order or "shuffling" the songs into a random order—hence its name. To change

FIGURE 1-3 The iPod shuffle clips onto your clothing. (Image used courtesy of Apple Inc.)

from playlist mode to shuffle mode, you move the switch at the top from the Play In Order position to the Shuffle Music position.

You control playback by using the five buttons (Play/Pause, Previous Track and Next Track, and Volume Up and Volume Down) laid out in a circular arrangement on its face (see Chapter 4 for details). You can switch from playlist to playlist by using the Voiceover feature, which also announces the current song name and artist.

Because the iPod shuffle has no screen, the only way you can navigate through your playlist is by using the Previous button and Next button and listening to the song that plays. The shuffle mode makes a virtue out of this limitation by offering to mix up the songs for you.

The iPod shuffle is great for exercise or extreme activities that would threaten a larger iPod, especially as the controls are easy to use without looking. But it's also great if you often get new music and want to focus your listening on it without being distracted by your existing collection, or if you want to force yourself to listen to artists or albums that you normally neglect.

Because of the iPod shuffle's limitations, much of what you'll read in the rest of this book doesn't apply to it. For example, you can't put your contacts, your calendar, or notes on the iPod shuffle, because it has no way to display them to you; likewise, you can't watch video on it. The iPod shuffle doesn't use equalizations, but it does support the Start Time and End Time options in iTunes, which allow you to skip part of the beginning or end of a track.

But the iPod shuffle isn't only for playing music. You can also use the iPod shuffle as a portable disk, and because of its diminutive size, the iPod shuffle is a great way to take your key documents with you.

Choose the iPod That's Best for You

By ruthlessly discontinuing earlier iPod models even when they were selling strongly, Apple has made the process of choosing among the different iPods pretty straightforward:

- If you need the smallest iPod possible, or an iPod for active pursuits, get an iPod shuffle.
- If you want the cutest medium-capacity iPod, go for an iPod nano. The iPod nano is great for smaller libraries, or for carrying only the newest or most exciting songs in your colossal library with you, but its lower capacity makes it a poor value alongside the iPod classic.
- If you want to carry as many songs and videos as possible with you, buy an iPod classic.
- If you need a mobile phone that includes an iPod (or vice versa), buy an iPhone.
- If you want to watch videos, send mail, surf the Web, and run applications on the iPod, but you don't want to pay for an iPhone contract, get an iPod touch.

Table 1-1 shows you how much music you can fit onto the current iPod models at widely used compression ratios for music. For spoken audio (such as audio books, plays, or talk radio), you can use lower compression ratios (such as 64 Kbps or even 32 Kbps) and still get acceptable sound with much smaller file sizes. The table

TABLE 1-1   iPod Capacities at Widely Used Compression Ratios

iPod Nominal Capacity	iPod Real Capacity	128 Kbps		160 Kbps		320 Kbps		Apple Lossless Encoder[1]	
		Hours	Songs	Hours	Songs	Hours	Songs	Hours	Songs
2GB	1.9GB	34	500	28	400	16	200	5	75
4GB	3.7GB	65	950	55	775	30	375	10	150
8GB	7.2GB	135	2,000	110	1,600	55	800	20	290
16GB	14.7GB	270	4,000	220	3,200	110	1,600	40	580
32GB	29.6GB	550	8,000	440	6,400	220	3,200	80	1,160
64GB	60GB	1100	16,000	880	12,800	440	6,400	160	2,320
160GB	148GB	2,700	40,000	1,000	32,000	1,100	16,000	400	5,500

[1]Apple Lossless Encoder encoding rates vary; these figures are approximations.

assumes a "song" to be about four minutes long and rounds the figures to the nearest sensible point. The table doesn't show less widely used compression ratios such as 224 Kbps or 256 Kbps. (For 256 Kbps, halve the 128 Kbps numbers.)

 The iPods and iTunes refer to tracks as "songs"—even if they're not music—so this book does the same. Similarly, Apple and this book refer to "artists" rather than "singers," "bands," or other terms.

How to...   **Buy an iPod for Less Than Full Price**

If you'd prefer not to pay full price for an iPod, consider these alternatives:

- **Buy a refurbished iPod from Apple**   Apple sells refurbished iPods at a discount—sometimes up to a third off the normal price. To find them, search the Apple Store (http://store.apple.com) for **refurbished iPod.** These iPods have a one-year limited warranty, which you should read before buying one (look for a link to the warranty on any page that offers a refurbished iPod). You can also buy AppleCare to extend the coverage, although this is typically worthwhile only for the most expensive models.
- **Buy a used or reconditioned iPod from another vendor**   eBay and other sites carry used or reconditioned iPods. The prices may be attractive, but even on a reconditioned model, you will not normally get a warranty—and it may be hard to determine the quality of the reconditioning.
- **Grab an old iPod when a relative or friend upgrades**   If you know someone who simply must have the latest technology, get ready to jump in line for their existing iPod.

2

Get Your Computer Ready to Work with Your iPod

HOW TO...

- Find out what your iPod needs your PC or Mac to have
- Get your PC ready to work with your iPod
- Get your Mac ready to work with your iPod

Once you've chosen your iPod, as discussed in the previous chapter, and brought it home, you'll need to connect it to your computer to set it up and load it with songs, videos, and other content.

This chapter shows you how to get your PC or Mac ready to work with an iPod. We'll start by going over what the iPod needs—the operating system, connection hardware, and so on. Then we'll look at what you may need to add to your PC to make the iPod happy. Finally, we'll look at what you may need to add to your Mac.

Know What Your iPod Needs Your Computer to Have

If your PC or Mac is a recent model, it probably is ready to work with whichever new iPod you choose. If it's older, or if it's a budget model, or if you've picked up an older iPod, you may need to add new components.

Here are the requirements for an iPod classic, an iPod nano, or an iPod shuffle:

- A PC running Windows 7 (Home Premium, Professional, Ultimate, or Enterprise Edition), Windows Vista (Home Premium, Business, Ultimate, or Enterprise Edition), or either Windows XP Home Edition or Windows XP Professional with Service Pack 2 or Service Pack 3; or a Mac running Mac OS X 10.7 (Lion), 10.6 (Snow Leopard), or 10.5 (Leopard).

Did You Know?

Why USB 2.0 Makes a Huge Difference to Using an iPod

USB 2.0 is up to 40 times faster than USB 1.x, so you'll definitely want USB 2.0 if you have the choice. USB 1.x has a top speed of 12 megabits per second (Mbps), which translates to a maximum transfer of about 1.5MB of data per second; USB 2.0 has a top speed of 400 Mbps, which gives a data transfer rate of about 60MB per second.

As a result of this difference, loading an iPod via a USB 2.0 port will go far faster than via a USB 1.x port. The difference is most painful when you're loading an iPod classic, but you'll feel the pinch of USB 1.x even with the lower capacity of an iPod shuffle or an iPod nano.

At this writing, the latest version of USB—USB 3.0, also called SuperSpeed USB—has been released, but Apple hasn't yet used it for either iPods or Macs. USB 3.0 provides up to 5 gigabits per second (Gbps) and is backward compatible with USB 2.0, so if your PC has a USB 3.0 port, you can plug the iPod into that port without problems.

Instead of adding USB 3.0 to Macs, Apple has added a technology called Thunderbolt, which is even faster and more capable.

- A USB port. It's best to have a high-power USB 2.0 port, although you can scrape by with a USB 1.x port if you're prepared to be patient. The USB port must deliver enough power to recharge the iPod. If your keyboard has a built-in USB port (as many Apple keyboards do), it may not deliver enough power for recharging.
- An optical drive (a CD drive or a DVD drive) if you want to be able to rip songs from CDs to put in iTunes and on the iPod.
- A CD burner if you want to burn CDs from iTunes, or a DVD burner if you want to be able to burn both DVDs and CDs. (Most modern optical drives include burning capabilities.)
- iTunes 10 or a later version. We'll look at how to get and install iTunes in Chapter 3.

Get Your PC Ready to Work with an iPod

If you bought your PC in 2003 or later, it most likely has everything you need to start using an iPod and iTunes:

- A USB 2.0 port.
- Windows 7 (Home Premium, Professional, Ultimate, or Enterprise Edition), Windows Vista (Home Premium, Business, Ultimate, or Enterprise Edition), or Windows XP (either Home Edition or Professional) with Service Pack 2 or Service Pack 3. (If you don't yet have Service Pack 3, you can download it from the Microsoft website for free.)

- A 500-MHz or faster processor. You can get away with a slower processor, but it won't be much fun.
- 1GB RAM (for Windows 7), 512MB RAM (for Windows Vista), or 128MB RAM (for Windows XP). Much more RAM is much better.
- Enough hard-disk space to contain your library, on either an internal hard disk or an external hard disk.
- A CD or DVD burner if you want to rip songs from CDs or burn songs to CDs or DVDs.

If your PC can't meet those specifications, read the following sections to learn about possible upgrades.

Add USB 2.0 if Necessary

Most PCs manufactured in 2003 or later include one or more USB 2.0 ports—some have a half-dozen or more USB ports. If your PC has one or more, you're all set. If your computer has only USB 1.*x*, you can add USB 2.0 by installing a PCI card in a desktop PC or by inserting a PC Card in a laptop PC.

If you don't know whether your computer's USB ports are USB 1.*x* or USB 2.0, simply plug in the iPod and set it up. Either iTunes or Windows itself will warn you if the device is using a USB 1.*x* port rather than a USB 2.0 port. The Windows warning is usually a notification-area pop-up saying "HI-SPEED USB Device Plugged into non-HI-SPEED USB Hub" or "This USB device can perform faster if you connect it to a Hi-Speed USB 2.0 port," while the iTunes warning is an easy-to-understand message box.

 If your PC has USB 2.0 but is short of ports, get a USB 2.0 hub to add extra ports. Small USB hubs have around four ports, while larger USB hubs have seven ports or more. Many larger USB hubs have their own power supplies. Plugging in an extra power brick for a USB hub can be awkward, but it makes sure that the hub has the power it needs to feed your iPod and other USB devices.

Check Your Operating System Version

Make sure your PC is running Windows 7, Windows Vista, or Windows XP with Service Pack 2 or Service Pack 3. If you're in doubt about which version of Windows your computer is running, press WINDOWS KEY–BREAK, and then look at the System window (on Windows 7 or Windows Vista; see Figure 2-1) or the General tab of the System Properties dialog box (on Windows XP; see Figure 2-2). If your keyboard doesn't have a BREAK key, click the Start button, right-click Computer (in Windows 7 or Windows Vista) or My Computer (in Windows XP), and then click Properties on the context menu.

If you don't have Windows 7, Windows Vista, or Windows XP, it's well past time to upgrade to one of them. It's possible to use an iPod with an older version of Windows (such as Windows 98 Second Edition, Windows Me, or Windows 2000 Professional) if you use third-party software such as XPlay (www.mediafour.com), but these versions of Windows aren't safe on the Internet anymore.

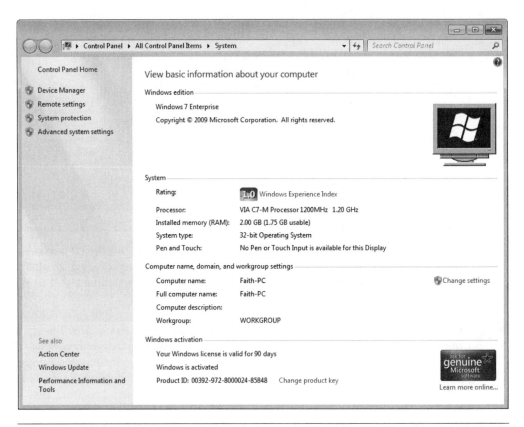

FIGURE 2-1 In Windows 7 and Windows Vista, the System window shows which version of Windows you're using, which Service Pack is installed (if any), and how much RAM the computer contains.

Check Memory and Disk Space

If you don't know how much memory your computer has, check it. As in the previous section, press WINDOWS KEY–BREAK (or click the Start button, right-click Computer or My Computer, and click Properties on the context menu), and then look at the System window (on Windows 7 or Windows Vista) or the General tab of the System Properties dialog box (on Windows XP).

To check disk space, follow these steps:

1. Open a Windows Explorer window to display all the drives on your computer:
   - **Windows 7 or Windows Vista** Choose Start | Computer.
   - **Windows XP** Choose Start | My Computer.
2. Right-click the drive you want to check, and then choose Properties from the shortcut menu to display the Properties dialog box for the drive.

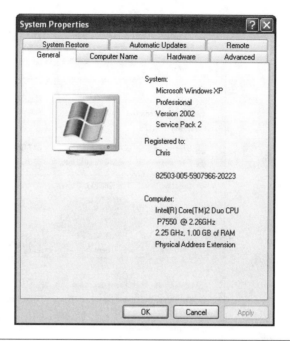

FIGURE 2-2   The readouts on the General tab of the System Properties dialog
box typically include the version of Windows, the latest Service Pack
installed, and the amount of RAM in your PC.

3. Look at the readout on the General tab of the Properties dialog box to see the
   amount of free space and used space on the drive. Figure 2-3 shows an example
   using Windows 7.
4. Click the OK button to close the Properties dialog box.

Add a Burner Drive if Necessary

If you want to be able to burn CDs or DVDs from iTunes, add a burner drive to your
computer. Which drive technology is most appropriate depends on your computer
type and configuration:

- For a desktop PC that has an open 5.25-inch bay and a spare internal drive connector,
  an internal burner drive is easiest.
- For a desktop PC that has no open 5.25-inch bay or no spare internal drive connector,
  or for a portable PC, get a USB 2.0 burner drive. If your PC has USB 3.0, go for a USB
  3.0 burner drive.

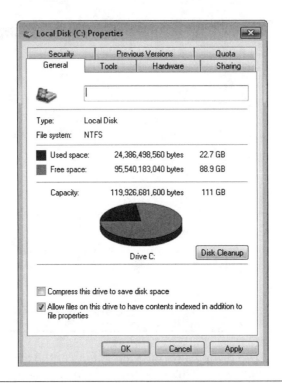

FIGURE 2-3 The General tab of the Properties dialog box for a drive shows you how much space has been used and how much remains free.

Get Your Mac Ready to Work with an iPod

If you bought your Mac in 2004 or later, chances are it's already all set to work with an iPod: It has one or more USB 2.0 ports, Mac OS X (Lion, Snow Leopard, or Leopard) with iTunes, and plenty of disk space and memory. Unless it's one of Apple's new models that lack an optical disc drive, it probably has a DVD burner drive as well.

But if you have an older Mac, it may lack a USB 2.0 port; that means you'll either need to add a USB 2.0 port or suffer slow USB 1.x transfer speeds instead. And if your Mac doesn't have a CD or DVD burner drive, you may need to add a burner drive to get the best out of iTunes.

Add USB 2.0 if Necessary

If your Mac lacks a USB 2.0 port, add one or more USB 2.0 ports:

- **Power Mac or Mac Pro** Insert a PCI card in a vacant slot.
- **PowerBook or MacBook** Insert a PC Card if your Mac has a PC Card slot.

If you have an iPod shuffle and your Mac has only a USB 1.*x* port, you probably don't need to upgrade, because the USB 1.*x* port will fill an iPod shuffle in a tolerably short time.

Check Your Operating System Version

Make sure your version of Mac OS is advanced enough to work with the iPod. You need Mac OS X 10.5 (Leopard), 10.6 (Snow Leopard), or 10.7 (Lion) to use current iPods. Upgrade if necessary, or use Software Update (choose Apple | Software Update) to download the latest point releases.

If you're not sure which version of Mac OS X you have, choose Apple | About This Mac to display the About This Mac window. Click the More Info button, and then look at the Software readout on the Overview tab of the larger About This Mac window.

 Apple frequently adds new features to iTunes and the iPods. To get the latest features and to make sure that iTunes and the iPod work as well as possible, keep Mac OS X, iTunes, and the device up to date. To check for updates, choose Apple | Software Update.

Check Disk Space and Memory

Make sure your Mac has enough disk space and memory to serve the iPod adequately.

In most cases, memory shouldn't be an issue: If your Mac can run Mac OS X and conventional applications at a speed you can tolerate without sedation, it should be able to handle iTunes and the iPod. Technically, Lion requires a minimum of 1GB of RAM, and either Leopard or Snow Leopard requires a minimum of 512MB, but you'll get far better performance with twice those amounts—preferably four or eight times the amounts.

Disk space is more likely to be an issue if you will want to keep many thousands of songs and videos in your library. The best situation is to have enough space on your hard drive to contain your entire library, both at its current size and at whatever size you expect it to grow to within the lifetime of your Mac. That way, you can easily synchronize your entire library with the iPod (if your library fits on the device) or just whichever part of your library you want to take around with you for the time being.

For example, to fill a 160GB iPod classic with music and video, you'll need 160GB of disk space to devote to your library. Recent Macs have hard disks large enough to spare 160GB without any hardship, but if you have an older desktop Mac, MacBook, or PowerBook, you may not be able to spare that much space.

If you have a Power Mac or Mac Pro, you can add another internal hard drive. If you have any other Mac, you can go for an external FireWire or USB drive. If your Mac has a Thunderbolt port, you can add a Thunderbolt external drive.

Add an Optical Drive if Necessary

If your Mac doesn't have an optical drive, you may want to add one so you can rip CDs from iTunes and burn CDs or DVDs from iTunes and other applications.

If you have a Power Mac or a Mac Pro that has a full-size drive bay free, you can add an internal DVD burner drive. For any other Mac, add a USB DVD drive.

How to...

Check the Speed of Your Mac's USB Ports

If you're not sure of the speed of your Mac's USB ports, check them like this:

1. Choose Apple | About This Mac to display the About This Mac window.
2. Click the More Info button to display a larger version of the About This Mac window, containing six tabs of information: Overview, Displays, Storage, Memory, Support, and Service. At first, the Overview tab appears at the front.
3. On the Overview tab, click the System Report button to display the System Information window. This window shows detailed information about your Mac's hardware, software, and network connections.
4. Expand the Hardware entry in the Contents pane if it's collapsed. Then click the USB item to display its contents.
5. Select one of the USB Bus items in the USB Device Tree pane and check the Speed readout in the lower pane, as shown here. If the readout says "Up to 12 Mb/sec," it's USB 1.*x*. If the readout says "Up to 480 Mb/sec," it's USB 2.0.

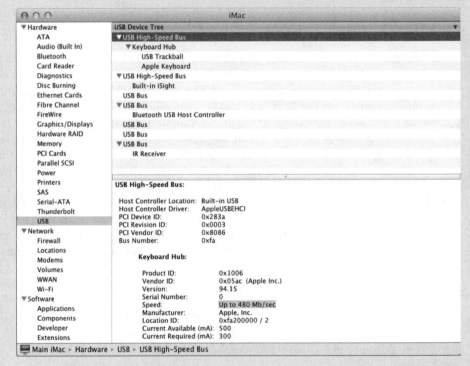

6. Press ⌘-Q or choose System Information | Quit System Information to close the System Information window.

3

Configure iTunes and Load Your iPod with Music, Video, and Data

HOW TO...

- Identify the different components included with your iPod
- Set up your iPod and connect it to your PC or Mac
- Install iTunes
- Start creating your library from existing files and CDs
- Load music, video, and data onto your iPod
- Eject and disconnect your iPod

In this chapter, you'll unpack your iPod (if you haven't already done so), give it an initial full charge if it needs one, and connect it to your PC or Mac. You'll install iTunes if you don't already have it installed. Then you'll start creating your library from any existing digital audio and video files you have and from your audio CDs. Finally, you'll load your iPod with songs, videos, contacts, calendars, and other information.

This chapter discusses how to proceed on both Windows and the Mac. Most of the way, the process is the same for both operating systems. Where they differ, the chapter presents Windows first and then the Mac, so you'll need to skip past the sections that cover the operating system that you're not using.

Unpack Your iPod

The iPod classic, iPod nano, and iPod shuffle include these components:

- The iPod itself
- A pair of ear-bud headphones
- A USB cable for connecting the iPod to your computer
- Booklets containing basic instructions and technical information

The iPod's standard way of recharging the battery is by taking power from your computer along the USB cable, but you can also plug the iPod into an electric socket. To do so, buy an Apple USB Power Adapter ($29) from the Apple Store (http://store.apple.com), or a third-party power adapter that gives the same output.

Install iTunes if It's Not Already Installed

Before you connect the iPod to your computer, you need to install iTunes—unless you have it installed already, as is likely on a Mac. The process is a little different on Windows and on the Mac, so the next two sections discuss the operating systems separately.

 Installing iTunes on Windows also installs helper programs that enable Windows to recognize the iPod and work with it.

Install iTunes on Your PC

To install iTunes on your PC, follow these steps:

1. Open your browser, go to the iTunes Download page on the Apple website (www.apple.com/itunes/download/), and then download the latest version of iTunes.

 The iTunes Download page encourages you to provide an e-mail address so that you can receive the New On iTunes newsletter, special iTunes offers, Apple news, and more. Unless you want to receive this information, be sure to clear the check boxes—in which case, you don't need to provide an e-mail address.

2. If Internet Explorer displays a File Download – Security Warning dialog box like the one shown here, verify that the name is iTunesSetup.exe. Then click the Run button.

3. If Internet Explorer displays an Internet Explorer – Security Warning dialog box like the one shown here, verify that the program name is iTunes and the publisher is Apple Inc. Then click the Run button.

4. On the Welcome To iTunes screen, click the Next button.
5. On the License Agreement screen, read the license agreement, select the I Accept The Terms In The License Agreement option button if you want to proceed, and then click the Next button.
6. On the Installation Options screen (see Figure 3-1), choose installation options:
   - **Add iTunes And QuickTime Shortcuts To My Desktop**   Select this check box only if you need shortcuts on your desktop. The installation routine creates shortcuts on your Start menu anyway. The Start menu is usually the easiest way to launch iTunes. In Windows 7, you may want to pin iTunes to the taskbar so that you can launch it quickly.

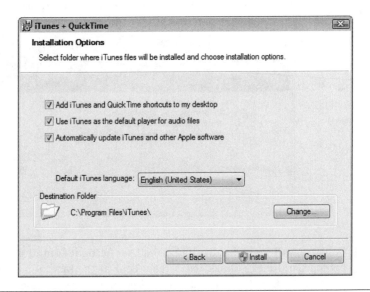

FIGURE 3-1   Choose whether to create shortcuts for iTunes and QuickTime on your Desktop, use iTunes as the default audio player, and update iTunes and QuickTime automatically.

- **Use iTunes As The Default Player For Audio Files** Select this check box if you plan to use iTunes as your main audio player. If you plan to use iTunes only for synchronizing the iPod and use another player (for example, Windows Media Player) for music, don't make iTunes the default player. iTunes associates itself with the AAC, MP3, Apple Lossless Encoding, AIFF, and WAV file extensions.
- **Automatically Update iTunes And Other Apple Software** Select this check box if you want to set Apple Software Update to check automatically for updates to iTunes, QuickTime, Safari, and other Apple software you install. Apple Software Update is a utility that installs in Control Panel. The automatic updating is an easy way to make sure you have the latest versions of the Apple software. The latest versions may contain bug fixes or extra features, so having them is usually helpful.
- **Default iTunes Language** In this drop-down list, choose the language you want to use—for example, English (United States).
- **Destination Folder** The installer installs iTunes in an iTunes folder in your Program Files folder by default. This is fine for most computers, but if you want to use a different folder, click the Change button, choose the folder, and then click the OK button.

7. Click the Install button to start the installation.
8. The installer displays the iTunes + QuickTime screen while it installs iTunes and QuickTime. On Windows XP, you need take no action until the Congratulations screen appears, telling you that iTunes and QuickTime have been successfully installed. But on Windows 7 and Windows Vista, you must go through several User Account Control prompts like the one shown here for different components of the iTunes installation (unless you've turned User Account Control off).

 On Windows 7 and Windows Vista, the User Account Control prompts may get stuck behind the iTunes + QuickTime screen. Look at the taskbar now and then to see if there's a flashing User Account Control prompt that you need to deal with before the installation can continue. Don't leave the installation unattended, because if you don't answer the User Account Control prompt, it times out and cancels the installation of the component.

9. When the Congratulations screen appears, leave the Open iTunes After The Installer Exits check box selected if you want to run iTunes immediately; otherwise, clear it. Then click the Finish button to close the installer.

Run iTunes

If you allowed the installer to run iTunes, the program now opens. If not, choose Start | iTunes | iTunes when you're ready to start running iTunes.

 The first time you launch iTunes, the program displays the iTunes Tutorial window, which contains tutorial videos showing you how to get started with iTunes and your iPod. Watch the videos that interest you, and then click the Close button (the × button) to close the iTunes Tutorial window.

You then see the iTunes window with the Music item selected in the Source list. Because you haven't yet added any music to the iTunes library, the Music item displays information on downloading music, importing your CDs, and finding the music files in your home folder. The home folder is the folder that opens when you click the Start button and then click your user name on the Start menu.

 If your computer is connected to the Internet, iTunes checks to see if an updated version is available. If one is available, iTunes prompts you to download it (which may take a few minutes, depending on the speed of your Internet connection) and install it. After updating iTunes, you may need to restart your PC.

Connect the iPod to Your PC

Next, connect the iPod to your PC. Connect the USB end of the iPod's cable to your computer, and then connect the other end to the iPod.

At this point, depending on the iPod and the version of iTunes you have, either or both of two things may happen:

- **Restore**   iTunes may prompt you to "restore" the device to change it from Macintosh formatting to PC formatting. Click the OK button and follow through the prompts. iTunes formats the iPod's hard disk or flash memory, reinstalls its operating system, and then displays a message box telling you it has done so.
- **Update**   iTunes may tell you that the device's software isn't up to date and prompt you to update it. Doing so is almost always a good idea, but be prepared to wait for a few minutes while iTunes downloads the update.

Install or Update iTunes on the Mac

If you have a Mac running Mac OS X, you most likely have iTunes installed already, because a default installation of Mac OS X includes iTunes.

Even if you explicitly exclude iTunes from the installation, Software Update offers you each updated version of iTunes that becomes available, so you need to refuse the updates manually or tell Software Update to ignore them. (To tell Software Update to ignore updates, select the iTunes item in the list, and then press ⌘-BACKSPACE or choose Update | Ignore Update.)

Get and Install the Latest Version of iTunes

If you've managed to refuse all these updates, the easiest way to install the latest version of iTunes is to use Software Update:

1. Choose Apple | Software Update to launch Software Update, which checks automatically for updates. (Your Mac must be connected to the Internet to use Software Update.)
2. If Software Update doesn't turn up a version of iTunes that you can install, choose Software Update | Reset Ignored Updates. Software Update then checks automatically for the latest versions of updates you've ignored and presents the list.
3. Make sure the iTunes check box is selected, and then click the Install Items button. Follow through the update process, entering your password in the authentication dialog box and accepting the license agreements.
4. Restart your Mac when Software Update prompts you to do so.

Launch iTunes

By this point, you should be ready to run iTunes on your Mac. To do so, click the iTunes icon on the Dock. If there's no iTunes icon on the Dock, click the Launchpad icon on the Dock, and then click the iTunes icon on the Launchpad screen.

 If you're using a version of Mac OS X before Mac OS X Lion, and the iTunes icon doesn't appear on the Dock, launch iTunes from the Applications folder. Click the Finder icon on the Dock (or simply click the desktop) to activate the Finder, choose Go | Applications or press ⌘-SHIFT-A to open your Applications folder, and then double-click the iTunes icon.

Connect Your iPod to Your Mac

Now connect the USB end of the cable that came with the iPod to your Mac, and then connect the other end to the Dock Connector port on the bottom of the device. For an iPod shuffle, slide the other end of the cable into the headphone socket.

Finish Setting Up the iPod

After you install iTunes and connect the iPod, iTunes recognizes the device, adds it to the Devices category in the Source list, and displays the Set Up Your iPod screen shown in Figure 3-2.

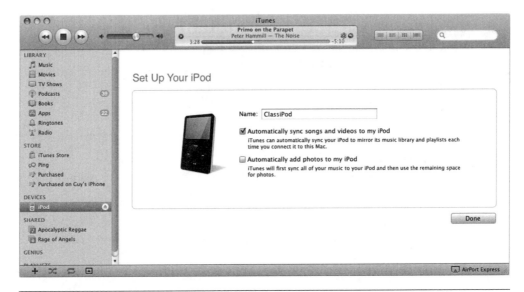

FIGURE 3-2   The Set Up Your iPod screen lets you name the iPod, choose whether to update it automatically from the start, and decide whether to synchronize pictures.

Follow these steps to finish setting up the iPod:

1. In the Name text box, you can change the name that iTunes has suggested for the iPod—for example, Max's iPod.
2. Choose what to synchronize on your iPod:
   - If the iPod has enough space to store your entire library, and you want to synchronize all items in your library with the iPod, select the Automatically Sync Songs And Videos To My iPod check box. If you want to update the iPod manually from the start, clear this check box.
   - If you want to synchronize photos automatically with the iPod, select the Automatically Add Photos To My iPod check box. On Windows, open the Sync Photos From drop-down list and select the source of the photos—for example, your Pictures folder on Windows 7 or Windows Vista, or your My Pictures folder on Windows XP.
3. Click the Done button to apply your choices.

Start Creating Your Library

Before you can add any songs or other items to the iPod, you must add them to your library in iTunes. This section gets you started with the basics of adding songs to your library from your home folder, from other folders, and from your CDs. Chapter 11 covers this topic in far greater depth, discussing how to plan, create, and manage an effective library for iTunes, your iPod, and your household.

Make Sure iTunes Has Suitable Settings

Before you add songs to your library, take a minute to check two important settings in iTunes. The first of these settings controls whether iTunes copies existing files into your library or adds references to their existing locations. The second controls whether iTunes automatically renames your files to match the tag information they contain.

These settings are both on the Advanced tab of the iTunes dialog box (on Windows) or the Preferences dialog box (on the Mac). Follow these steps to reach the Advanced tab:

1. Display the iTunes dialog box or the Preferences dialog box:
   - In Windows, choose Edit | Preferences or press CTRL-COMMA or CTRL-Y to display the iTunes dialog box.
   - On the Mac, choose iTunes | Preferences or press ⌘-COMMA or ⌘-Y to display the Preferences dialog box.
2. Click the Advanced tab to display its contents (see Figure 3-3).

Now choose which settings you want, as discussed in the following subsections.

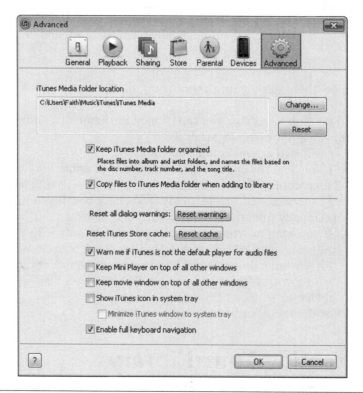

FIGURE 3-3 On the Advanced tab of the iTunes dialog box or the Preferences dialog box, clear the Copy Files To iTunes Media Folder When Adding To Library check box if you don't want to store a copy of each song file on your hard disk. Clear the Keep iTunes Media Folder Organized check box if you don't want iTunes to rename your files.

Decide Whether to Copy All Song Files to Your Library

The ideal setup is to store all your songs and videos within your Music folder (on Windows 7 or Windows Vista), your My Music folder (on Windows XP), or the Music folder in your Home folder (on the Mac). Typically, this folder is on your computer's hard drive (or on its primary hard drive, if it has more than one hard drive).

That means your hard drive must have enough space for all your songs, videos, and other items (for example, podcasts and TV shows), not to mention the operating system, your applications, and all your other files (such as documents, pictures, and video files). For a modest-sized library, this is easy enough. But for the kind of library that most music enthusiasts accumulate over the years, it means your computer must have a huge hard drive. Most modern desktop computers do, but at this writing laptop hard drives are limited to around 1TB—and most laptops have hard drives that are far smaller than this.

If your computer does have a huge hard drive, all is well. But if it doesn't, you'll have to either make do with only some of the songs and videos you want or store some of the files on other drives or other computers. You can tell iTunes to store references to where files are located rather than store a copy of each file in the library folder on your hard drive.

Even if your computer has enough hard drive space for all your songs, you may prefer not to store them in your Music folder, My Music folder, or the Music folder in your Home folder so that you can more easily share them through the file system with other members of your household. iTunes' Sharing features (discussed in Chapter 11) enable you to share even files stored in your private folders, but they limit other users to playing the songs (rather than adding them to their music libraries) and work only when iTunes is running. For more flexibility, you may prefer to store shared songs on a server or in a folder that all members of your household can access.

If you want iTunes to copy the files, select the Copy Files To iTunes Media Folder When Adding To Library check box. If you want iTunes to leave the files where they are, and simply add to your library the references to the files, clear this check box.

Storing references is great when you have too little space free on your hard disk to accommodate your colossal library. For example, if you have a laptop whose hard disk is bulging at the seams, you might choose to store in your library only references to songs located on an external hard disk rather than trying to import a copy of each song. But—obviously enough—you won't be able to play any song stored on the external hard disk when your laptop isn't connected to it.

Decide Whether to Let iTunes Organize Your Media Folder

Take a moment to think about the Keep iTunes Media Folder Organized setting, because it decides whether you or iTunes controls the organization of the files in your library.

If you turn this feature on, iTunes stores a song in a file named after the track number (if you choose to include it). iTunes places the song in a folder named after the album; this folder is stored within a folder named after the artist, which is placed in your iTunes Media folder.

For example, if you rip the album *Brothers* by The Black Keys, iTunes stores the first song as\The Black Keys\Brothers\01 Everlasting Light.aac on Windows or as/The Black Keys/Brothers/01 Everlasting Light.aac on Mac OS X. If you then edit the artist field in the tag to "Black Keys" instead of "The Black Keys," iTunes changes the name of the artist folder to "Black Keys" as well.

This automatic renaming is nice and logical for iTunes, but you may dislike the way folder and file names change when you edit the tags. If so, clear the Keep iTunes Media Folder Organized check box on the Advanced tab of the iTunes dialog box (in Windows) or the Preferences dialog box (on the Mac). You can change this setting at any time, but it's least confusing to make a choice at the beginning and then stick with it.

Add Your Existing Song Files to Your Library

If you haven't yet added any songs to your library, the best place to start is by having iTunes add all the songs in your home folder. You can then add other folders as needed.

Make iTunes Add the MP3 and AAC Files from Your Home Folder

The quick way to start creating your library is to have iTunes add all the MP3 files and AAC files stored in your home folder. To do this, follow these steps:

1. In iTunes, click the Music item in the Library category of the Source list on the left. The Music screen appears, showing a screen of information rather than a list of songs because you haven't yet added any songs to your library.
2. Click the Find MP3 And AAC Files In My Home Folder link. iTunes automatically searches your home folder for MP3 files and AAC files, and adds all those it finds to your library.

Add Songs from Other Folders

To add songs to your library, follow these instructions:

- In Windows, to add a folder of songs, choose File | Add Folder To Library. In the Browse For Folder dialog box, navigate to and select the folder you want to add. Click the OK button, and iTunes either copies the song files to your library (if you selected the Copy Files To iTunes Media Folder When Adding To Library check box) or adds references to the song files (if you cleared this check box).
- In Windows, to add a single file, choose File | Add File To Library or press CTRL-O. In the Add To Library dialog box, navigate to and select the file you want to add. Click the OK button, and iTunes adds it.
- On the Mac, choose File | Add To Library or press ⌘-O. In the Add To Library dialog box, navigate to and select the folder or the file you want to add, and then click the Choose button to add the folder or file.

On either Windows or the Mac, you can drag files to the Library section of the Source list and drop them there. On Windows, select the files on your Desktop or in a Windows Explorer window first; on the Mac, select the files on your desktop or in a Finder window.

Add WMA Files on Windows

If you have files in the WMA format on your Windows PC, you can have iTunes convert them to AAC or another iTunes-friendly format for you.

To convert the WMA files, either drag them to the Library section of the Source list from a Windows Explorer window (or your Desktop) or use the Add Folder To Library dialog box to pick them. When iTunes displays the dialog box shown here, warning you that it will convert the files, click the Convert button.

How to... # Decide Whether to Convert Your WMA Files to AAC Files

Converting your unprotected WMA files to AAC files is usually a good idea. WMA files can be protected with digital rights management (DRM) restrictions that control which computers can play the files. iTunes can't convert protected WMA files to AAC files.

Technically, the AAC files you end up with contain all the flaws of the original WMA files plus any flaws that the AAC encoding introduces. This is because all "lossy" audio formats lose audio quality, introducing flaws into the resulting audio files.

In practice, however, if the WMA files sound great to you, the AAC files will probably sound at least acceptable—and you can play them on your iPod, which you cannot do with the WMA files.

In any case, the conversion process leaves the original WMA files untouched, so if you don't like the resulting AAC files, you can simply delete them. The AAC files will probably take up around the same amount of space on your computer's hard disk as the WMA files, so make sure you have plenty of free space before you convert the files.

Converting the WMA files to AAC gives you the best quality, but you can create MP3 files instead if you prefer. Before you import the files, set the file format you want. Follow the instructions in the section "Check iTunes' Settings for Importing Music," later in this chapter.

Then import the files. When iTunes warns you that it will convert the files, click the Convert button.

WMA is the abbreviation for Windows Media Audio, Microsoft's preferred file format for audio on Windows.

Copy CDs to Your Library

The other way to add your existing digital music to your library is to copy it from CD. iTunes makes the process as straightforward as can be, but you should first verify that the iTunes settings for importing music are suitable.

Check iTunes' Settings for Importing Music

Follow these steps to check iTunes' settings for importing music:

1. Display the iTunes dialog box or the Preferences dialog box:
   - In Windows, choose Edit | Preferences or press CTRL-COMMA or CTRL-Y to display the iTunes dialog box.
   - On the Mac, choose iTunes | Preferences or press ⌘-COMMA or ⌘-Y to display the Preferences dialog box.
2. Click the General tab if it's not already displayed.
3. In the When You Insert A CD drop-down list, choose the action you want iTunes to take when you insert a CD: Show CD, Begin Playing, Ask To Import CD, Import CD, or Import CD And Eject. When you're building your library, Show CD is usually the best choice, as it gives you the chance to scan the CD information for errors that you need to correct before you import the CD. This section assumes you're using the Show CD setting.
4. Click the Import Settings button to open the Import Settings dialog box (see Figure 3-4).

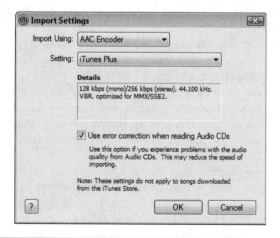

FIGURE 3-4   Before importing music, open the Import Settings dialog box and make sure that iTunes is configured with suitable settings.

5. Verify that AAC Encoder is selected in the Import Using drop-down list.
6. In the Setting drop-down list, choose High Quality if you want good audio quality with a compact file size—for example, if you have an iPod shuffle or a low-capacity iPod nano. Choose iTunes Plus if you're prepared to use twice as much disk space to improve the audio quality.
7. Click the OK button to close the Import Settings dialog box.
8. Click the OK button to close the iTunes dialog box or Preferences dialog box.

iTunes can store the music extracted from CDs in several different formats, including Advanced Audio Coding (AAC, the default), MP3, and Apple Lossless Encoding. Chapter 7 discusses the pros and cons of the various formats and how to choose which will suit you best. For the moment, this book assumes that you are using AAC.

Add a CD to Your Library

To add a CD to your library, follow these steps:

1. Start iTunes if it's not already running.
2. Insert the CD in your computer's optical drive (CD drive or DVD drive). iTunes loads the CD and displays an entry for it in the Source list. If your computer is connected to the Internet, iTunes retrieves the CD's information and displays it (see Figure 3-5).

FIGURE 3-5 Load a CD, check that the data is correct, and then click the Import CD button to import its songs into your library.

If you selected the Ask To Import CD item in the When You Insert A CD drop-down list, iTunes displays a dialog box asking if you want to import the CD. Click the Yes button or the No button, as needed. If you selected the Import CD item, iTunes goes ahead and imports the CD without asking you. If you selected the Import CD And Eject item, iTunes imports the CD and then spits it out.

3. Look at the CD's information and make sure that it is correct. If not, click twice (with a pause between the clicks) on the piece of information you want to change, type the correction, and then press ENTER (Windows) or RETURN (Mac).

You can also change CD or song information in other ways. See Chapters 7 and 10 for the details.

4. Clear the check box for any song you don't want to import.
5. Click the Import CD button. iTunes extracts the audio from the CD, converts it to the format you chose, and saves the files to your library.

If you want Windows 7 or Windows Vista to prompt you to show or import songs every time you insert an audio CD, choose Start | Control Panel, choose Large Icons in the View By drop-down list (on Windows 7) or click the Classic View button link (in Windows Vista), and then double-click the AutoPlay icon. In the Audio CD drop-down list, choose Show Songs Using iTunes or Import Songs Using iTunes (as appropriate), and then click the Save button.

How to... Associate Your Music Files with iTunes on Windows

If iTunes notices that it's not the default player for the audio file types it normally plays, it displays the dialog box shown here telling you about the problem (as iTunes sees it). On Windows 7 or Windows Vista, iTunes prompts you to go to the Default Programs control panel to set it up, as shown on the left here. On Windows XP, iTunes simply suggests you make iTunes the default player, as shown on the right here.

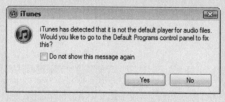
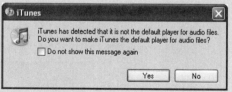

If you've set up another program to play these audio files, select the Do Not Show This Message Again check box and click the No button. Otherwise, click the Yes button. On Windows XP, iTunes simply grabs the file associations. On Windows 7 or Windows Vista, iTunes opens the Set Program Associations window, shown here.

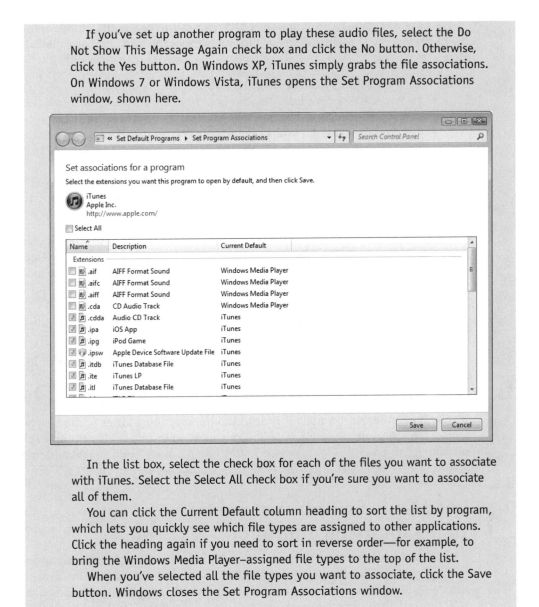

In the list box, select the check box for each of the files you want to associate with iTunes. Select the Select All check box if you're sure you want to associate all of them.

You can click the Current Default column heading to sort the list by program, which lets you quickly see which file types are assigned to other applications. Click the heading again if you need to sort in reverse order—for example, to bring the Windows Media Player–assigned file types to the top of the list.

When you've selected all the file types you want to associate, click the Save button. Windows closes the Set Program Associations window.

Check That the Songs You've Added Sound Okay

After adding the first CD, click the Music item under the Library category in the Source list, double-click the first song you imported from the CD, and listen to it to make sure there are no obvious defects (such as clicks or pauses) in the sound. If you have time, listen to several songs, or even the entire CD.

If the songs sound fine, you probably don't need to use error correction on your CD drive. But if you do hear defects, turn on error correction and copy the CD again. Here's how:

1. Display the iTunes dialog box or the Preferences dialog box:
   - In Windows, choose Edit | Preferences or press CTRL-COMMA or CTRL-Y to display the iTunes dialog box.
   - On the Mac, choose iTunes | Preferences or press ⌘-COMMA or ⌘-Y to display the Preferences dialog box.
2. Click the General tab if it's not already displayed.
3. Click the Import Settings button to open the Import Settings dialog box.
4. Select the Use Error Correction When Reading Audio CDs check box.
5. Click the OK button to close each dialog box.

In your library, click the first song that you ripped from the CD, hold down SHIFT, and click the last song from the CD to select all the songs. Press DELETE or BACKSPACE on your keyboard, click the Yes button in the confirmation dialog box, and then click the Yes button in the dialog box that asks whether you want to move the files from your Music folder to the Recycle Bin (on Windows) or the Trash (on the Mac).

Click the CD's entry in the Source list, and then click the Import CD button to import the songs again. Check the results and make sure they're satisfactory before you import any more CDs.

Load Your iPod with Music, Video, and Data

If you chose to let iTunes update your iPod automatically, iTunes performs the first update after you connect it. If your library will fit on the iPod, iTunes copies all the songs to it. All you need to do is wait until the songs have been copied and then disconnect it (see "Eject and Disconnect the iPod," later in this chapter).

Load Only Some Songs from Your Library on Your iPod

If your library is larger than the capacity of the iPod, iTunes warns you of the problem (see Figure 3-6). Click the OK button (there's no other choice) to let iTunes put an automatic selection of songs on the iPod; iTunes creates a playlist named *device's name* Selection (where *device's name* is the name you've given the iPod), assigns a selection of songs to it, and copies them to the iPod.

Configure How Your iPod Is Loaded

Instead of having iTunes load your iPod automatically, you can choose custom settings. Follow these steps:

1. Click the iPod's entry in the Source list.
2. Click the Summary tab to display its contents (see Figure 3-7).

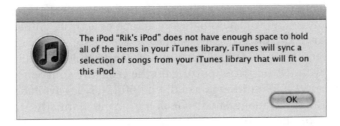

FIGURE 3-6 If your library is too large to fit on the iPod, iTunes will choose a selection of songs for it automatically.

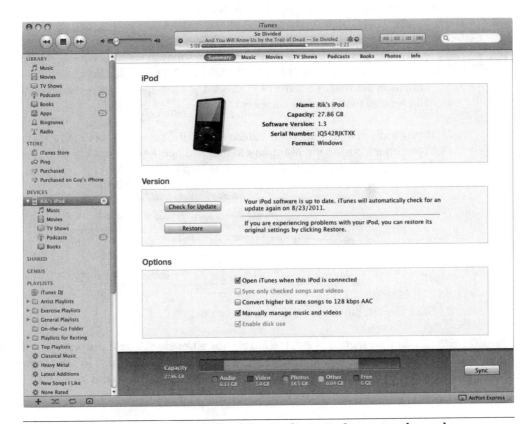

FIGURE 3-7 On the Summary tab of the iPod's control screens, choose how to load the iPod.

3. Select the Open iTunes When This iPod Is Connected check box if you want your computer to automatically launch or activate iTunes when you connect your iPod. This is usually handy.
4. Select the Sync Only Checked Songs And Videos check box if you want to prevent iTunes from putting on the iPod any song whose check box you've cleared. This setting is usually helpful; it's not available if you select the Manually Manage Music check box or the Manually Manage Music And Videos check box.
5. For an iPod shuffle, select the Enable Sound Check check box if you want to use the Sound Check feature to "normalize" the volume on the iPod. This helps prevent wide variations in the volume of songs, but it tends to make them sound less interesting because it squashes down the dynamic range—the difference in volume between the quietest bits and the loudest bits.
6. Select the Convert Higher Bit Rate Songs To 128 Kbps AAC check box if you want to get as many songs as possible on the iPod.

 Converting songs to 128 Kbps prevents iTunes from loading higher-bitrate songs on your iPod. This setting is a great help if the songs in your library use high bitrates and your iPod's capacity is too low to hold all the songs at that quality. The drawbacks are that the conversion slows down the loading process considerably and reduces sound quality somewhat.

7. If you want to load songs and videos manually, select the Manually Manage Music check box or the Manually Manage Music And Videos check box. iTunes displays a confirmation dialog box, as shown here.

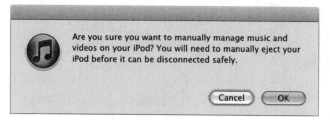

Are you sure you want to manually manage music and videos on your iPod? You will need to manually eject your iPod before it can be disconnected safely.

Cancel   OK

8. Click the OK button to close the dialog box.

 For an iPod shuffle, select the Enable VoiceOver check box if you want to use the VoiceOver feature to announce the names of songs and artists. In the Language drop-down list, choose the language you want VoiceOver to use for status messages (such as "Battery low").

9. Click each of the other tabs in turn, and choose the items you want to sync. We'll discuss the other tabs later in this chapter.
10. Click the Apply button.

Did You
Know?

Why Your First-Ever iPod Synchronization May Take Much Longer than Subsequent Synchronizations

USB 2.0 connections are fast, but your iPod's first-ever synchronization may take several hours if your library contains many songs or videos. This is because, on the first synchronization, iTunes must copy each song or video to the iPod.

Subsequent synchronizations are much quicker, because iTunes needs only to transfer new songs and videos you've added to your library, remove songs you've deleted, and update the data on items whose tags (information such as the artist name and song name) you've changed.

If you're using USB 1.*x* rather than USB 2.0 to synchronize your iPod, the first synchronization will take several hours if your library contains many songs and videos. You might plan to perform the first synchronization sometime when you can leave your computer and iPod to get on with it—for example, overnight, or when you head out to work.

Load Music on Your iPod Manually

If you decided against automatic updating of either your entire library or iTunes' automatic selection from it, you need to load your iPod manually. You can perform either of the following actions:

- Connect your iPod to your computer, wait until its entry appears in the Source list, and then drag songs, artists, albums, or playlists to its entry. When you drop the items, iTunes copies the songs to your iPod, which takes a few seconds.
- Create a playlist for your iPod by choosing File | New Playlist, typing the name in the text box, and then pressing ENTER (Windows) or RETURN (Mac). Drag songs, albums, or artists to the playlist to add them. When you're ready to load the playlist, connect your iPod to your computer, wait until its entry appears in the Source list, and then drag the playlist to the entry. iTunes then copies the songs to the iPod all at once.

To force iTunes to copy to your iPod any song files that lack the tag information the device normally requires, add the songs to a playlist. Doing so can save you time over retagging many files manually and can be useful in a pinch. (In the long term, you'll probably want to make sure all your song files are tagged properly.)

Choose Custom Synchronization Settings

Setting up synchronization of songs, videos, and maybe photos with your iPod is a good start, but you'll probably want to choose custom synchronization settings so that you can get exactly the files and data you want on the iPod.

To choose custom settings, connect your iPod, click its entry in the Devices category in the Source list, and then set options on the iPod's settings tabs (discussed next). Click the Apply button in the lower-right corner of the window to apply your changes.

Choose Which Contacts and Calendars to Synchronize with the iPod classic

For the iPod classic, click the Info tab to display its contents (see Figure 3-8), and then choose which information you want to synchronize with the iPod:

- **Contacts**   On Windows, select the Sync Contacts From check box and choose the source in the drop-down list: Yahoo! Address Book, Windows Address Book or Windows Contacts, Google Contacts, or Outlook. On Mac OS X, select the Sync Address Book Contacts check box. On either OS, either select the All Contacts

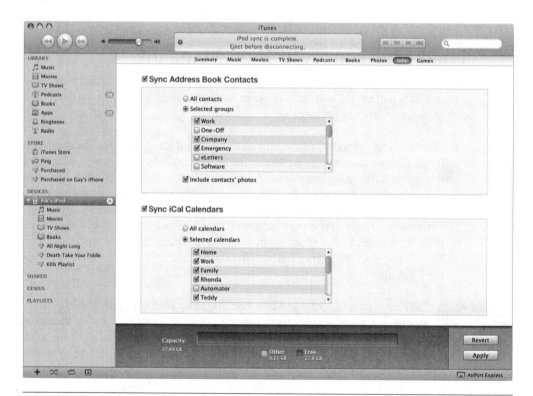

FIGURE 3-8   For an iPod classic, use the Info tab to choose which contacts and calendars to synchronize.

option button, or select the Selected Groups option button and select the check box for each group of contacts you want to synchronize. Select the Include Contacts' Photos check box if you want to include photos.

 The choices available in the Sync Contacts From drop-down list and the Sync Calendars From drop-down list depend on the programs and accounts you've installed on your PC.

- **Calendars**   On Windows, select the Sync Calendars From check box and choose Outlook in the drop-down list. On the Mac, select the Sync iCal Calendars check box. On either OS, either select the All Calendars option button, or select the Selected Calendars option button and select the check box for each calendar you want to synchronize.

Choose Music Synchronization Settings

On the Music tab (see Figure 3-9), choose whether to synchronize music and, if so, which music:

1. Select the Sync Music check box. This enables the other controls.
2. Select the Entire Music Library option button to synchronize your entire library. Select the Include Music Videos check box if you want to include music videos with the songs.
3. Select the Selected Playlists, Artists, Albums, And Genres option button if you want to synchronize the iPod with the items whose check boxes you select in the Playlists list box, Artists list box, Genres list box, and Albums list box that appear. This is a good choice when the iPod doesn't have enough capacity to hold your entire library.

Choose Photos Synchronization Settings for the iPod classic and iPod nano

To tell iTunes which photos to put on the iPod, click the Photos tab, select the Sync Photos From check box, and then choose the source in the drop-down list. For example, in Mac OS X, choose iPhoto or a particular folder in the Sync Photos From drop-down list.

Once you've done that, choose which photos to include:

- **Windows**   Select the All Photos option button to add all the photos. To add just some, select the Selected Folders option button, and then select the check box for each folder you want to synchronize.
- **Mac OS X**   Select the All Photos And Albums option button if you want to include all the photos. To choose by Events, select the Events option button, and then choose which Events from the pop-up menu: All, 1 Most Recent, 3 Most Recent, 5 Most Recent, 10 Most Recent, or 20 Most Recent. (An *Event* is a group of photos in iPhoto that are organized by date or by topic.)

FIGURE 3-9 To choose which items iTunes syncs to your iPod, click the Selected Playlists, Artists, Albums, And Genres option button, and then select the check box for each item you want to include.

Select the Include Full-Resolution Photos check box if you want to put the full-resolution versions of the pictures on the iPod as well as the smaller versions that iTunes prepares for you. Select this check box only if you want to have the original photos with you—for example, because you may need to share the photo files with people by connecting your iPod to their computer and transferring the files.

Choose Podcasts Synchronization Settings

On the Podcasts tab, select the Sync Podcasts check box, and then choose which episodes to synchronize:

- All the episodes (the simple choice)
- 1, 3, 5, or 10 of the most recent episodes
- 1, 3, 5, or 10 of the most recent unplayed episodes

- 1, 3, 5, or 10 of the least recent unplayed episodes
- All the new episodes
- 1, 3, 5, or 10 of the most recent new episodes
- 1, 3, 5, or 10 of the least recent new episodes

Then use the controls in the Podcasts list box, the Episodes list box, and the Include Episodes From Playlists list box to choose which podcasts to synchronize.

Choose Video Synchronization Settings for an iPod classic

On the Movies tab and TV Shows tab, choose which movies and TV shows you want to synchronize with the device. Select the Sync Movies check box or the Sync TV Shows check box, and then choose the details of the movies or shows to include.

Choose Books Synchronization Settings

On the Books tab, select the Sync Audiobooks check box if you want to put your audiobooks on your iPod. Select the All Audiobooks option button if you want to load all your audiobooks. Otherwise, select the Selected Audiobooks option button, and use the Audiobooks list box, the Parts list box, and the Include Audiobooks From Playlists list box to specify which audiobooks and parts you want.

 For an iPod classic, you can also synchronize games you've downloaded from the iTunes Store. Click the Games tab to reach these settings.

Recharge the iPod

As with most devices, the battery icon on the iPod's display shows you the status of the device's battery power.

The easiest way to recharge the iPod is to plug it into a high-power USB port on a computer. If the USB port provides enough power, you will see the battery indicator add a charging symbol. (If the port doesn't provide enough power, try another port.)

Alternatively, you can use the Apple USB Power Adapter, an optional accessory. See Chapter 5 for details. The Power Adapter is useful when you need to recharge the iPod away from any computer. You can also run the iPod from the Power Adapter even while the battery is charging.

 Using the Apple USB Power Adapter to charge an iPod is more reliable than using the USB cable, and the Power Adapter is useful for troubleshooting problems such as the device becoming nonresponsive. For this reason, a Power Adapter is a great accessory to have, even if you normally charge directly from the computer.

Most batteries take between three and five hours to recharge. After about half of the charging time, the battery should be at about 80 percent of its charge capacity—enough for you to use the iPod for several hours. (This is because the battery charges quickly at first, up to around the 80 percent level, and then charges more slowly the remainder of the way so as not to overcharge.)

Eject and Disconnect the iPod

When iTunes has finished loading songs onto the iPod, you can disconnect it unless it's in disk mode (or you need to continue recharging its battery). iTunes displays the message saying that the update is complete and "OK to disconnect." The iPod displays the message "OK to disconnect." When you see this message, you can unplug the iPod from the cable or from your computer.

But if you're using an iPod in disk mode, iTunes doesn't prepare the iPod for disconnection after it finishes loading songs. Instead, it leaves the iPod mounted on your computer as a disk so that you can transfer files to and from it manually. When the iPod is in disk mode like this, it displays the message "Do Not Disconnect." In Mac OS X, an icon for the iPod appears on the desktop unless you have specifically chosen to exclude it (see the "Prevent the iPod from Appearing on the Desktop in Mac OS X" sidebar). See Chapter 14 for more information about disk mode.

 If you forget to eject the iPod before you log out of Mac OS X, you shouldn't need to log back in to eject the device. If it's an iPod classic or an iPod nano, make sure that the screen is displaying the "OK to disconnect" message, and then disconnect the iPod. If it's an iPod shuffle, make sure that the orange or amber light isn't blinking.

How to...

Prevent the iPod from Appearing on the Desktop in Mac OS X

When the iPod is mounted in disk mode, it appears on the Mac OS X desktop by default. You can prevent it from appearing, but doing so also prevents CDs and DVDs from appearing. Here's how:

1. Click the desktop to activate the Finder.
2. Choose Finder | Preferences to display the Finder Preferences window.
3. Click the General tab if it isn't already displayed.
4. Clear the CDs, DVDs, And iPods check box.
5. Click the Close button on the Finder Preferences window, or choose File | Close Window or press ⌘-w, to close the window.

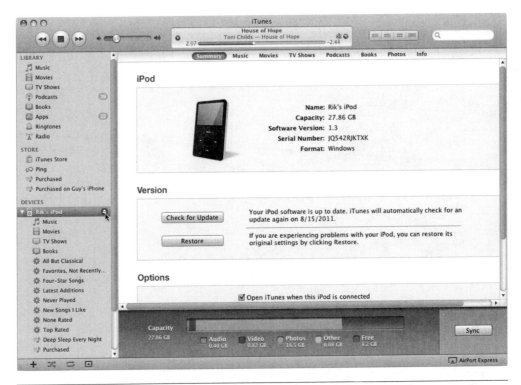

FIGURE 3-10 The easiest way to eject the iPod is to click its Eject button in the Source list.

You can eject the iPod in any of the following ways:

- Click the Eject button that appears next to the device's entry in the Source list (see Figure 3-10).
- Right-click (or CTRL-click on the Mac) the device's entry in the Source list and then click the Eject item on the shortcut menu.
- Click the device's entry in the Source list and then choose Controls | Eject *device's name* or press CTRL-E (Windows) or ⌘-E (Mac).

4

Enjoy Music and Video on Your iPod

HOW TO...

- Connect your headphones or speakers to your iPod
- Play music and video on an iPod classic
- Play music on an iPod nano
- Choose settings to make your iPod easier to use
- Use key extra features
- Play music on the iPod shuffle

This chapter shows you the essentials of using your iPod. You'll start by connecting your headphones or speakers, and then quickly get the hang of playing music, first on the iPod classic and then on the iPod nano. You'll also learn to play video on the iPod classic. The chapter also explains how to choose settings on the iPod classic and the iPod nano and how to use their other key features, such as the sleep timer, stopwatch, passcode lock (on the iPod classic), and radio (on the iPod nano).

At the end of the chapter, we'll look at how to play music on the iPod shuffle.

Connect Your Headphones or Speakers

The easiest way to get sound out of an iPod is to connect your headphones or speakers to the headphones port. The headphones port is on the top of the iPod classic and the iPod shuffle and on the bottom of the iPod nano. You can't miss it: a $\frac{1}{8}$-inch (3.5mm) round hole, into which you slide a miniplug of the corresponding size.

Connecting the miniplug and the port couldn't be easier, but a couple of things are worth mentioning:

- The headphone port delivers up to 60 milliwatts (mW) altogether—30 mW per channel. To avoid distortion or damage, turn down the volume when connecting your iPod to a different pair of headphones, powered speakers, or an amplifier. Make the connection, set the volume to low on the speakers or amplifier, and then start playing the audio.
- If you have a dock for the iPod classic or iPod nano, you can play music from the device when it's docked. Plug a cable with a stereo miniplug into the line-out port on the dock, and then connect the other end of the cable to your powered speakers or your stereo. Use the iPod's controls to navigate to the music, play it, pause it, and so on. Use the volume control on the speakers or the receiver to control the volume at which the songs play.

 The line-out port delivers a standard volume and better audio quality than the headphone port, so it's well worth using a dock if you have one. Similarly, most speakers designed specifically for use with iPods have a Dock Connector port that enables them to receive audio at line-out quality and a constant volume.

Use Headphones with Your iPod

Each iPod comes with a pair of ear-bud headphones—the kind that fit in your ear rather than sit on your ear or over your ear. The headphones are designed to look good with the iPod—and in fact their distinctive white has helped muggers in many countries target victims with iPods (and iPhones) rather than those with less desirable audio players and phones.

Beyond that, these are good-quality headphones with a wide range of frequency response: from 20 Hz (hertz) to 20 kHz (kilohertz; 1,000 hertz), which is enough to cover most of the average human's hearing spectrum. Apple emphasizes that the headphones have drivers (technically, *transducers*) made of neodymium, a rare earth magnet that provides better frequency response and higher sound quality than alternative materials (such as cobalt, aluminum, or ceramics).

A wide range of frequency response and high sound quality are desirable, but what's more important to most people is that their headphones be comfortable and that they meet any other requirements, such as shutting out ambient sound or enhancing the wearer's charisma. See the sidebar "Choose Headphones to Suit You" for suggestions on evaluating and choosing headphones.

 If you're looking for the ultimate sound quality, look into having custom earphones molded to fit your ears. You can find these online (terms vary, but try searching for "in-ear monitors"), but you may also want to consult your local musical instruments store.

How to...   # Choose Headphones to Suit You

If you don't like the sound your iPod's headphones deliver, or if you just don't find them comfortable, use another pair of headphones instead. Any headphones with a standard miniplug will work; if your headphones have a quarter-inch jack, get a good-quality miniplug converter to make the connection to your iPod. You don't need to break the bank by buying the most expensive converter, but those with gold-plated contacts tend to give noticeably better audio quality than ones with base metals, as well as costing more.

Headphones largely break down into three main types, although you can find plenty of exceptions:

- **Ear-bud headphones**   The most discreet type of headphones and the easiest to fit in a pocket. Most ear buds wedge in your ears like the iPod's ear buds do, but others sit on a headband and poke in sideways.
- **Supra-aural headphones**   These headphones sit on your ears but don't fully cover them. Supra-aural headphones don't block out all ambient noise, which makes them good for situations in which you need to remain aware of the sounds happening around you. They also tend not to get as hot as circumaural headphones, because more air can get to your ears.
- **Circumaural headphones**   These headphones sit over your ears, usually enclosing them fully. *Open* circumaural headphones allow external sounds to reach your ears, whereas *sealed* circumaural headphones block as much external sound as possible. Sealed headphones are good for noisy environments, but even better are noise-canceling circumaural headphones such as Bose's QuietComfort headphones (www.bose.com), which use electronics to reduce the amount of ambient noise that you hear.

Headphones can cost anywhere from a handful of dollars to many hundred dollars. Even ear buds can be impressively expensive: Shure's top-of-the-line set, the SE535 ear buds, cost $549 (www.shure.com), and Etymotic Research, Inc.'s hf5 in-ear phones go for $149 (www.etymotic.com). When choosing headphones, always try them on for comfort and listen to them for as long as possible, using a variety of your favorite music on the iPod, to evaluate their sound as fully as you can.

Whichever type of headphones you choose to use, don't turn the volume up high enough to cause hearing damage. Instead, if you use an iPod often with a high-end pair of headphones, get a headphone amplifier to improve the sound. A headphone amplifier plugs in between the sound source and your headphones to boost and condition the signal. You don't necessarily have to listen to music *louder* through a headphone amplifier—the amplifier can also improve the sound at a lower volume. Many headphone amplifiers are available from various manufacturers, but HeadRoom's Total AirHead and Total BitHead seem especially well regarded (www.headphone.com). You can also find plans on the Web for building your own headphone amplifier.

Use Speakers with Your iPod

Instead of using headphones, you can also connect an iPod to a pair of powered speakers, a receiver or amplifier, or your car stereo. Chapter 6 discusses this topic in detail, but briefly, there are two main ways of making such a connection:

- **Direct connection**   Use a standard cable with a $\frac{1}{8}$-inch stereo headphone connector at the iPod end and the appropriate type of connector at the other end. For example, to connect an iPod to a conventional amplifier, you need two phono plugs on the other end of the cable.
- **Dock connection**   If you have a dock for the iPod, you can get higher-quality sound by connecting the receiver or amplifier to the dock's line-out port instead of the player's headphone port. The line-out port on the dock also gives a consistent level of signal, so you won't need to adjust the volume on the iPod.

Powered speakers are speakers that contain an amplifier, so you don't need to use an external amplifier. Many speaker sets designed for use with portable CD players, MP3 players, and computers are powered speakers. Usually, only one of the speakers contains an amplifier, making one speaker far heavier than the other. Sometimes the amplifier is hidden in the subwoofer, which lets you put the weight on the floor rather than on the furniture.

Your iPod will work with any pair of speakers or stereo that can accept input, but you can also get various speakers designed specifically for iPods. Chapter 5 discusses some of the options and suggests how to choose among them.

Play Music and Video on the iPod classic

This section shows you how to get up to speed with an iPod classic, play music and video, choose settings, and make the most of the iPod's extra features.

Read the iPod classic's Display

The iPod classic has an LCD display that shows nine lines of text and icons as needed. For example, in Figure 4-1, the battery indicator appears in the upper-right corner.

The title bar at the top of the display shows the title of the current screen—for example, "iPod" for the main menu (the top-level menu), "Settings" for the Settings screen, "Now Playing" when the iPod's playing a song, "Cover Flow" when you're browsing using Cover Flow, or "Artists" when you're browsing by artist.

To turn on the display's backlight, hold down the Menu button for a moment. The backlight uses far more power than the LCD screen, so don't use the backlight unnecessarily when you're trying to extract the maximum amount of playing time from a single battery charge. You can configure how long the iPod keeps the backlight on after you press a button (see "Set the Backlight Timer or Auto-Lock," later in this chapter).

FIGURE 4-1   The iPod classic's LCD display contains nine lines of text, graphics, and status icons, such as the battery-status indicator shown here.

Use the iPod classic's Controls

Below the iPod classic's display are the main controls, which you use for accessing songs and playing them back. The control buttons are integrated into the Click wheel, as you see in Figure 4-2.

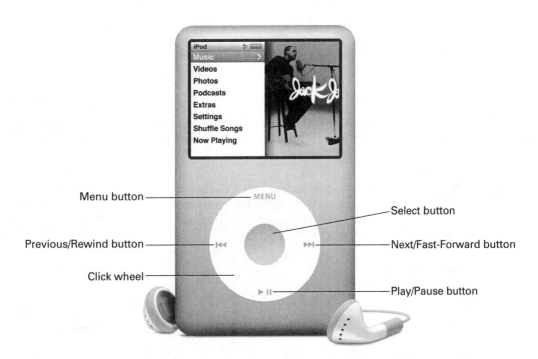

FIGURE 4-2   The control buttons on the iPod classic are integrated into the Click wheel. (Image used courtesy of Apple Inc.)

Use the buttons and the Click wheel as follows:

- Press any button to switch on the iPod classic.
- Press the Menu button to move up to the next level of menus.
- Press the Previous/Rewind button or the Next/Fast-Forward button to navigate from one song to another and to rewind or fast-forward the playing song. Press one of these buttons once (and release it immediately) to issue the Previous command or the Next command. Hold down the button to issue the Rewind command or the Fast-Forward command. The iPod rewinds or fast-forwards slowly at first, but then speeds up if you keep holding down the button.
- Press the Play/Pause button to start playback or to pause it. Hold down the Play/Pause button for three seconds or so to switch off the iPod.
- Press the Select button to select the current menu item.
- Scroll your finger around the Click wheel to move up and down menus, change the volume, or change the place in a song.

The Click wheel adjusts the scrolling speed in response to your finger movements on the Click wheel and the length of time you scroll for: When you're scrolling a long list, it speeds up the scrolling as you continue the scroll, and then slows down as you ease back on the scroll. This behavior makes scrolling even long lists (such as the Songs list, which lists every song on the iPod) swift and comfortable once you get used to it.

Browse and Access Your Music

The iPod classic's menu-driven interface makes browsing and accessing your music as easy as possible on the device's compact display.

Once you've accessed a list of songs—a playlist, an album, or a listing of all songs by an artist or composer—press the Play button to play the list from the start. Alternatively, scroll down to another song, and then press the Play button to start playing from that song.

 You can customize the main menu on the iPod classic (see the "Customize the Main Menu and Music Menu for Quick Access to Items" sidebar for details). This chapter assumes you're using the default menu layout.

Play a Playlist

To access your playlists, choose the Music item and press the Select button, then scroll to the Playlists item and press the Select button again. On the resulting screen, scroll down to the playlist you want to play, and then press the Select button.

Browse Your Music

To browse your music, select the Music item on the main menu. The iPod classic displays the Music menu, which contains entries for the various ways you can browse the songs and other audio items on the iPod.

How to... **Customize the Main Menu and Music Menu for Quick Access to Items**

You can customize the iPod classic's main menu by controlling which items appear on it. By removing items you don't want, and adding items you do want, you can give yourself quicker access to the items you use most. For example, you might want to promote the Playlists item from the Music menu to the main menu, or you might want to put the Screen Lock item on the main menu so that you can lock the iPod's screen more easily.

To customize the main menu, follow these steps:

1. Choose Settings | Main Menu to display the Main Menu screen.
2. Scroll to the item you want to affect.
3. Press the Select button to toggle the item's setting between on (with a check mark next to it) and off (without a check mark).
4. Make further changes as necessary. Then press the Menu button twice to return to the main menu and see the effect of the changes you made.

To reset your main menu to its default settings, choose the Reset Main Menu item at the bottom of the Main Menu screen, and then choose Reset from the Menus screen.

Another way of resetting your main menu is to reset all settings on the iPod by choosing the Reset Settings item at the bottom of the Settings screen. Resetting all settings includes the main menu.

You can also customize the Music menu in a similar way by selecting the Music Menu item on the Settings screen, and then working on the Music Menu screen.

If you listen to many compilation albums—*Ultimate Aerosmith Hits, Lost Stoner Rock of the Desert*, and so on—you may want to add the Compilations item to the Main menu. This makes it much easier to browse your compilations.

Scroll to the browse category you want to use, and then press the Select button to access that category. Here's what you need to know about the browse categories:

- **Cover Flow**   Displays the songs as a sequence of CD covers, as shown here. You can move from one cover to the next by pressing the Previous button or the Next button. To flick through the covers faster, scroll to the left or to the right. When you've highlighted the cover you want, press the Play button to start it playing.

Temple of the Dog
Temple of the Dog

- **Playlists** Displays an alphabetical list of the playlist folders and playlists you have created. To access a playlist within a folder, choose the folder, and then press the Select button to display its contents. Once you've chosen the playlist you want, press either the Select button or the Play button to start it playing.
- **Artists** Displays an alphabetical list of all the songs on the iPod sorted by artist. The first entry, All Albums, displays an alphabetical list of all the albums on the iPod. Otherwise, scroll down to the artist and press the Select button to display a list of the albums by the artist. (If there's only one album, the iPod displays that album's songs immediately.) This menu also has a first entry called All Songs that displays an alphabetical list of all songs by the artist.
- **Albums** Displays an alphabetical list of all the albums on the iPod. Scroll down to the album you want, and then press the Select button to display the songs it contains.

 The data for the artist, album, song title, genre, composer, and so on comes from the tag information in the song file. (See Chapter 7 for instructions on editing the tag information.) An album shows up in the Artists category, the Albums category, the Genre category, or the Composers category even if only one file on the iPod has that album entered in the Album field on its tag. So the entry for an album doesn't necessarily mean that you have that entire album on the iPod—you may have only one song from that album.

- **Songs** Displays an alphabetical list of every song on the iPod. Scroll down to the song you want to play, and then press the Select button to start playing the song.
- **Genres** Displays a list of the genres you've assigned to the music on the iPod. (The iPod builds the list of genres from the Genre field in the tags in AAC files, Apple Lossless Encoding files, and MP3 files.) Scroll to a genre, and then press the Select button to display the artists whose albums are tagged with that genre. You can then navigate to albums and songs by an artist.
- **Composers** Displays a list of the composers for the songs on the iPod. (The iPod builds the list of composers from the Composer field in the tags in the song files.) Scroll to a composer, and then press the Select button to display a list of the songs by that composer.
- **Audiobooks** Displays a list of the audiobooks on the iPod. (The iPod can play audiobooks in the Audible format, which you can buy either from the iTunes Store or from the Audible.com website.) Scroll down to the audiobook you want, and then press the Select button to start it playing.
- **Search** Displays a screen for searching by strings of text you dial in using the Click wheel—for example, the key word in a song title. Searching initially seems clumsy, but once you get the hang of it, you may find it a handy way to find songs whose full names escape you.

| How to... | **Use the Composers Category Effectively to Find Music** |

The Composers category is primarily useful for classical music, because these songs may be tagged with the name of the recording artist rather than that of the composer. For example, an album of The Fargo Philharmonic playing Beethoven's *Ninth Symphony* might list The Fargo Philharmonic as the artist and Beethoven as the composer. By using the Composers category, you can access the works by composer: Bach, Beethoven, Brahms, and so on.

But there's no reason why you shouldn't use the Composers category to access nonclassical songs as well. For example, you could use the Composers category to quickly access all your Nick Drake cover versions as well as Drake's own recordings of his songs. The only disadvantage to doing so is that the tag information for many CDs in the online CD Database (CDDB) that iTunes uses doesn't include an entry in the Composer field, so you'll need to add this information if you want to use it. In this case, you may be better off using iTunes to create a playlist that contains the songs you want in the order you prefer.

There's also no reason why you should confine the contents of the Composer field to information about composers. By editing the tags manually, you can add to the Composer fields any information by which you want to be able to sort songs on your iPod.

Create a Playlist on the iPod classic

As well as synchronizing playlists from iTunes, you can create a playlist directly on the iPod classic. This is called the On-The-Go playlist, and you create it like this:

1. If you've previously created an On-The-Go playlist, decide whether to clear it or add to it. To clear it, choose Music | Playlists | On-The-Go | Clear Playlist | Clear.
2. Navigate to the song, album, artist, or playlist you want to add to the playlist.
3. Press the Select button and hold it down until the item's name starts flashing.
4. Repeat Steps 2 and 3 for each additional item that you want to add to the On-The-Go playlist.

To play your On-The-Go playlist, choose Playlists | On-The-Go. (Until you create an On-The-Go playlist, selecting this item displays an explanation of what the On-The-Go playlist does.)

To save your On-The-Go playlist under a different name, choose Playlists | On-The-Go | Save Playlist. The iPod saves the playlist under the name *New Playlist 1* (or *New Playlist 2*, or the next available number). After synchronizing the iPod with iTunes, click the playlist in the Source list, wait a moment and click it again, type the new name, and then press ENTER (Windows) or RETURN (Mac).

Play Songs

Playing songs on the iPod classic is straightforward. The following sections tell you what you need to know.

Start and Pause Play

To start playing a song, take either of the following actions:

- Navigate to the song, and then press the Play/Pause button or the Select button.
- Navigate to a playlist or an album, and then press the Play/Pause button or the Select button.

To pause, press the Play/Pause button. Press again to resume playback.

Change the Volume

To change the volume, scroll counterclockwise (to reduce the volume) or clockwise (to increase it) from the Now Playing screen. The volume bar at the bottom of the screen shows the volume setting as it changes (see Figure 4-3).

Change the Place in a Song

As well as fast-forwarding through a song by using the Next/Fast-Forward button, or rewinding through a song by using the Previous/Rewind button, you can *scrub* through a song to quickly change the location.

FIGURE 4-3   Scroll counterclockwise or clockwise to change the volume from the Now Playing screen.

Scrubbing can be easier than fast-forwarding or rewinding because the iPod displays a readout of how far through the song the playing location currently is. Scrubbing is also more peaceful, because whereas Next/Fast-Forward and Previous/Rewind play blips of the parts of the song you're passing through (to help you locate the passage you want), scrubbing keeps the song playing until you indicate you've reached the part you're interested in.

To scrub through a song, follow these steps:

1. Display the Now Playing screen.
2. Press the Select button to display the scroll bar (see Figure 4-4).
3. Scroll counterclockwise to move backward through the song or clockwise to move forward through the song.
4. Press the Select button to cancel the display of the scroll bar, or wait a few seconds for the iPod to cancel its display automatically.

To display the lyrics for the currently playing song (if it contains lyrics), press the Select button twice from the Now Playing screen. Scroll down to see more lyrics (if there are more). Press the Select button again to access the Ratings screen, again to reach the repeat-mode screen, and press it once more to return to the Now Playing screen. Some artists include lyrics in song files distributed online, but you'll need to add them yourself to other files or to files you rip from your CDs.

Rate a Song as You Play It

To assign a rating to the song that's currently playing, follow these steps:

1. Display the Now Playing screen if it's not currently displayed. For example, from the main screen, scroll to the Now Playing item, and then press the Select button.

FIGURE 4-4   To "scrub" forward or backward through the current song, press the Select button, and then scroll clockwise (to go forward) or counterclockwise (to go backward).

2. Press the Select button three times. (If the song has no CD cover art, you need only press twice.) The iPod displays five hollow dots under the song's name on the Now Playing screen.
3. Scroll to the right to display the appropriate number of stars in place of the five dots. Then press the Select button to apply the rating.

The iPod synchronizes the rating with iTunes at the next synchronization.

Use the Hold Switch

The Hold switch (also called the Lock switch), located on the top of the iPod classic, locks the iPod controls in their current configuration. The Hold switch helps protect the controls against being bumped in active environments—for example, when you're exercising at the gym or barging your way onto a packed bus or subway train. When the Hold switch is pushed to the Hold side so that the orange underlay shows, the iPod is on hold.

The Hold switch is equally useful for keeping music playing without unintended interruptions and for keeping your iPod locked in the Off position, which prevents the battery from being drained by the iPod being switched on accidentally when you're carrying it.

If your iPod seems to stop responding to its other controls, check first that the Hold switch isn't on.

Navigate the Extras Menu

The Extras menu provides access to the iPod classic's Clocks, Calendars, Contacts, Alarms, Games, Notes, Screen Lock, and Stopwatch features:

- To use the iPod's clock features, scroll to the Clocks item on the Extras menu, and then press the Select button. On the first Clock screen, which lists the clocks already configured, select the clock you want, or press the Select button to pop up a panel that allows you to add a new clock or either edit or delete an existing clock.
- To use the calendars, scroll to the Calendars item on the Extras menu, and then press the Select button. The iPod displays the list of calendars you've synchronized with the iPod (see Chapter 3 for instructions on how to do this). Scroll to the calendar you want and press the Select button to display the calendar in month view. Scroll to access the day you're interested in, and then press the Select button to display the events listed for that day. The one-month display shows empty squares for days that have no events scheduled and dots for days that have one or more events. If the day contains more appointments than will fit on the iPod's display, scroll up and down.
- To access a contact, scroll to the Contacts item on the Extras menu, and then press the Select button. On the Contacts screen, scroll to the contact, and then press the Select button.

- To play the games included with the iPod, scroll to the Games item on the Extras menu, and then press the Select button. From the Games menu, scroll to the game you want, and then press the Select button.

 You can buy further games for your iPod from the iTunes Store. Not all games work on all iPod models, so before you buy a game, verify that it supports your iPod model.

- To access your text notes, scroll to the Notes item on the Extras menu, and then press the Select button.

Choose Settings for the iPod classic

This section shows you how to choose settings on an iPod classic. Start by displaying the Settings screen like this:

1. Press the Menu button however many times it takes to display the main menu.
2. Scroll down to the Settings item.
3. Press the Select button.

Check the "About" Information

To see the iPod's details, scroll to the About item, and then press the Select button. Press the Select button to move on to the second About screen, and then press again to display the third About screen.

The About screen (or screens) includes the following information:

- The number of songs, videos, photos, podcasts, games, contacts, and other items the iPod contains
- The device's capacity and the amount of space available
- The device's name, serial number, and model
- The version number of the device's software
- Whether the iPod is formatted for Windows or for the Mac (at the end of the Version readout)

Apply Shuffle Settings to Randomize Songs or Albums

Instead of playing the songs in the current list in their usual order, you can tell the iPod to shuffle them into a random order. To do so, scroll to the Shuffle setting on the Settings menu and press the Select button to choose the Shuffle setting you want:

- **Off**   This is the default setting. The songs play in the order they appear in the album or playlist.
- **Songs**   Choose Songs to shuffle the songs in the album or playlist you're playing.
- **Albums**   Choose Albums to shuffle the albums by your chosen artist or composer into a random order.

Repeat One Song or All Songs

Instead of playing each song just once, you can either repeat a single song or repeat all the songs in the current album or playlist. Scroll to the Repeat items on the Settings menu, and then press the Select button to choose One (to repeat the current song), All (to repeat all the songs in the current list), or Off (to turn repeating off).

Set the Volume Limit

To prevent the iPod classic from playing back audio too loudly, follow these steps:

1. Connect the headphones that you (or the listener) will use. Different headphones give different levels of output, so it's best to use the same set you or the listener will use.
2. Set a song playing.
3. Display the Settings screen.
4. Scroll to the Volume Limit item, and then press the Select button to display the Volume Limit screen.
5. Scroll to set the maximum audio volume, and then press the Play button. The Enter Combination screen appears.
6. Dial each of the four digits to create the combination number for locking the volume limit, pressing the Select button after choosing each digit.
7. After you press the Select button for the last digit, the iPod applies the volume limit and displays the Settings screen again.

Set the Backlight Timer or Auto-Lock

To customize the length of time that the display backlight stays on after you press one of the iPod's controls, follow these steps:

1. Display the Settings screen.
2. Scroll to the Backlight option.
3. Press the Select button to display the Backlight screen.
4. Select the option you want:
   - **Off**   Keeps the backlight off until you turn it on manually by holding down the Menu button for a second.
   - **2 Seconds, 5 Seconds, 10 Seconds, 20 Seconds, or 30 Seconds**   Keeps the backlight on for this length of time.
   - **Always On**   Keeps the backlight on until you turn it off.

   The Always On setting is useful when you're using your iPod as a sound source in a place that's too dark to see the display without the backlight and when you need to change the music frequently—for example, when you're DJing. The disadvantage is that the iPod gets through battery power surprisingly quickly.

Set the Screen Brightness

To control the screen brightness, scroll to the Brightness item, press the Select button, and then select the brightness you want on the Brightness screen.

Change the Speed at Which Audiobooks Play

If you listen to audiobooks on an iPod, you may want to make them play faster or slower. To do so, scroll to the Audiobooks item, press Select, and then choose Slower, Normal, or Faster, as needed.

Choose Equalizations to Make Your Music Sound Better

The iPod classic contains a graphical equalizer—a device that alters the sound of music by changing the level of different frequency bands. Here are two examples of how equalizations work:

- A typical equalization for rock music boosts the lowest bass frequencies and most of the treble frequencies, while reducing some of the midrange frequencies. The normal effect of this arrangement is to punch up the drums, bass, and vocals, making the music sound more dynamic.
- A typical equalization for classical music leaves the bass frequencies and midrange frequencies at their normal levels while reducing the treble frequencies, producing a mellow effect overall and helping avoid having the brass section blast the top off of your head.

The iPod classic includes the following equalizations, which are also built into iTunes: Acoustic, Bass Booster, Bass Reducer, Classical, Dance, Deep, Electronic, Flat, Hip Hop, Jazz, Latin, Loudness, Lounge, Piano, Pop, R & B, Rock, Small Speakers, Spoken Word, Treble Booster, Treble Reducer, and Vocal Booster. You might long for a Vocal Reducer setting for some artists or for karaoke, but the iPod doesn't provide one.

The names of most of these equalizations indicate their intended usage clearly, but Flat and Small Speakers deserve a word of explanation:

- Flat is an equalization with all the sliders at their midpoints—an equalization that applies no filtering to any of the frequency bands. If you don't usually use an equalization, there's no point in applying Flat to a song, because the effect is the same as not using an equalization. But if you *do* use an equalization for most of your songs, you can apply Flat to individual songs to turn off the equalization while they play.
- Small Speakers is for use with small loudspeakers. This equalization boosts the frequency bands that are typically lost by smaller loudspeakers. If you listen to the iPod through portable speakers, you may want to try this equalization for general listening. Its effect is to reduce the treble and enhance the bass.

Don't take the names of the equalizations too literally, because those you find best will depend on your ears, your earphones or speakers, and the type of music you listen to. For example, if you find trip-hop sounds best played with the Classical equalization, don't scorn the Classical equalization because of its name. Or you may prefer to use different equalizations even for different songs that belong to the same genre—or even to the same CD.

To apply an equalization, follow these steps:

1. Display the Settings menu.
2. Scroll to the EQ menu item.
3. Press the Select button to display the EQ screen.
4. Scroll to the Equalization you want. A graphical representation of the equalization appears on the right, giving you an idea of the frequency settings.
5. Press the Select button to apply the equalization.

Choose Off at the top of the EQ list if you want to turn equalizations off.

Specifying an equalization like this works well enough when you need to adjust the sound balance for the music you're playing during a listening session. But if you want to use different equalizations for the different songs in a playlist, set the equalization for each song in iTunes, as described in the section "Specify an Equalization for an Individual Item" in Chapter 10. iTunes and the iPod then apply this equalization each time you play back the song.

Use Sound Check to Standardize the Volume

Sound Check is a feature for normalizing the volume of different songs so you don't have to crank up the volume to hear a song encoded at a low volume and then suffer ear damage because the next song was recorded at a far higher volume.

To set Sound Check, scroll to the Sound Check item on the Settings menu, and then press the Select button to toggle Sound Check on or off.

For Sound Check to work on the iPod, you must also turn on the Sound Check feature in iTunes. Press CTRL-COMMA or choose Edit | Preferences to display the iTunes dialog box in Windows, or press ⌘-COMMA or choose iTunes | Preferences on the Mac to display the Preferences dialog box. Click the Playback tab to display its controls. Select the Sound Check check box, and then click the OK button to close the dialog box. iTunes then scans through the songs in your library and determines the loudest point of each, so that it knows how much to damp them down during playback.

Turn the Clicker Off

By default, the iPod classic plays a clicking sound as you move the Click wheel, to give you feedback. You can turn off this clicking sound if you don't like it. Choose Settings | Clicker | Off.

Set the Date and Time

You can set the date and time, or switch between using the 12-hour clock and the 24-hour clock, by choosing Extras | Date And Time.

 On the iPod classic, you can display the time in the title bar by setting the Time In Title item on the Date & Time screen to On.

Choose How to Sort and Display Your Contacts

The iPod classic can sort your contacts either by first name or by last name. Usually, you'll want to sort by "Last, First" so that your contacts appear in alphabetical order by last name, but you can also sort by "First, Last" if you prefer to have the contacts in alphabetical order by first name.

To control how the iPod classic sorts your contacts, scroll to the Sort By item on the Settings screen, and then press the Select button to toggle between First (sorting the contacts by their first names) and Last (sorting them by their last names).

Lull Yourself to Sleep with a Sleep Timer

Here's how to set music to play for a length of time and then switch off—for example, when you're going to sleep:

1. Choose Extras | Alarms to display the Alarms screen.
2. Choose Sleep Timer and press the Select button.
3. Scroll to the number of minutes (15, 30, 60, 90, or 120), and then press the Select button.
4. The Sleep Timer starts running. Set your music running, and it will play until the timer runs out.

 To turn off the Sleep Timer, access the Sleep screen again, and then select the Off setting.

Set an Alarm to Wake You Up or Remind You of an Appointment

Before you lull yourself to sleep, you may also want to set an alarm to blast yourself awake using a playlist of your choice. Or you may simply want to set an alarm for a mustn't-miss appointment.

To use the Alarm Clock on the iPod classic, follow these steps:

1. Create a custom playlist for waking up if you like (or create several—one for each day of the week, maybe). If you don't have your computer at hand, and the iPod doesn't contain a suitable playlist, create an On-The-Go playlist on the iPod.
2. Choose Extras | Alarms, and then choose Create Alarm to display the Alarm Clock screen.
3. Scroll to the Alarm item, and then press the Select button to toggle the alarm on or off, as appropriate.
4. Scroll to the Date item, and then press the Select button to access a screen on which you can set the date for the alarm.
5. Scroll to the Time item, and then press the Select button to access a screen on which you can set the time for the alarm.
6. If you want the alarm to repeat, scroll to the Repeat item, and then press the Select button to access a screen on which you can set up repeating. The default is Once (in other words, without repeating), but you can also choose Every Day, Weekdays, Weekends, Every Week, Every Month, or Every Year.
7. Scroll to the Sound item, and then press the Select button to display a screen on which you can choose between Tones and Playlists. If you just want a beep, select the Tones item, and then select the Beep item on the following screen. More likely, you'll want a playlist—in which case, select the Playlists item, and then choose the playlist on the resulting screen.
8. If you want to name the alarm, scroll to the Label item, and then press the Select button to access a screen on which you can choose from various predefined labels—for example, Wake Up, Work, Class, or Prescription.
9. If you're setting an alarm to wake you, connect the iPod to your speakers or stereo (unless you sleep with headphones on), and then go to sleep. Otherwise, use the iPod as normal.

When the appointed time arrives, the iPod wakes itself (if it's sleeping) and then unleashes the alarm.

 The iPod classic can remind you of appointments in your calendar when their times arrive. Choose Extras | Calendars, scroll down to the Alarms item, and then press the Select button. Choose the Beep setting for Alarms to receive a beep and a message on the screen. Choose the None setting to receive only the message. Choose the Off setting to receive neither the beep nor the message.

Use the iPod classic as a Stopwatch

You can also use the iPod classic as a stopwatch. To access the Stopwatch feature, choose Extras | Stopwatch, and then press the Select button.

Lock the iPod classic with a Passcode

To protect the contents of the iPod classic, you can lock it with a four-digit passcode. Follow these steps:

1. Choose Extras | Screen Lock to display the Screen Lock screen.
2. Dial the four-digit code you want by scrolling each number in turn to the appropriate digit, and then pressing the Select button.
3. Reenter the passcode on the Confirm Combination screen, and then press the Select button. The iPod returns you to the Screen Lock screen.
4. Select the Lock button, and then press the Select button to lock the iPod.

Now you must enter the passcode before you can use the iPod again.

 If you forget your combination, all shouldn't be lost: Just connect the iPod to its home computer, and it unlocks. But if this doesn't work (don't ask why not), you'll need to restore the device's software to unlock it. See Chapter 15 for instructions on restoring the software.

Play Music on the iPod nano

The iPod nano has an LCD touch screen that you use to navigate the iPod's contents and control playback. When you start the iPod nano by pressing the Sleep/Wake button on the top for a few seconds, the iPod nano displays the first home screen.

The home screen shows four icons at a time, as you see in Figure 4-5. To reach other icons, you swipe your finger from right to left (displaying the next home screen) or from left to right (displaying the previous home screen). The black dots

FIGURE 4-5   The iPod nano displays the home screen. Tap an icon to access that feature, or swipe your finger to the left or the right to access other features.

at the bottom of the display show how many home screens there are. The white dot indicates the home screen you're viewing at the moment.

To open an item, you tap its icon on the home screen. For example, tap the Artists icon to display the list of artists, and then tap the artist whose works you want to browse. Flick your finger up to scroll down the list of items, or flick down to scroll back up. Tap an album to open it, and then tap the song you want to play.

Apart from Artists, you can browse your songs and other audio content by the following categories:

- **Playlists**   Playlists you've synced to the iPod nano from iTunes and playlists you create on the iPod nano itself, as discussed in the section "Create a Playlist on the iPod nano," later in this chapter.
- **Genius Mixes**   Genius Mixes you've synced to the iPod nano from iTunes or created on the iPod nano, as discussed in the section "Create a Genius Mix on the iPod nano," later in this chapter.
- **Podcasts**   Podcasts you've synced from iTunes.
- **Songs**   The full list of songs on the iPod nano, in alphabetical order.
- **Albums**   The full list of albums on the iPod nano, in alphabetical order.
- **Genres**   The genres of the songs the iPod nano contains.
- **Composers**   The composers of the songs. A song is assigned to a composer only if the song file has an entry in the Composer tag. See the sidebar "Use the Composers Category Effectively to Find Music," earlier in this chapter, for more information on using the Composer tag.
- **iTunes U**   Any iTunes U collections you've synced from iTunes. This icon appears only when you've synced one or more iTunes U collections.
- **Audiobooks**   Any audiobooks you've synced from iTunes. This icon appears only when you've synced audiobooks.

To control the playback volume, you press the Volume Up button or the Volume Down button on the top of the iPod nano. To control other aspects of playback, tap the screen to display the playback controls. You can then control playback as follows:

- **Pause and resume playback**   Tap the Pause button to pause playback. Tap the Play button to resume playback.
- **Fast-forward through the song**   Tap and hold the Fast-Forward/Next button until you reach the point in the song you want to play from.
- **Play the next song**   Tap the Fast-Forward/Next button once.
- **Rewind through the song**   Tap and hold the Rewind/Previous button until you reach the point in the song you want to play from.
- **Play the previous song**   Tap the Rewind/Previous button once.

To move to a different point in the song, swipe your finger left across the screen again to display the next screen of playback controls. Tap the playhead on the scrubber bar, and then drag the playhead to the right or to the left.

When you drag the playhead on the scrubber bar, it moves in large increments at first. To make the playhead move in smaller increments, slide your finger up so that it is above the scrubber bar. The farther your finger is above the scrubber bar, the smaller the increments as you drag the playhead to the right or to the left.

To view the song's lyrics (if they are in the song file), swipe your finger left across the screen again to display the next screen of playback information.

After you start a song playing, the iPod nano automatically turns off its backlight to save power. When you need to see the screen again, press the Sleep/Wake button briefly. When the backlight is on, you can press the Sleep/Wake button briefly to turn it off.

How to... Rearrange the Icons on the iPod nano's Home Screens

To make your iPod nano work your way, you can rearrange the icons on the home screen, putting the icons you use the most right at your fingertips.

To rearrange the icons, follow these steps:

1. Display the home screen.
2. Tap and hold any icon on the home screen until the icons start to jiggle.
3. Drag the icons into your preferred arrangement. You can drag an icon off the side of the screen to reach another home screen.
4. When you've finished rearranging the icons, press the Sleep/Wake button. The iPod nano saves your new arrangement.

If you want to restore the icons to their original positions on the home screens, reset all the iPod nano's settings. Follow these steps:

1. Display the home screen.
2. Tap Settings to display the Settings screen.
3. Scroll up to reach the bottom of the screen.
4. Tap Reset Settings. A confirmation screen appears.
5. Tap Reset to reset the settings. The iPod nano displays the screen for choosing your language.
6. Tap the language you want to use.
7. Tap Done.

Use the Equalizer

To change the sound of music, you can apply a graphical equalization. To do so, follow these steps:

1. Display the home screen.
2. Tap Settings to display the Settings screen.
3. Tap Music to display the Music screen.
4. Tap EQ to display the EQ screen.
5. Tap the equalizer preset you want to use.

Use Sound Check to Standardize the Volume

Sound Check is a feature for normalizing the volume of different songs so that you don't have to keep turning the volume up and down. Sound Check can help you avoid getting your ears blasted by louder songs, but you may find that it robs the songs of their dynamic range and appeal.

To turn Sound Check on or off, follow these steps:

1. Display the home screen.
2. Tap Settings to display the Settings screen.
3. Tap Music to display the Music screen.
4. Move the Sound Check switch to the On position or the Off position, as needed.

For Sound Check to work on the iPod, you must also turn on the Sound Check feature in iTunes. Press CTRL-COMMA or choose Edit | Preferences to display the iTunes dialog box in Windows, or press ⌘-COMMA or choose iTunes | Preferences on the Mac to display the Preferences dialog box. Click the Playback tab to display its controls. Select the Sound Check check box, and then click the OK button to close the dialog box. iTunes then scans through the songs in your library and determines the loudest point of each, so that it knows how much to damp them down during playback.

Create a Playlist on the iPod nano

The easiest way to create playlists for the iPod nano is by working in iTunes and then synchronizing the playlists to the iPod nano. But you can also create playlists on the iPod nano when you need to. Follow these steps:

1. Display the home screen.
2. Tap Playlists to open the Playlists screen.
3. Flick your finger down to display the top of the screen.

4. Tap the Add button to start the new playlist. The iPod names the playlist New Playlist 1.

You can't rename the new playlist while it's on the iPod nano. But when you synchronize the iPod with your computer, the playlist appears in iTunes. You can then rename the playlist in iTunes. The change carries through to the playlist on the iPod nano at the next sync.

5. Tap each item you want to add to the playlist. For example, tap Songs to display the list of songs, and then tap each song. You can also add entire albums or existing playlists if you want.
6. Tap the Done button.

You can edit a playlist by opening it from the Playlists screen, flicking your finger down, and then tapping the Edit button. Tap the Remove (–) button next to each item you want to remove, and then tap the Delete button. Tap the Done button when you have finished editing the playlist.

Create a Genius Mix on the iPod nano

As long as you've turned on Genius in iTunes, you can also create Genius Mixes on the iPod nano. Follow these steps:

1. Start playing the song on which you want to base the Genius Mix.
2. Tap the album artwork to display the play controls.
3. Swipe your finger to the left, and then tap the Genius symbol. The iPod nano creates the Genius Mix.
4. Flick your finger up to look at the list of songs the Genius has produced.
5. If you want the Genius to try again, tap the Refresh button at the top of the screen.
6. When the Genius Mix is to your satisfaction, tap the Save button.

Rate a Song as You Play It

To assign a rating to the song that's currently playing, follow these steps:

1. Display the Now Playing screen if it's not currently displayed. For example, tap the Now Playing icon on the home screen.
2. Tap the album artwork to display the play controls.
3. Tap the Info button to display the information screen.
4. Tap the rating at the top of the screen.

The iPod synchronizes the rating with iTunes at the next synchronization.

Play Radio on the iPod nano

The iPod nano includes a built-in radio tuner, so you can listen to radio stations whenever you've got the iPod with you. To play a radio station, follow these steps:

1. Connect the headphone cord. This acts as the radio antenna, so you can't listen to radio stations without it.
2. Go to the home screen that contains the Radio icon.
3. Tap the Radio icon. The radio controls appear.
4. Tap the right-arrow button to tune to your next favorite station or the next tunable station up the dial. Tap the left-arrow button to tune to your previous favorite or the next tunable station down the dial.

 To tune manually to a particular station, tap the tuner dial, and then drag the red line to the left or right until you reach the station's frequency.

5. When you find a radio station that you want to make a favorite, tap the star button.
6. Tap the Stop button when you want to stop playback.
7. Press the Sleep/Wake button twice in quick succession to skip to the next radio station the iPod can find.

 The radio screen displays HD radio information (such as the artist's name and the song title) if it's available.

Use the Clock Feature

To keep track of time with your iPod nano, use the Clock feature. Apart from telling the time, the Clock includes a stopwatch and a timer.

Display the Time

Tap the Clock icon on the home screen to display the Clock feature. At first, you see the Clock screen, which shows the time, day, and date.

 If you want to use your iPod nano as a clock, you can set it to display the clock on waking. Go to the home screen, tap Settings, and then tap General. On the General screen, tap Date & Time to display the Date & Time screen. Move the Time On Wake switch to the On position. You can also tap the Clock Face item and choose between White and Black for the color of the clock face.

FIGURE 4-6   The iPod nano's stopwatch includes lap times.

Use the Stopwatch

From the Clock screen, swipe your finger left to display the Stopwatch controls (shown on the left in Figure 4-6). You can then record times and laps:

1. Tap the Start button to start timing. The timer runs, as shown on the right in Figure 4-6.
2. Tap the Lap button to record a lap time. You can then tap the button in the upper-right corner to display the lap time.
3. Tap the Stop button to stop timing.
4. Tap the Reset button to reset the stopwatch to zero.

Use the Timer

From the Clock screen, swipe your finger left twice to display the Timer screen (shown here). You can then set a timer like this:

1. Spin the dials to set the length of time.
2. Tap the i button in the lower-right corner to display the list of alert sounds.
3. Tap the sound you want to use.
4. Tap the Set button to return to the Timer screen.
5. Tap the Start button to set the timer running.

Play Music on the iPod shuffle

With no screen, the iPod shuffle needs only a limited set of controls for playing music (see Figure 4-7). These are largely intuitive but have a couple of hidden tricks:

- To start playing the songs on the iPod shuffle in the order of the playlist, move the mode switch on the top of the iPod shuffle to play mode, and then press the Play/Pause button.

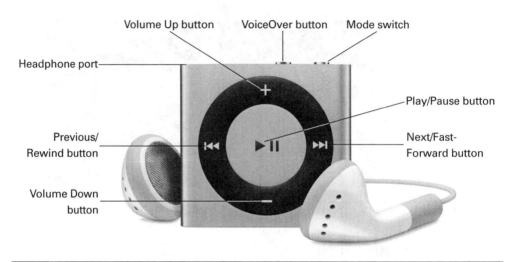

Volume Up button   VoiceOver button   Mode switch

Headphone port

Previous/
Rewind button

Volume Down
button

Play/Pause button

Next/Fast-
Forward button

FIGURE 4-7   The iPod shuffle's limited set of controls includes a couple of hidden tricks. (Image used courtesy of Apple Inc.)

    If the iPod shuffle blinks green and amber several times in succession when you press the Play/Pause button, it probably contains no songs. Move the mode switch to the Off position, wait for five seconds or more, move the switch back to the On position, and press the Play/Pause button again. If you see green and amber blinking again, connect the iPod shuffle to your computer and make sure that some songs are loaded on it.

- To start playing the songs in random order, move the mode switch to shuffle mode, and then press the Play/Pause button. When you hit a part of the playlist that you want to hear in sequence, you can move the mode switch to play mode to continue in sequence.
- Press the Play/Pause button three times in immediate succession to move to the start of the playlist. To get to the end of the playlist, press the Play/Pause button three times, and then press the Previous/Rewind button once.

    When the iPod shuffle is in shuffle mode and you move to the beginning of the playlist, it shuffles the playlist again.

- Press the Next/Fast-Forward button to skip to the next song. Hold it down to fast-forward through the song.

    When the iPod shuffle is paused, you can press the Next/Fast-Forward button to start the next song playing, or press the Previous/Rewind button to start the previous song playing. The iPod shuffle doesn't remain paused when you press the Next/Fast-Forward button or the Previous/Rewind button, unlike other iPod models.

- Press the Previous/Rewind button to return to the start of the current song; press it again to go to the start of the previous song. Hold the button down to rewind through the current song.
- Press the Volume Up button to increase the volume, or press the Volume Down button to decrease the volume.
- To put the iPod shuffle on hold, hold down the Play/Pause button for several seconds. The top light gives three orange blinks to indicate that hold is applied. To remove hold, press the Play/Pause button for several seconds again until the status light blinks green.
- To reset the iPod shuffle, turn it off, wait five seconds, and then turn it on again.

 If, when you press a button on the iPod shuffle, you see only the top light blink orange, it means that the iPod shuffle is on hold. Hold down the Play/Pause button for several seconds until the orange light blinks three times to take it off hold.

- The iPod shuffle's lights give you feedback on the battery's status, as explained in the following table.

Battery Light Color	Battery Status
Green (when in dock)	30 percent or more charge
Amber (bottom light, when in dock)	10 to 30 percent charge
Red (bottom light, when in dock)	Critically low (less than 10 percent)—needs more charging
No light (bottom light, when in dock)	No charge
Blinking red (top light, while playing)	Critically low—recharge at once

- To announce the current song and artist, press the VoiceOver button, the button in the middle of the top of the iPod shuffle.
- To change the playlist, hold down the VoiceOver button so that the iPod shuffle announces the current song and artist, but keep holding the button down until the iPod announces the current playlist. Release the button. Wait until the iPod announces the playlist you want, and then press the VoiceOver button again.

5

Get More Out of Your iPod with Hardware Accessories

HOW TO...

- Approach buying accessories the right way
- Select cases for your iPod
- Learn about power adapters and car adapters for your iPod
- Choose iPod stands, docks, and speakers
- Choose a radio transmitter

Like many consumer products that have been a runaway success, the iPods have spawned a huge market for accessories—from cases to stands, from microphones for input to speakers or radio transmitters for output. Apple makes some of the accessories, and third-party companies make far more. Some of these accessories are widely useful (although you may not need any of them yourself). Others are niche products, some of which are for very small niches.

This chapter discusses the major categories of accessories (leaving you to choose the types you need) and highlights some of the less obvious and more innovative accessories that you might want to know about for special needs. This chapter focuses on the iPod classic, sixth-generation iPod nano, and fourth-generation iPod shuffle.

Approach Buying Accessories for Your iPod

Before you buy any accessory for your iPod, run a quick reality check:

- *Do you really need the accessory, or is it just cool or cute?* These are your dollars, so this is your decision.
- *Is there a less expensive alternative?* For some types of accessories, such as power adapters and cassette adapters, you don't need to restrict your horizons to iPod-specific accessories—you can choose generic accessories as well. Often, generic

accessories are substantially less expensive than custom accessories, give you much more flexibility, or both.

- *Will this accessory work only with your current iPod, or will it work with other devices you may buy in the future?* (You can be sure that Apple will release such compelling new iPods, iPads, and iPhones that you'll want to upgrade sooner or later.) For example, if you get a radio transmitter designed for the iPod nano only, you'll need to upgrade the transmitter as well if you buy an iPod touch or an iPhone. In this case, buying a perhaps less stylish but more flexible accessory might make better financial sense.

Cases

Your iPod is built to be carried, so it's hardly surprising that a wide variety of cases has been developed for the various models—everything from bifold cases to armband cases to armored cases and waterproof cases. Early iPod models came with sturdy cases in the box—those were the days!—but Apple has dropped the cases along with the prices, so the first accessory you might need is a protective case for your iPod.

 Many stores sell iPod cases, but at this writing, the prime sources are the Apple Store (http://store.apple.com), Amazon.com (www.amazon.com), eBay (www.ebay.com), and the stores searchable through iLounge (http://ilounge.pricegrabber.com).

The Apple Store has user ratings for most cases, which can help you weed out superficially attractive losers.

Choosing a Case

Choosing a case is as fiercely personal as choosing comfortable underwear or choosing a car. Different aspects of cases are important to different people, and although one size may suit many, it doesn't fit all. As with underwear (or a car), you may prefer not to use a case at all—but the iPod's shiny surfaces will tend to get scratched, and you'll need to be careful not to drop the device onto any unforgiving surface.

But as with underwear (and, to a lesser extent, a car), it's vital to make sure the case you choose is the right size for the model of iPod you have. For example:

- **iPod classic** The latest version is slimmer than some of its predecessors that used the same name.
- **iPod nano** Each of the six generations has a different size and shape.
- **iPod shuffle** Each of the four generations has a different size and shape.

Beyond getting the size right, the remaining choices are yours. The following paragraphs summarize the key ways in which the cases differ. You get to decide which points are important for you:

- **How the case attaches to you (if at all)**   Many cases attach to your belt, whereas some hook on to a lanyard that goes around your neck or a strap that goes over your shoulder. Still others attach to an armband, which some people find better for performing vigorous activities. Some cases come with a variety of attachments—for example, a belt clip and an armband, or a mounting for sticking the iPod to a flat surface. Other cases are simply protective, designed to be carried in a pocket or a bag.
- **The amount of protection the case provides**   In general, the more protection a case provides, the larger and uglier it is, the more it weighs, and the more it costs. Balance your need for style against the iPod's need for protection when gravity gets the better of your grip.
- **Whether or not the case is waterproof**   If you plan to take the iPod outdoors for exercise, you may want to get a case that's water-resistant or waterproof. Alternatively, carry a sturdy plastic bag in your pocket for weather emergencies. Either way, protect the device's Dock Connector port and headphone port.
- **Whether or not the case lets you access the iPod's controls**   Access to the controls is pretty vital unless you have a remote control for the iPod, in which case your need to access the controls once you've set the music playing will be much less. Generally speaking, the more waterproof the case, the less access it offers to the controls—although some case makers have been more successful than others at letting you reach the iPod's buttons and sensitive parts.
- **Whether or not the case can hold your iPod's headphones and remote control**   If you'll be toting your iPod in a bag or pocket, a case that can hold the ear-bud headphones and remote control as well as the player itself may be a boon. You may even want a case that can accommodate a USB cable and power adapter for traveling. But if you're more interested in a case that straps firmly to your body and holds your iPod securely, you probably won't want the case to devote extra space to store other objects.

If you're looking for an inexpensive case that'll take your iPod's complete entourage, consider the type of case designed for portable CD players and built into a padded belt.

- **Whether or not you need to take your iPod out of the case to dock or recharge it**   Some cases are designed to give you access to the Dock Connector port, so you can leave the iPod in the case unless you need to admire it. With more protective cases, usually you need to remove the iPod more often.
- **What the case is made of and how much it costs**   Snug cases tend to be made of silicone or neoprene. Impressive cases tend to be made of leather or armor. Leather and armor cost more than lesser materials.
- **Whether the case is single-purpose or multipurpose**   Most cases are designed for carrying, either in your pocket or attached to your belt or clothing. Some cases convert to mount the iPod in your car or home.

When shopping for a case, look for special-value bundles that include other accessories you need—for example, a car cassette adapter or cables for connecting the iPod to a stereo.

Examples of Cases

Most manufacturers who make cases worth having produce a range of them for most or all current models of iPod. Here are examples of interesting cases you may want to look at.

Rugged-Lifestyle Cases

When delicate electronics meet a rugged lifestyle, the results are often unfortunate— but who can leave their communications and entertainment behind just because reality can be harsh?

If you take your iPod classic anyplace you and it may get dunked in water, look at waterproof cases such as the MP3 Case + Headphones from Aquapac International (http://store.aquapac.net/explore-product-range/waterproof-ipod-mp3-cases.html).

If you're looking for protection against drops and bangs, you can find many cases that offer varying degrees of protection. For heavy-duty protection, look for the OtterBox Armor for the iPod classic. The manufacturer has discontinued this product, but you can still pick it up online—for example, at Amazon.com.

For everyday rough-and tumble protection for the iPod classic, try the ToughSkin from Speck Products (www.speckproducts.com), a polymer case with rubber bumpers.

Sports Cases

If you need to take your iPod out for a jog or a hike, an iPod shuffle or an iPod nano can be a great solution, because you can clip it firmly to your least sweaty piece of clothing. Alternatively, you can get a case that's snug on both the iPod and you—and preferably comfortable on you both. Normally, this means an armband. Here are three examples of cases to look at:

- **AeroSport Armband** The Griffin AeroSport series (www.griffintechnology.com) includes low-profile sport armbands that keep an iPod firmly attached to your upper arm. You can also clip the case onto a belt or—for gentler activities—a strap.
- **Belkin Sport Armband Plus** The Sport Armband Plus from Belkin (www .amazon.com and other stores) is a series of lightweight neoprene armbands that bind the iPod firmly to your quivering muscles.
- **AeroSport Active-Use Armband** The AeroSport Active-Use Armband from Griffin Technology (www.griffintechnology.com and various stores) straps the sixth-generation iPod nano to your upper arm for exercise.
- **iWatchz Q Series watchband** The iWatchz Q Series (http://store.apple.com) is a holder with a built-in watch strap (or the other way around, depending on how you look at it). Either way, the iWatchz Q Series lets you strap your sixth-generation iPod nano to your wrist and wear it there. You can display the Clock app for bonus points.

The iWatchz Q Series is a nice idea if you're wearing long sleeves that you can run the headphone cable along. Otherwise, having a dangling cable can be a salutary reminder why you don't normally have your ears attached to your wrist.

Everyday Cases

For everyday use, you probably won't want your iPod armored to the teeth or clamped immovably to your bulging biceps. Here are examples of cases that protect the iPod from minor dings but slip into your pocket without leaving an awkward bulge:

- **Reflect**   The Reflect series from Griffin Technology (www.griffintechnology.com and various stores) includes tough polycarbonate cases for iPods and the iPhone. The front of each Reflect has a mirrored chrome finish that hides the device's screen until you turn the device on. If you wear mirror shades, you'll want one of these.
- **DecalGirl Skins**   The DecalGirl Skins (www.decalgirl.com) are thin, soft cases that come in various flashy designs and hug the iPod classic like a friendly anaconda.
- **Incase Leather Sleeve**   The Incase Leather Sleeve series (www.goincase.com) is a protective leather case that lets you easily access your iPod classic's controls and ports. The Sleeve includes a belt clip.

Stands and Docks

Cases can be great, but you won't always want to carry your iPod. Sometimes, you'll want to park it securely so that you can use it without worrying about knocking it down, or so that you can crank up the volume on an external speaker—either one with a dock built right in or one to which you connect the iPod with a cable.

Another option for docking your iPod is to get a set of portable speakers with a built-in stand for the device. See "Portable Speakers for the iPod," later in this chapter, for examples.

Early iPods included docks, but Apple has gradually phased them out in the interests of economy and streamlined packaging. But you can get plenty of iPod docks from Apple and from third-party manufacturers.

Playing audio from an iPod dock that includes a line-out port has two advantages. First, the Dock Connector and line-out port give higher audio quality than the headphone socket. Second, the Dock Connector and line-out port deliver a standard volume rather than a variable volume. The standard volume means that you're less likely to damage your receiver or speakers by putting too great a volume through them. It also means that you can't adjust the volume on the iPod, only on the receiver or speakers.

Apple Universal Dock

If you want standard dock features for an iPod classic, start by looking at the Apple Universal Dock (http://store.apple.com). This dock works with not only the iPod classic but also the iPhone, the iPod touch, and iPod nano models up to the fifth generation. The Universal Dock includes assorted Dock Adapters to make these differently shaped devices fit well. The Universal Dock includes an Apple Remote, a line-out port for producing high-quality audio (via the Dock Connector port), and an S-video out port for displaying photos, videos, or slideshows on a TV.

Third-Party Stands and Docks

If you decide that an Apple Universal Dock isn't what your iPod needs, you should be able to find third-party alternatives that offer an appealing design, extra features, or both. Here are a couple of the possibilities:

- **Simplifi** The Simplifi from Griffin Technology (www.griffintechnology.com) is an iPod or iPhone dock that incorporates a media-card reader and a USB hub. This means you can plug into the Simplifi not only the iPod or iPhone but also your memory cards and other USB devices—a neat idea that can reduce the clutter on your desk by several cables and devices. Simplifi includes Universal Dock adapters to fit the iPod classic, the iPod touch, and the iPhone.
- **reviveLITE II** The reviveLITE II from Scosche (http://store.apple.com) is a dock built into a wall charger. This enables you to recharge an iPod without using a cable, which can be a boon for cluttered desks. The reviveLITE II works for any iPod with a Dock Connector.

Car and Bike Mounting Kits

The iPod on your body or desk gets you only so far. To get further, you'll probably want to use the iPod in your car or on your bike. To prevent it from shifting around as you shift gears, you'll probably want to secure it.

Car Mounts and All-in-One Adapters

The ideal way of securing an iPod in a car is one of the "iPod-integration" units that car manufacturers are increasingly building into cars. If your car came without an iPod-integration unit, you can add a third-party one easily enough—see the next chapter for details—but in many cases you will need to replace your existing stereo.

If all you need is to mount your iPod in your car, you can find various types of car mounts on sites such as Amazon.com and eBay. These range from windshield mounts and dash mounts to foam inserts that turn a cup holder into a snug nest for an iPod (or iPhone, or other mobile phone).

But usually mounting the iPod is only part of the problem. You'll also need to get your music from the iPod to the stereo, and you may also want to power the iPod from the car rather than run it from the battery. So normally, after an iPod-integration unit, the next best choice for securing an iPod in a car is an all-in-one adapter that gives you these features:

- A power adapter that connects to your car's 12-volt accessory outlet or cigarette-lighter socket.
- A means of piping the iPod's output to your stereo. This can use a direct cable connection, a cassette adapter, or a radio transmitter.
- A cradle or other device for holding the iPod, either built onto the power adapter (using the power adapter as its support) or fitting into a cup holder or onto the dash.

Many different all-in-one gadgets are available. Here are a couple of examples:

- **TuneBase and TuneCast**   The TuneBase and TuneCast series from Belkin (www.belkin.com) provide a variety of ways to play audio from an iPod or iPhone through a car stereo. For example, the TuneBase FM with ClearScan powers the iPod from the accessory outlet, holds the iPod on a stand, and transmits audio wirelessly to the car stereo.
- **TuneFlex Aux HandsFree**   The TuneFlex Aux HandsFree from Griffin Technology (www.griffintechnology.com) holds the iPod classic (or iPhone, or iPod touch) on a flexible steel neck, powers it from the accessory outlet, and sends its output to your stereo's auxiliary port.

How to... **Use Your iPod with Your Bike**

Almost everyone who pronounces on the subject of road safety is adamant that you shouldn't listen to audio using earphones when riding a bike lest you fail to hear the vehicles thundering past with their own music shaking the scenery.

One solution is to get a bike-mounted speaker for al-fresco audio. Some bike speakers, like the CycleSound (www.cyclesound.com), attach under the seat and include a built-in compartment for your iPod. Other bike speakers mount in a bike-bottle holder and need the iPod to be mounted either on the bike or on you.

But even a powerful and well-designed bike speaker can have a hard time competing with traffic—so you may decide that earphones are the only way to go. If so, keep your eyes on the road rather than on the iPod's screen. An iPod shuffle is great for biking, because there's no screen to distract you, you can easily attach the player to your clothing rather than to your bike, and you can work the buttons by touch.

Power Adapters and Battery Packs

Each iPod comes with a USB cable that allows you to recharge it from a computer. You may want to get a power adapter so that you can recharge the device from an electrical outlet, or you may need to prolong your AC-free playing time by using a backup battery pack.

Battery Packs

When you don't have easy access to an electrical socket, a battery pack is a great way to keep the music going. This section shows you three examples of battery packs for iPods.

JumpStart

The JumpStart (http://store.apple.com and other stores) from Philips is an attachable battery pack that can double the playback time for an iPod classic. The JumpStart also works with the iPhone and the iPod touch.

TuneJuice

The TuneJuice products from Griffin Technology (www.griffintechnology.com) are external backup batteries for any iPod with a Dock Connector port (or an iPhone). The basic model runs off four AAA batteries; the higher-end model runs off three AA batteries. Each TuneJuice not only gives you more run time but also recharges the iPod's battery.

JBoxMini

The JBoxMini from Macally (www.macally.com) is an external lithium-ion battery that connects to any iPod or iPhone via a Dock Connector or a USB socket. The JBoxMini gives up to four hours extra battery life.

Basic AC Power Adapters

If you want to be able to recharge your iPod without connecting it to a USB port, you can buy an Apple USB Power Adapter (http://store.apple.com). Alternatively, you can find a third-party USB power adapter for less.

Car Adapters

If you drive extensively (or live in a vehicle), you may need to bolster your iPod's battery life. To recharge the iPod in your car, you need either an iPod-integration unit or a power adapter that'll run from your car's 12-volt accessory outlet or cigarette-lighter socket.

Technically, such an adapter is an *inverter*, a device that converts DC into AC, but we'll stick with the term *adapter* here.

You can choose between a generic USB car adapter, a generic car adapter for heavier power requirements, and a custom car adapter for the iPod. Another option is an all-in-one device that combines a power adapter with a radio transmitter or auxiliary cable and (in some cases) a means of mounting the device, as discussed in the section "Car Mounts and All-in-One Adapters," earlier in this chapter.

Generic USB Car Adapter

If the only thing you need to power from your car is your iPod, and you have a USB-to–Dock Connector cable to spare, you can get away with an inexpensive car adapter that provides one or more USB sockets. You can pick these up for just a few dollars on eBay, Amazon.com, and other sites.

Generic Car Adapter

If you need to power your iPod and other devices from your car, consider getting a generic car adapter that plugs into your car's 12-volt accessory outlet or cigarette-lighter socket. Models vary, but the most effective types give you one or more conventional AC sockets. You plug an iPod power adapter into one of these AC sockets, just as you would any other AC socket, and then plug the USB cable into the power adapter.

The advantage to these adapters is that you can run any electrical equipment off them that doesn't draw too heavy a load—a laptop, your cell phone charger, a portable TV, or whatever. The disadvantage is that such adapters can be large and clumsy compared with custom adapters.

Cost usually depends on the wattage the adapter can handle; you can get 50-watt adapters from around $20 and 140-watt adapters for around $50, whereas 300-watt adapters cost more like $80. A 50-watt adapter will take care of an iPod and portable computer easily enough.

iPod-Specific Adapters

If your iPod is the only thing you'll need to power from your car's accessory socket, but you don't have a spare USB-to–Dock Connector cable, you can get a car adapter designed especially for the iPod. Many different models are available, including the following:

- The Incase Car Charger (http://store.apple.com) is a charger with a USB port and a cable for connecting to your iPod's Dock Connector. The USB port delivers 2 amps for fast charging.
- The Belkin MicroCharge + ChargeSync In-Car (www.belkin.com) includes a charger for iPods with the Dock Connector port and a three-foot cable for connecting to your computer.
- The Griffin PowerJolt for iPad, iPhone, and iPod (http://store.apple.com) is an adapter with a USB socket and a USB-to–Dock Connector cable.

World Travel Adapters

If you travel abroad with an iPod, the lightest and easiest way to recharge it is from your laptop—provided that you have your computer with you, and you have access to an electric socket so that you don't flatten your computer's battery by charging the iPod.

If you need to recharge your iPod directly from the electric socket, get an adapter that lets you plug the iPod's power adapter into electric sockets in different countries. The adapter can handle multiple voltages, so you can plug it in safely even in countries that think 240 volts is just a refreshing tingle.

For such adapters, you have the choice between a set of cheap and ugly adapters and a set of stylish and sophisticated adapters. You can get the cheap and ugly adapters from any competent electrical-supply shop; they consist of an assortment of prong-converter receptacles into which you plug the power adapter U.S. prongs. The resulting piggyback arrangement is clumsy, and sometimes you have to jiggle the adapters to get a good connection. But these adapters are inexpensive (usually from $5 to $10) and functional, and they work for any electrical gear that can handle the different voltages.

The stylish and sophisticated adapters are designed by Apple and are (collectively) called the World Travel Adapter Kit. You can get the kit from the Apple Store (http://store.apple.com) or an authorized reseller. You slide the U.S. prongs off the iPod power adapter and replace them with a set of prongs suited to the country you're in. The kit includes six prongs that'll juice up any iPod (except the iPod shuffle) in continental Europe, the United Kingdom, Australia, Hong Kong, South Korea, China, and Japan, as well as in the United States. These adapters also work with Apple laptops, but they won't help you plug in any of your other electrical equipment.

 If you're going somewhere sunny that lacks electricity, or you live somewhere sunny that suffers frequent power outages, consider a solar charger such as the Solio Bolt (www.solio.com).

Microphones

If you have an iPod classic, you may want to add a microphone so that you can use the iPod to take audio notes.

 You can record on the iPod nano by using the Apple Earphones with Remote and Mic (http://store.apple.com). After connecting the earphones, tap the Voice Memos icon on the Home screen to display the Voice Memos screen, which contains recording controls.

At this writing, your best bet is the TuneTalk Stereo from Belkin (www.belkin.com or other stores). The TuneTalk Stereo is a digital recorder that clips onto the iPod's base and enables you to record CD-quality audio (16-bit, 44.1 KHz).

The TuneTalk Stereo has a real-time gain control. You can also plug in an external microphone and record through that instead of through the TuneTalk Stereo's two built-in microphones.

Portable Speakers for the iPod

You can use the iPod as the sound source for just about any stereo system, as you'll see in "Connect an iPod to a Stereo" in the next chapter. But if you travel with an iPod, or simply prefer a compact lifestyle, you may want portable speakers that will treat the iPod as the center of their universe. You can find a variety of iPod-specific speakers to meet most constraints of budgets and portability.

Choosing Portable Speakers for the iPod

If you've decided that you need portable speakers specifically for your iPod, you've already narrowed down your choices considerably. Bear the following in mind when choosing portable speakers:

- *How much sound do the speakers make?* The best design in the world is useless if the speakers deliver sound too puny for your listening needs.
- *Do the speakers recharge the device?* Some speakers recharge the iPod as it plays. Others just wear down the battery.
- *Do the speakers work with various iPods or only with a single model?* Some speakers are designed only to work with a particular model. Others can recharge various iPods (for example, all models with the Dock Connector port) but can accept input from other players via a line-in port.
- *How are the speakers powered?* Some speakers are powered by replaceable batteries; others by rechargeable batteries; and others by AC power. A pairing of rechargeable batteries and AC power gives you the most flexibility.
- *Do the speakers include a remote control?* If you're planning to use the speakers from across the room, look for speakers that include a remote control.

Examples of Speakers for the iPod

As with many iPod accessories, there are far more speakers than you could shake even a large and threatening stick at. But here are a handful of speakers worth looking at—for assorted reasons:

- **Bowers & Wilkins Zeppelin Air** The Zeppelin Air from Bowers & Wilkins (http://store.apple.com) is a zeppelin-shaped speaker that hides four 25-watt midrange/tweeter speakers and a 50-watt bass unit. With an iPod classic or iPod nano, you connect the iPod directly to the Zeppelin Air via the Dock Connector. With an iPod touch, iPhone, or iPad, you can play music wirelessly via AirPlay.

The Zeppelin Air's look is clearly driven by design considerations, but the sound gets rave reviews too.

- **Bose SoundDock**   The SoundDock speakers from Bose (www.bose.com) are a series of speakers for iPods. The SoundDock 10 is the largest and most powerful, and is capable of shaking up your neighbors. The SoundDock Portable is designed for portability and has a built-in carrying handle. Finally, the SoundDock II delivers enough sound to fill even large rooms.
- **JBL On Stage and OnBeat**   The On Stage IV speaker from JBL (www.jbl.com) is a round-ish speaker unit that gives up to 16 hours of playback on battery power. It also charges the iPod at the same time. The On Stage IV is designed for iPods with the Dock Connector port, but you can also use other sound sources through an auxiliary audio input cable. JBL also makes the OnBeat speakers (www.jbl.com) and the smaller On Stage Micro III (www.jbl.com), both also for iPods with the Dock Connector port.
- **Altec Lansing inMotion**   The inMotion series from Altec Lansing (www.alteclansing.com) includes portable and ultraportable stereo systems designed for iPods with Dock Connector ports. The larger models are AC powered, while the smaller models can run from batteries.

Radio Transmitters

Portable speakers are a great way of getting a decent amount of audio out of your iPod when you're at home or traveling with a moderate amount of kit. But where portable speakers aren't practical, or when you need to travel light, you can use a radio transmitter to play audio from your iPod through a handy radio. This is useful in hotels, in cars, in friends' houses—and even in your own home.

Choosing a Radio Transmitter

Many models of radio transmitters are available. Apart from price and esthetics, consider the following when choosing between them:

- *Does the transmitter fit only one model, or will it work for any device?* You may find that the choice is between a transmitter designed to fit only your current model of iPod or a less-stylish transmitter that will work with any model—or indeed any sound source.
- *Is the transmitter powered by the iPod, or does it have its own power source?* Drawing power from the iPod's battery is a neater arrangement, because you don't have to worry about keeping the battery in the transmitter charged (or putting in new batteries) or connecting an external power supply. But drawing power from the iPod's battery tends to limit the transmitter to working with certain models only, and drains the iPod's battery that much more sooner.
- *Is the transmitter powerful enough for your needs?* Even among low-power transmitters that are legal for unlicensed use, power and range vary widely.

- *How many frequencies can the transmitter use?* Avoid any transmitters set to broadcast on a single frequency, because you'll be straight out of luck if a more powerful local station happens to be using that frequency. Instead, get either a transmitter with several preset frequencies among which you can switch or a transmitter that you can tune to exactly the frequency you want. Some transmitters have "auto-tune" features to help you find a frequency that's free amid the radio storm.
- *Does the transmitter have other tricks?* Some transmitters are designed for use in your car or another vehicle, whereas others are general purpose.

 Low-power radio transmitters are legal in the United States and the United Kingdom, but some other countries don't permit them. If you don't know whether your country permits radio transmitters, check before buying one.

Examples of Radio Transmitters

Here are three examples of radio transmitters:

- **TuneFM**   The TuneFM from Belkin (www.belkin.com) is a compact radio transmitter that offers two preset buttons that you can program to frequencies you find to be empty in your area.
- **iTrip**   The iTrip family from Griffin Technology (www.griffintechnology.com) consists of compact radio transmitters designed to work with most iPods. The iTrip models connect to the Dock Connector port, adding an extra section to the bottom of the iPod. Some draw power from the iPod's battery rather than using batteries of their own, while others connect to a car accessory socket to power themselves and recharge your iPod. You can set the iTrip to broadcast on any frequency between 87.7 and 107.9 FM, so you should be able to get the signal through even in a busy urban area.
- **iBreath**   If you suspect your iPod has had too much to drink—just a second, let me try that again. If you want to ask your iPod if you've had too much to drink, consider getting the iBreath Breathalyzer & FM Transmitter (www.davidsteele .com/). If you're too well oiled to drive, you can simply listen to the FM transmitter instead.

6

Use an iPod as Your Home Stereo or Car Stereo

HOW TO...

- Equip an iPod with speakers
- Connect an iPod to your stereo
- Play music throughout your house from an iPod
- Play music through an AirPort Express network
- Connect an iPod to your car stereo
- Use your computer to play songs directly from an iPod

By the time you've loaded hundreds or thousands of songs onto your iPod, you'll probably have decided that headphones only get you so far. To enjoy your music the rest of the time, chances are that you'll want to play it from the iPod and through your home stereo or your car stereo. This chapter shows you the various ways of doing so, from using cables to using radio waves.

Equip an iPod with Speakers

The simplest way to get a decent volume of sound from an iPod is to connect it to a pair of powered speakers (speakers that include their own amplifier). You can buy speakers designed especially for the iPod (see the section "Portable Speakers for the iPod" in Chapter 5), but you can also use any iPod with any powered speakers that accept input via a miniplug connector (the size of connector used for the iPod's headphones).

Speakers designed for the iPod tend to be smaller and more stylish than general-purpose speakers, but also considerably more expensive.

To get the highest sound quality possible from an iPod, together with a consistent volume, use a dock rather than the headphone port. Various models are available, from the utilitarian to the decorative. Connect the dock's line-out port to the speakers or receiver, and you're in business any time you've docked the iPod. Similarly, most speakers designed for the iPod include a Dock Connector, both to get the best sound quality from the iPod and to be able to charge it.

Connect an iPod to a Stereo

If you already have a stereo that produces good-quality sound, you can play songs from an iPod through the stereo. There are three main ways of doing this:

- Connect the iPod directly to the stereo with a cable, either via the device's headphone port or (better) via a dock.
- Use a radio transmitter to send the music from the iPod to your radio, which plays it.
- Use your computer to play the music from an iPod through an AirPort Express wireless access point that's connected to your stereo.

Connect an iPod to a Stereo with a Cable

The most direct way to connect an iPod to a stereo system is with a cable. For a typical receiver, you'll need a cable that has a miniplug at one end and two RCA plugs at the other end. Figure 6-1 shows an example of an iPod connected to a stereo via the amplifier.

 Some receivers and boom boxes use a single stereo miniplug input rather than two RCA ports. To connect an iPod to such devices, you'll need a stereo miniplug-to-miniplug cable. Make sure the cable is stereo, because mono miniplug-to-miniplug cables are common. A stereo cable has two bands around the miniplug (as on most headphones), whereas a mono cable has only one band.

If you have a high-quality receiver and speakers, get a high-quality cable to connect the iPod to them. After the amount you've presumably spent on the iPod and stereo, it'd be a mistake to degrade the signal between them by sparing a few bucks on the cable.

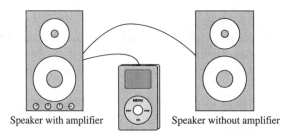

Speaker with amplifier   Speaker without amplifier

FIGURE 6-1   A miniplug-to-RCA-plugs cable is the most direct way of connecting an iPod to your stereo system.

You can find various home-audio connection kits that contain a variety of cables likely to cover your needs. These kits are usually a safe buy, but unless your needs are peculiar, you'll end up with one or more cables you don't need. So if you do know which cables you need, make sure a kit offers a cost savings before buying it instead of the individual cables.

Connect the iPod to your receiver as follows:

1. Connect the miniplug to the player's headphone port. If you have a dock, connect the miniplug to the dock's line-out port instead, because this gives a consistent volume and better sound quality than the headphone port.
2. If you're using the headphone port, turn down the volume on the iPod all the way.
3. Whichever port you're using, turn down the volume on the amplifier as well.
4. Connect the RCA plugs to the left and right ports of one of the inputs on your amplifier or boom box—for example, the AUX input or the Cassette input (if you're not using a cassette deck).

 Don't connect the iPod to the Phono input on your amplifier. The Phono input is built with a higher sensitivity to make up for the weak output of a record player. Putting a full-strength signal into the Phono input will probably blow it.

5. Start the music playing. If you're using the headphone port, turn up the volume a little.
6. Turn up the volume on the receiver so that you can hear the music.
7. Increase the volume on the two controls in tandem until you reach a satisfactory sound level.

 Too low a level of output from the player may produce noise as your amplifier boosts the signal. Too high a level of output from the player may cause distortion.

If you plug a player directly into your stereo, get a remote control for the player so that you don't need to march over to it each time you need to change the music. See "Remote Controls" in Chapter 5 for details of some of the remote controls available for the iPod.

Use a Radio Transmitter Between an iPod and a Stereo

If you don't want to connect the iPod directly to your stereo system, you can use a radio transmitter to send the audio from the player to the radio on your stereo. See "Radio Transmitters" in Chapter 5 for examples of radio transmitters designed for the iPod.

The sound you get from this arrangement typically will be lower in quality than the sound from a wired connection, but it should be at least as good as listening to a conventional radio station in stereo. If that's good enough for you, a radio transmitter can be a neat solution to playing music from the iPod throughout your house.

Using a radio transmitter has another advantage: You can play the music on several radios at the same time, giving yourself music throughout your dwelling without complex and expensive rewiring.

Use an AirPort Express, a Computer, and an iPod

If you have an AirPort Express (a wireless access point that Apple makes), you can use it not only to network your home but also to play music from your computer or iPod through your stereo system.

To play music through an AirPort Express, follow these general steps:

1. Connect the AirPort Express to the receiver via a cable. The line-out port on the AirPort Express combines an analog port and an optical output, so you can connect the AirPort Express to the receiver in either of two ways:
   - Connect an optical cable to the AirPort Express's line-out socket and to an optical digital-audio input port on the receiver. If the receiver has an optical input, use this arrangement to get the best sound quality possible.
   - Connect an analog audio cable to the AirPort Express's line-out socket and to the RCA ports on your receiver.
2. If your network has a wired portion, connect the Ethernet port on the AirPort Express to the switch or hub using an Ethernet cable. If you have a DSL that you will share through the AirPort Express, connect the DSL via the Ethernet cable.
3. Plug the AirPort Express into an electric socket.
4. Install on your computer the software that accompanies the AirPort Express. Then use AirPort Admin Utility for Windows or AirPort Utility (on Mac OS X) to configure the network.
5. Connect the iPod to your computer.
6. Launch iTunes if it isn't already running.
7. If the iPod is set for automatic updating of songs and playlists, click its entry in the Source list to display the device's screens. On the Summary tab, select the Manually Manage Music and Videos option button, click the OK button in the confirmation dialog box, and then click the Apply button to apply the changes.
8. Click the Choose Which Speakers To Use button (the button at the bottom of the iTunes window that shows a rectangle with a triangle through its lower side) and choose the entry for the AirPort Express from the drop-down list. (This button appears only if iTunes has detected an AirPort Express within striking distance.) You can also choose Multiple Speakers to open the Multiple Speakers dialog box (shown here), and then choose which speakers to use and set their relative volumes.

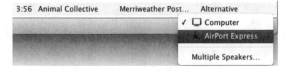

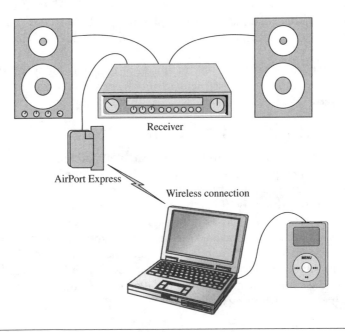

FIGURE 6-2 If you have an AirPort Express, you can play music on your computer or iPod through your stereo system across the wireless network.

9. Click the iPod's entry in the Source list to display its contents. You can then play the songs on the iPod back via your computer to the speakers connected to the AirPort Express.

10. To switch back to playing through the computer's speakers, click the Choose Which Speakers To Use button at the bottom of the iTunes window again. This time, choose the Computer entry from the drop-down list.

 If you changed the iPod's updating preferences in Step 7, remember to change updating back to your preferred setting before you disconnect the device.

Figure 6-2 shows a typical setup for playing music from an iPod through an AirPort Express.

Connect an iPod to a Car Stereo

You can connect an iPod to a car stereo in any of the following ways:

- Get a car with a built-in iPod connection or add an after-market iPod-integration device.
- Use a cassette adapter to connect the iPod to the car's cassette player.

- Use a radio-frequency device to play the iPod's output through the car's radio.
- Wire the iPod directly to the car stereo and use it as an auxiliary input device.

Each of these methods has its pros and cons. The following sections tell you what you need to know to choose the best option for your car stereo.

Use a Built-in iPod Connection

At this writing, Apple claims that more than 90 percent of new cars sold in the United States have an option for connecting an iPod. (See the list at www.apple.com/ipod/car-integration.) So if you're in the market for a new car, add iPod connectivity to your list of criteria. Similarly, if you're buying a used car that's only a few years old, you may be able to get iPod connectivity built in.

If your car doesn't have its own means of integrating an iPod, look for a third-party solution. Some adapters not only let you play back music from the iPod through the car's stereo and control it using the stereo system's controls, but also let you display the song information from the iPod on the stereo's display, making it easier to see what you're listening to.

Use a Cassette Adapter

If the car stereo has a cassette player, your easiest option is to use a cassette adapter to play audio from the iPod through the cassette deck. You can buy such adapters for between $10 and $20 from most electronics stores or from an iPod specialist.

The adapter is shaped like a cassette and uses a playback head to input analog audio via the head that normally reads the tape as it passes. A wire runs from the adapter to the iPod.

A cassette adapter can be an easy and inexpensive solution, but it's far from perfect. The main problem is that the audio quality tends to be poor, because the means of transferring the audio to the cassette player's mechanism is less than optimal. But if your car is noisy, you may find that road noise obscures most of the defects in audio quality.

If the cassette player's playback head is dirty from playing cassettes, audio quality will be that much worse. To keep the audio quality as high as possible, clean the cassette player regularly using a cleaning cassette.

 If you use a cassette adapter in an extreme climate, try to make sure you don't bake it or freeze it by leaving it in the car.

Use a Radio Transmitter

If the car stereo doesn't have a cassette deck, your easiest option for playing music from an iPod may be to get a radio transmitter. This device plugs into the iPod and broadcasts a signal on an FM frequency to which you then tune your radio to play the music. Better radio transmitters offer a choice of frequencies to allow you easy access to both the iPod and your favorite radio stations.

 See the section "Radio Transmitters" in Chapter 5 for a discussion of how to choose among the many radio transmitters offered and examples of transmitters designed for the iPod.

Radio transmitters can deliver reasonable audio quality. If possible, try before you buy by asking for a demonstration in the store (take a portable radio with you, if necessary).

The main advantages of these devices are that they're relatively inexpensive (usually between $15 and $50) and they're easy to use. They also have the advantage that you can put the iPod out of sight (for example, in the glove compartment—provided it's not too hot) without any telltale wires to help the light-fingered locate it.

On the downside, most of these devices need batteries (others can run off the 12-volt accessory outlet or cigarette-lighter socket), and less expensive units tend not to deliver the highest sound quality. The range of these devices is minimal, but at close quarters, other radios nearby may be able to pick up the signal—which could be embarrassing, entertaining, or irrelevant, depending on the circumstances. If you use the radio transmitter in an area where the airwaves are busy, you may need to keep switching the frequency to avoid having the transmitter swamped by the full-strength radio stations.

How to... Find a Suitable Frequency for a Radio Transmitter

In most areas, the airwaves are busy these days—so to get good reception on your car's radio from your iPod's radio transmitter, you need to pick a suitable frequency. To do so, follow these steps:

1. With the iPod's radio transmitter turned off, turn on your car radio.
2. Tune the car radio to a frequency on which you get only static, and for which the frequencies one step up and one step down give only static as well. For example, if you're thinking of using the 91.3 frequency, make sure that 91.1 and 91.5 give only static as well.
3. Tune the radio transmitter to the frequency you've chosen, and see if it works. If not, identify and test another frequency.

This method may sound obvious, but what many people do is pick a frequency on the radio transmitter, tune the radio to it—and then be disappointed by the results.

If you decide to get a radio transmitter, you'll need to choose between getting a model designed specifically for the iPod and getting one that works with any audio source. Radio transmitters designed for the iPod typically mount on the iPod, making them a neater solution than general-purpose ones that dangle from the headphone socket. Radio transmitters designed for use with iPods in cars often mount on the accessory outlet or dash and secure the device as well as transmitting its sound.

A radio-frequency adapter works with radios other than car radios, so you can use one to play music through your stereo system (or someone else's). You may also want to connect a radio-frequency adapter to a PC or Mac and use it to broadcast audio to a portable radio. This is a great way of getting streaming radio from the Internet to play on a conventional radio.

Wire an iPod Directly to a Car Stereo

If neither the cassette adapter nor the radio-frequency adapter provides a suitable solution, or if you simply want the best audio quality you can get, connect the iPod directly to your car stereo. How easily you can do this depends on how the stereo is designed:

- If your car stereo has a miniplug input built in, get a miniplug-to-miniplug cable, and you'll be in business.
- If your stereo is built to take multiple inputs—for example, a CD player (or changer) and an auxiliary input—you may be able to simply run a wire from unused existing connectors. Plug the iPod into the other end, press the correct buttons, and you'll be ready to rock-and-roll down the freeway.
- If no unused connectors are available, you or your local friendly electronics technician may need to get busy with a soldering iron.

If you're buying a new car stereo, look for iPod integration or at least an auxiliary input that you can use with an iPod.

PART II

Create and Manage Your Library

7

Create Audio Files,
Edit Them, and Tag Them

HOW TO...

- Choose where to store your library
- Choose suitable audio-quality settings in iTunes
- Convert audio files from other audio formats to AAC or MP3
- Create AAC files or MP3 files from cassettes, vinyl, or other sources
- Remove scratches, hiss, and hum from audio files
- Trim or split song files
- Rename song files efficiently
- Save audio streams to disk

In Chapter 3, you learned how to start creating your library by copying music from your CDs and importing your existing music files. This is a great way to put songs on an iPod quickly, but to get the most enjoyment out of your music, you may well want to customize iTunes' settings rather than use the defaults.

You may also want to do things with AAC files and MP3 files that iTunes doesn't support. For example, you may receive (or acquire) files in formats the iPod can't handle, so you'll need to convert the files before you can use them on an iPod. You may want to create song files from cassettes, LPs, or other media you own, and you may need to remove clicks, pops, and other extraneous noises from such recordings you make. You may want to trim intros or outros off audio files, split files into smaller files, or retag batches of files in ways iTunes can't handle. Last, you may want to record streaming audio to your hard disk.

Choose Where to Store Your Library

Because your library can contain dozens—or even hundreds—of gigabytes of files, you must store it in a suitable location if you choose to keep all your files in it.

By default, iTunes stores your library in a folder named iTunes Media. This folder, the library folder, contains several folders:

- **Audiobooks**   This folder contains any audiobooks you've downloaded.
- **iTunes U**   This folder contains any iTunes U podcasts you've downloaded.

 If you have an iPhone, iPad, or iPod touch, your iTunes Media folder may contain other folders, such as Books and Mobile Applications.

- **Movies**   This folder contains your movies, in subfolders named with the movie names.
- **Music**   This folder contains your songs, in subfolders named after the artists.
- **Podcasts**   This folder contains the podcasts you've downloaded, in subfolders named with the podcast names.
- **Ringtones**   This folder contains the ringtones you've bought or created.
- **TV Shows**   This folder contains the TV shows you've downloaded, in subfolders named with the show names.

 Instead of keeping all your song files in your library, you can store references to where the files are located in other folders. Doing so enables you to minimize the size of your library. But for maximum flexibility and to make sure you can access all the tracks in your library all the time, keeping all your song files in your library folder is best—if you can do so.

To change the location of your library from now on, follow these steps:

1. Display the iTunes dialog box or the Preferences dialog box:
   - In Windows, choose Edit | Preferences or press CTRL-COMMA or CTRL-Y to display the iTunes dialog box.
   - On the Mac, choose iTunes | Preferences or press ⌘-COMMA or ⌘-Y to display the Preferences dialog box.
2. Click the Advanced tab to display its contents. Figure 7-1 shows the Advanced tab of the iTunes dialog box in Windows.
3. Click the Change button to display the Change iTunes Media Folder Location dialog box.
4. Navigate to the folder that will contain your library, select the folder, and then click the Select Folder button (Windows 7), OK button (Windows Vista), Open button (Windows XP), or Choose button (Mac). iTunes returns you to the iTunes dialog box or Preferences dialog box.

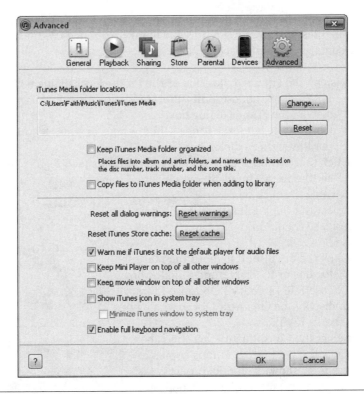

FIGURE 7-1   You may need to move your library folder from its default location to a folder that has more disk space available.

5. Click the OK button to close the iTunes dialog box or the Preferences dialog box. iTunes displays a message box as it updates your iTunes library, as shown here.

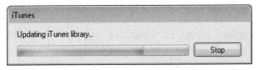

6. If iTunes prompts you to decide whether to let iTunes move and rename the files in your new iTunes Media folder, as shown here, click the Yes button.

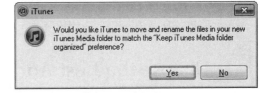

To reset your library folder to its default location, click the Reset button on the Advanced tab of the iTunes dialog box or the Preferences dialog box. On Windows, the default location is the \Music\iTunes\iTunes Media folder in your user folder. On the Mac, the default folder is the ~/Music/iTunes Media folder, where ~ represents your Home folder.

When you change the location of your library like this, iTunes doesn't actually move the files that are already in your library. To move the files, make sure the new folder contains enough space, and then follow these steps:

1. Display the iTunes dialog box or the Preferences dialog box again:
   - In Windows, choose Edit | Preferences or press CTRL-COMMA or CTRL-Y to display the iTunes dialog box.
   - On the Mac, choose iTunes | Preferences or press ⌘-COMMA or ⌘-Y to display the Preferences dialog box.
2. Click the Advanced tab to display its contents (see Figure 7-1).
3. Select the Keep iTunes Media Folder Organized check box.
4. Select the Copy Files To iTunes Media Folder When Adding To Library check box.
5. Click the OK button to close the iTunes dialog box or the Preferences dialog box.
6. Choose File | Library | Organize Library to display the Organize Library dialog box (shown here).
7. Select the Consolidate Files check box.
8. Click the OK button. iTunes copies the files, showing you its progress (as shown here) until it has finished.

Configure iTunes for the Audio Quality You Want

Before you rip and encode your entire CD collection, check that the settings in iTunes are suitable for your needs. iTunes' default is to encode to AAC files at 256 Kbps in stereo. This is a fair choice for defaults, but you may well want to change them. Spend some time choosing the right settings for ripping and encoding so that you don't waste time ripping your CDs more than once.

First, decide which music format and audio quality you want. Then choose the appropriate settings in iTunes.

Choose the Best Audio Format for Your Needs

iTunes can encode audio in five formats: AAC, MP3, Apple Lossless Encoding, WAV, and AIFF. AAC, MP3, and Apple Lossless Encoding are compressed audio formats, whereas WAV and AIFF are not compressed.

How to...

Understand CD-Quality Audio and Lossy and Lossless Compression

CD-quality audio samples audio 44,100 times per second (a sampling rate of 44.1 KHz) to provide coverage across most of the human hearing range. Each sample contains 16 bits (2 bytes) of data, which is enough information to convey the full range of frequencies. There are two tracks (for stereo), doubling the amount of data. CD-quality audio consumes around 9MB (megabytes) of storage space per minute of audio, which means that around 74 minutes of music fits on a standard 650MB CD and 80 minutes on a 700MB CD. The data on audio CDs is stored in *pulse code modulation* (PCM), a standard format for uncompressed audio.

To make more music fit on your computer or iPod, you can compress it so that it takes up less space. AAC and MP3 use *lossy compression*, compression that discards the parts of the audio data that your ears won't be able to hear or that your brain won't be able to pick out even though your ears hear it. Lossy audio codecs use *psychoacoustics*, the science of how the human brain processes sound, to select which data to keep and which to discard. As a basic example, when one part of the sound is masked by another part of the sound, the encoder discards the masked part, because you wouldn't hear it even if it were there.

How much data the encoder keeps depends on a setting called the *bitrate*. Almost all encoders let you choose a wide range of bitrates. In addition, most MP3 encoders can encode either at a constant bitrate (CBR) or a variable bitrate (VBR). To learn the pros and cons of CBR and VBR, see the sidebar "Choose Between CBR and VBR, and a Suitable Stereo Setting, for MP3," later in this chapter.

The advantage of lossy compression is that a well-designed codec can produce good-sounding audio at a fraction of the file size of uncompressed audio. For example, AAC and MP3 sound good to most people at a bitrate of 128 Kbps, which produces files around a tenth of the size of the uncompressed audio. The disadvantage of lossy compression is that the audio can never sound perfect, because some data has been discarded.

Better than lossy compression is *lossless compression*, which reduces the file size without discarding any of the audio data. Apple Lossless Encoding is lossless compression and produces extremely high-quality results.

The advantage of lossless compression is that it produces audio that is as high in quality as the uncompressed audio. The disadvantage is that lossless compression reduces the file size by much less than lossy compression, because it doesn't discard audio data.

AAC

AAC is the abbreviation for Advanced Audio Coding, a *codec* (*coder/deco*der) for compressing and playing back digital audio. AAC was put together by a group of heavy hitters in the audio and digital audio fields, including Fraunhofer IIS-A (the German company that developed MP3), Sony Corporation, Dolby Laboratories, AT&T, Nokia, and Lucent.

AAC is newer than MP3 (which is discussed in the next section), is generally agreed to deliver better sound than MP3, and is more tightly controlled than MP3. It is one of the key audio components of the MPEG-4 specification, which covers digital audio and video.

AAC files can be either protected with digital rights management (DRM) technology or unprotected.

The iTunes Store (discussed in Chapter 8) uses AAC for its songs, so if you buy songs from it, you won't have any choice about using AAC. You can convert unprotected AAC songs to other formats (for example, to MP3) but you lose audio quality in the conversion.

QuickTime includes an AAC codec. iTunes uses QuickTime's capabilities to encode audio and play back audio and video.

AAC can work with up to 48 full-frequency audio channels. This gives it a huge advantage over MP3, which can work with only two channels (in stereo) or a single channel (in mono). If you're used to listening to music in stereo, 48 channels seems an absurd number. But typically, only a small subset of those channels would be used at the same time. For example, conventional surround-sound rigs use 5.1 or 7.1 setups, using six channels or eight channels, respectively. Other channels can be used for different languages, so that an AAC player can play a different vocal track for differently configured players. Other tracks yet can be used for synchronizing and controlling the audio.

Advantages of AAC   For music lovers, AAC offers higher music quality than MP3 at the same file sizes, or similar music quality at smaller file sizes. Apple claims that 128-Kbps AAC files sound as good as 160-Kbps MP3 files—so you can either save a fair amount of space and get the same quality or enjoy even higher quality at the same bitrate. Around 24 Kbps, AAC streams provide quite listenable sound for spoken audio, whereas MP3 streams sound quite rough. (*Streaming* is the method of transmission used by Internet radio, in which you can listen to a file as your computer downloads it.)

Small file sizes are especially welcome for streaming audio over slow connections, such as modem connections. AAC streamed around 56 Kbps sounds pretty good (though not perfect), whereas MP3 sounds a bit flawed.

The main advantage of AAC for the music industry is that the format supports DRM. This means that AAC files can be created in a protected format with custom limitations built in. For example, most of the song files you can buy from the iTunes Store used to be protected by DRM so that, even if you distributed them to other people, those people couldn't play them. Happily, at this writing, Apple has phased out the iTunes Store's use of DRM for songs.

To tell whether an AAC file is protected, click it in iTunes, choose File | Get Info (or right-click or CTRL-click and then click Get Info), and then check the Kind readout on the Summary tab of the Item Information dialog box. If the file is protected, the Kind readout reads "Protected AAC Audio File." If not, Kind reads "AAC Audio File" or "Purchased AAC Audio File." Alternatively, check the file extension: The .m4p extension indicates a protected file, whereas the .m4a extension indicates an unprotected file.

Disadvantages of AAC   If you use iTunes and an iPod, you'll probably find AAC's disadvantages easy enough to bear:

- AAC files are not widely available except by using iTunes and the iTunes Store. Even though Apple has made AAC the default format for iTunes and the iTunes Store, most other sources of digital audio files use other formats—typically either WMA or MP3.
- Encoding AAC files takes more processor cycles than encoding MP3 files. But any computer built in the last few years should be plenty fast enough.
- DRM can prevent you from playing AAC files on the computers or devices you want to. Even worse, whoever applied the DRM can change its conditions after you buy a song—for example, further restricting your rights.

MP3

Like AAC, MP3 is a file format for compressed audio. MP3 became popular in the late 1990s and largely sparked the digital music revolution by making it possible to carry a large amount of high-quality audio with you on a small device and enjoy it at the cost of nothing but the device, battery power, and time.

Among Mac users, MP3 has been overshadowed recently by AAC since Apple incorporated the AAC codec in iTunes, QuickTime, and the iPod (and later the iPhone and iPad). But MP3 remains the dominant format for compressed audio on computers running Windows (where its major competition comes from WMA, Microsoft's proprietary Windows Media Audio format) and computers running Linux.

MP3's name comes from the Moving Picture Experts Group (MPEG; www .chiariglione.org/mpeg/—not www.mpeg.org), which oversaw the development of the MP3 format. MP3 is both the extension used by the files and the name commonly used for them. (Technically, MP3 is the file format for MPEG-1 Layer 3.)

MP3 can deliver high-quality music in files that take up as little as a tenth as much space as uncompressed CD-quality files. For speech, which typically requires lower fidelity than music, you can create even smaller files that still sound good, enabling you to pack that much more audio in the same amount of disk space.

Apple Lossless Encoding

Apple Lossless Encoding is an encoder that gives results that are mathematically lossless—there is no degradation of audio quality in the compressed files. The amount that Apple Lossless Encoding compresses audio depends on how complex the audio is. Some songs compress to around 40 percent of the uncompressed file size, whereas others compress to only 60–70 percent of the uncompressed file size.

Apple Lossless Encoding is a great way to keep full-quality audio on your computer—at least, if it has a large hard disk (or several large hard disks). Apple Lossless Encoding gives great audio quality on the iPod as well, but it's not such a great solution for most people. This is for three reasons:

- The large amount of space that Apple Lossless Encoding files consume means that you can't fit nearly as many songs on an iPod as you can using AAC or MP3.
- The Apple Lossless Encoding files are too large for the memory chip in the iPod classic to buffer effectively. As a result, the iPod has to read the hard drive more frequently, which reduces battery life. (This isn't a concern for the iPod nano or iPod shuffle, which use flash memory rather than a hard drive.)
- Most non-Apple hardware and software players can't play Apple Lossless Encoding files. If you want to be able to play your song files on various devices, either now or in the future, choose a format other than Apple Lossless Encoding.

WAV and AIFF

WAV files and AIFF files both contain uncompressed PCM audio, which is also referred to as "raw" audio. WAV files are PCM files with a WAV header, whereas AIFF files are PCM files with an AIFF header. The *header* is a section of identification information placed at the start of the file.

 AIFF tends to be more widely used on the Mac than in Windows, which favors WAV. But iTunes can create and play both AIFF files and WAV files on both Windows and Mac OS X.

If you want the ultimate in audio quality, you can create AIFF files or WAV files from your CDs and use them on your computer and iPod. But there are three reasons why you probably won't want to do this:

- Each full-length CD will take up between 500MB and 800MB of disk space, compared to the 50MB to 80MB it would take up compressed at 128 Kbps. Apple Lossless Encoding gives a better balance of full audio quality with somewhat reduced file size.
- An iPod classic won't be able to buffer the audio effectively, will need to access the hard drive more frequently, and will deliver poor battery life. Other iPods don't have this limitation.
- Neither AIFF files nor WAV files have containers for storing tag information, such as the names of the artist, the CD, and the song. iTunes does its best to help by maintaining the tag information for AIFF files or WAV files in its database, but if you move the files (for example, if you copy them to a different computer), the tag information doesn't go with them. By contrast, Apple Lossless Encoding files have containers for their tag information.

That all sounds pretty negative—yet if you need the highest quality for music, WAV or AIFF is the way to go. Another advantage is that WAV files are widely playable—all versions of Windows, Mac OS X, and most other operating systems have WAV players. The AIFF format is not as widely used on Windows (although iTunes for Windows can play AIFF), as it is primarily a Mac format.

Choose the Best Format for iTunes and the iPod

Choosing the best audio format for iTunes and the iPod can be tough. You'll probably be torn between having the highest-quality audio possible when playing audio on your computer and packing the largest possible number of good-sounding songs on your iPod—and making sure it has enough battery life for you to listen to plenty of those songs each day.

For the highest possible audio quality on your computer, use Apple Lossless Encoding. (WAV and AIFF are also possible, but they use more space, have no tag containers, and offer no advantage over Apple Lossless Encoding.) For the largest possible number of songs on an iPod, use AAC.

Unless your library has space for you to keep two copies of each song that you want to be able to play both on your computer and on the iPod, you'll probably be best off going with AAC at a high enough bitrate that you don't notice the difference in quality between the AAC files and Apple Lossless Encoding files.

AAC delivers high-quality audio, small file size, and enough flexibility for most purposes. But if you want to use the files you rip from a CD on a portable player that doesn't support AAC, or you need to play them using a software player that doesn't support AAC, choose MP3 instead. Similarly, if you want to share your music files with other people in any way other than sharing your library via iTunes, MP3 is the way to go—but remember that you need the copyright holder's explicit authorization to copy and distribute music.

Check or Change Your Importing Settings

To check or change the importing settings, follow these steps:

1. Display the iTunes dialog box or the Preferences dialog box:
   - In Windows, choose Edit | Preferences or press CTRL-COMMA or CTRL-Y to display the iTunes dialog box.
   - On the Mac, choose iTunes | Preferences or press ⌘-COMMA or ⌘-Y to display the Preferences dialog box.
2. Click the General tab if it's not already displayed.
3. In the When You Insert A CD drop-down list, choose what you want iTunes to do when you insert a CD: Show CD, Begin Playing, Ask To Import CD, Import CD, or Import CD And Eject.
   - Show CD, Import CD, and Import CD And Eject all involve looking up the song names on the Internet (unless you've already played the CD and thus caused iTunes to look up the names before), so iTunes will need to use your Internet connection.

Did You Know?

Digital Audio Formats iTunes and the iPod Can't Play

For most of the music you store on your computer and enjoy via iTunes or an iPod, you'll want to use AAC, MP3, or whichever combination of the two you find most convenient. Both iTunes and the iPod can also use WAV files and AIFF files.

For you as a digital audio enthusiast, other formats that may be of interest include the following:

- WMA is an audio format developed by Microsoft. It's the preferred format of Windows Media Player, the Microsoft audio and video player included with all desktop versions of Windows. WMA supports DRM, but its DRM is incompatible with iTunes and the iPod.
- mp3PRO was designed to be a successor to MP3, delivering higher audio quality at the same bitrates, but it has now been discontinued.
- Ogg Vorbis is an open-source format that's patent free but not yet widely used. To play Ogg Vorbis files on an iPod, you'll need to convert them to AAC or MP3. (You can also convert them to Apple Lossless Encoding, WAV, or AIFF, but doing so makes little sense, because Ogg Vorbis is a lossy format.) You can convert Ogg Vorbis files to WAV by using the freeware program Audacity (discussed later in this chapter) and then use iTunes to convert the WAV files to AAC or MP3, or convert them directly to AAC or MP3 by using Total Audio Converter (www.coolutils.com).
- FLAC, Free Lossless Audio Codec, is an open-source audio codec that creates lossless compressed files comparable in quality to Apple Lossless Encoding. To play FLAC files on an iPod, you'll need to convert them to AAC or MP3. For Windows, the best tool is Total Audio Converter (www.coolutils.com). To convert FLAC files to iPod-friendly formats on the Mac, use X Lossless Decoder (free; http://tmkk.pv.land.to/xld/index_e.html) or X Audio Compression Toolkit (xACT; free; http://download.cnet.com and other sites).

- Avoid the Import CD And Eject setting unless your computer's optical drive can always open (or eject a CD) safely without hitting anything.

4. Click the Import Settings button to display the Import Settings dialog box. Figure 7-2 shows the Import Settings dialog box on iTunes for the Mac. The Import Settings dialog box on iTunes for Windows has the same controls.

5. In the Import Using drop-down list, choose the encoder for the file format you want:
   - The default setting is AAC Encoder, which creates compressed files in AAC format. AAC files combine high audio quality with compact size, making AAC a good format for both iTunes and the iPod.
   - The other setting you're likely to want to try is MP3 Encoder, which creates compressed files in the MP3 format. MP3 files have marginally lower audio quality than AAC files for the same file size, but you can use MP3 files with a wider variety of software applications and hardware players.

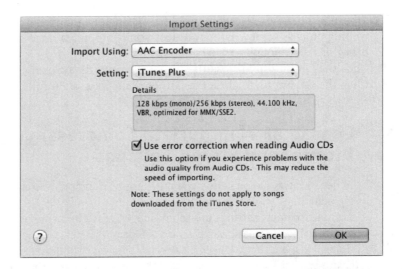

FIGURE 7-2   Configure your audio quality settings in the Import Settings dialog box.

- Apple Lossless Encoding files have full audio quality but a relatively large file size. They're good for iTunes but typically too large for the iPod.
- AIFF files and WAV files are uncompressed audio files, so they have full audio quality (and are widely playable, as noted earlier) but take up a huge amount of space. You'll seldom need to use either of these formats.

6. In the Setting drop-down list, choose the setting you want to use:
   - For the AAC Encoder, the Setting drop-down list offers the settings High Quality (128 Kbps), iTunes Plus (which uses the 256-Kbps bitrate), Spoken Podcast, and Custom. When you select Custom, iTunes displays the AAC Encoder dialog box so you can specify custom settings. See the next section, "Choose Custom AAC Encoding Settings," for a discussion of these options.
   - For the MP3 Encoder, the Setting drop-down list offers the settings Good Quality (128 Kbps), High Quality (160 Kbps), Higher Quality (192 Kbps), and Custom. When you select Custom, iTunes displays the MP3 Encoder dialog box so you can specify custom settings. See "Choose Custom MP3 Encoding Settings," later in this chapter, for a discussion of these options.
   - The Apple Lossless Encoder has no configurable settings. (The Setting drop-down list offers only the Automatic setting.)
   - For the AIFF Encoder and the WAV Encoder, the Setting drop-down list offers the settings Automatic and Custom. When you select Custom, iTunes displays the AIFF Encoder dialog box or the WAV Encoder dialog box (as appropriate) so you can specify custom settings. See "Choose Custom AIFF and WAV Encoding Settings," later in this chapter, for a discussion of these options.

7. Select the Use Error Correction When Reading Audio CDs check box if you want to turn on the error-correction feature. Usually, you need error correction only if you get clicks or skips in your imported files without it, but you may want

to turn it on anyway to avoid problems. Using error correction slows down the ripping process somewhat, but unless you're ripping a huge pile of CDs in a hurry, it's not enough to worry about.

8. Click the OK button to close the Import Settings dialog box.
9. Click the OK button to close the iTunes dialog box or Preferences dialog box.

How to...

Choose an Appropriate Compression Rate, Bitrate, and Stereo Settings

To get suitable audio quality, you must use an appropriate compression rate for the audio files you encode with iTunes.

iTunes' default settings are to encode AAC files in stereo at the 256-Kbps bitrate using automatic sample-rate detection. iTunes calls those settings iTunes Plus, and they deliver great results for most purposes. If you need to create smaller song files with acceptable quality, choose High Quality (128 Kbps) instead. For podcasts, choose the Spoken Podcast setting to create smaller files with lower quality. Alternatively, you can specify custom AAC settings for the files you create. With AAC you can change the bitrate, the sample rate, and the channels.

iTunes' MP3 Encoder gives you more flexibility. The default settings for MP3 are to encode MP3 files in stereo at the 160-Kbps bitrate, using CBR and automatic sample-rate detection. iTunes calls those settings High Quality, and they deliver results almost as good as the High Quality settings with the AAC Encoder, although they produce significantly larger files because the bitrate is higher.

For encoding MP3 files, iTunes also offers preset settings for Good Quality (128 Kbps) and Higher Quality (192 Kbps). Beyond these choices, you can choose the Custom setting and specify exactly the settings you want: bitrates from 16 Kbps to 320 Kbps, CBR or VBR, sample rate, channels, the stereo mode, whether to use Smart Encoding Adjustments, and whether to filter frequencies lower than 10 Hz.

If possible, invest a few days in choosing a compression rate for your library. Choosing the wrong compression rate can cost you disk space (if you record at too high a bitrate), audio quality (too low a bitrate), and the time it takes to rip your entire collection again at the bitrate you prefer.

Choose a representative selection of the types of music you plan to listen to using your computer and iPod. Encode several copies of each test track at different bitrates, and then listen to them over several days to see which provides the best balance of file size and audio quality. Make sure some of the songs test the different aspects of music that are important to you. For example, if your musical tastes lean to female vocalists, listen to plenty of those types of songs. If you prefer bass-heavy, bludgeoning rock, listen to that. If you go for classical music as well, add that to the mix. You may need to use different compression rates for different types of music to achieve satisfactory results and keep the file size down.

Choose Custom AAC Encoding Settings

To choose custom AAC encoding settings, follow these steps:

1. In the Import Settings dialog box, choose AAC Encoder in the Import Using drop-down list.
2. In the Setting drop-down list, choose the Custom item to display the AAC Encoder dialog box:

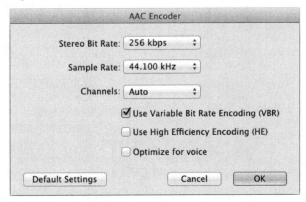

3. In the Stereo Bit Rate drop-down list, choose the bitrate. You can use from 16 Kbps to 320 Kbps. The default is 256 Kbps.
   - The 256 Kbps setting provides high-quality audio suitable for general music listening. You may want to experiment with higher bitrates to see if you can detect a difference. If not, stick with 256 Kbps as the best compromise between getting high audio quality and getting enough music on your iPod.
   - The 128 Kbps setting provides acceptable audio quality. You may want to use this setting for lower-capacity iPods to fit more songs on them.
   - If you listen to spoken-word audio, experiment with the bitrates below 64 Kbps to see which bitrate delivers suitable quality for the material you listen to, and select the Optimize For Voice check box.
4. In the Channels drop-down list, select Auto, Stereo, or Mono, as appropriate. In most cases, Auto (the default setting) is the best bet, because it makes iTunes choose stereo or mono as appropriate to the sound source. But you may occasionally need to produce mono files from stereo sources.
5. If you want to use VBR encoding rather than CBR encoding, select the Use Variable Bit Rate Encoding (VBR) check box.
6. If you want to use the High Efficiency Encoding format, select the Use High Efficiency Encoding (HE) check box. High Efficiency Encoding is a relatively new feature in AAC that creates smaller files. Audiophiles disagree as to whether it maintains the same quality; try it for yourself and see what you think.
7. If you want to optimize the encoding for voice instead of music, select the Optimize For Voice check box. Normally, you'd do this only for podcasts and other spoken-word audio.
8. Click the OK button to close the AAC Encoder dialog box.

Choose Custom MP3 Encoding Settings

To choose custom MP3 encoding settings, follow these steps:

1. In the Import Settings dialog box, choose MP3 Encoder in the Import Using drop-down list.
2. In the Setting drop-down list, choose the Custom item to display the MP3 Encoder dialog box:

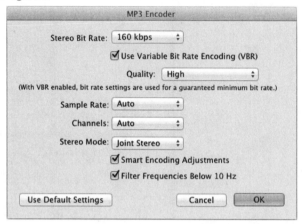

3. In the Stereo Bit Rate drop-down list, select the bitrate you want to use.
   - The choices range from 16 Kbps to 320 Kbps. 16 Kbps produces shoddy-sounding audio even for the spoken word, but it may be useful when you need to get long passages of low-quality audio into a small file. At the other extreme, 320 Kbps produces audio high enough in quality that most people can't distinguish it from CD-quality audio.
   - iTunes uses the bitrate you select as the exact bitrate for CBR encoding and as the minimum bitrate for VBR encoding.
   - See the section "Understand CD-Quality Audio and Lossy and Lossless Compression" earlier in this chapter for a discussion of CD-quality audio. "Choose an Appropriate Compression Rate, Bitrate, and Stereo Settings," also earlier in this chapter, offers advice on choosing a compression rate that matches your needs.
4. Select the Use Variable Bit Rate Encoding (VBR) check box if you want to create VBR-encoded files instead of CBR-encoded files.
   - See the sidebar "Choose Between CBR and VBR, and a Suitable Stereo Setting, for MP3" later in this chapter for a discussion of CBR and VBR.
   - If you select this check box, choose a suitable setting in the Quality drop-down list. The choices are Lowest, Low, Medium Low, Medium, Medium High, High, and Highest. iTunes uses the bitrates specified in the Stereo Bit Rate drop-down list as the guaranteed minimum bitrates. The Quality setting controls the amount of processing iTunes applies to making the file sound as close to the original as possible. More processing requires more processor cycles, which will make your computer work harder. If your computer is already working at full throttle, encoding will take longer.

5. In the Sample Rate drop-down list, set a sample rate manually only if you're convinced you need to do so.
   - You may want to use a lower sample rate if you're encoding spoken-word audio rather than music and don't need such high fidelity.
   - Choices range from 8 KHz to 48 KHz (higher than CD-quality audio, which uses 44.1 KHz).
   - The default setting is Auto, which uses the same sample rate as does the music you're encoding. Using the same sample rate usually delivers optimal results.
6. In the Channels drop-down list, select Auto, Mono, or Stereo. The default setting is Auto, which uses mono for encoding mono sources and stereo for stereo sources.
7. In the Stereo Mode drop-down list, choose Normal Stereo or Joint Stereo. See the sidebar "Choose Between CBR and VBR, and a Suitable Stereo Setting, for MP3" for a discussion of the difference between normal stereo and joint stereo. If you select Mono in the Channels drop-down list, the Stereo Mode drop-down list becomes unavailable because its options don't apply to mono.
8. Select or clear the Smart Encoding Adjustments check box and the Filter Frequencies Below 10 Hz check box, as appropriate. These check boxes are selected by default. In most cases, you'll do best to leave them selected.
   - Smart Encoding Adjustments allows iTunes to tweak your custom settings to improve them if you've chosen an inappropriate combination.
   - Frequencies below 10 Hz are infrasound and are of interest only to animals such as elephants, so filtering them out makes sense for humans.

 To restore iTunes to using its default settings for encoding MP3 files, click the Use Default Settings button in the MP3 Encoder dialog box.

9. Click the OK button to close the MP3 Encoder dialog box.

How to... Choose Between CBR and VBR, and a Suitable Stereo Setting, for MP3

After choosing the bitrate at which to encode your MP3 files, you must choose between constant bitrate (CBR) and variable bitrate (VBR). You must also choose whether to use joint stereo or normal stereo.

CBR simply records each part of the file at the specified bitrate. CBR files can sound great, particularly at higher bitrates, but generally VBR delivers better quality than CBR. This is because VBR can allocate space more intelligently as the audio needs it. For example, a complex passage of a song will require more data to represent it accurately than will a simple passage, which in turn will require more data than the two seconds of silence before the massed guitars come crashing back in.

The disadvantage to VBR, and the reason why most MP3 encoders are set to use CBR by default, is that many older decoders and hardware devices can't play it. If you're using iTunes and an iPod, you don't need to worry about this. But if you're using an older decoder or hardware device, check that it can manage VBR.

(Continued)

So VBR is probably a better bet. A harder choice is between the two different types of stereo that iTunes offers: joint stereo and normal stereo. (iTunes also offers mono—a single channel that gives no separation among the sounds. The only reason to use mono is if your sound source is mono; for example, a live recording that used a single mono microphone.)

Stereo delivers two channels: a left channel and a right channel. These two channels provide positional audio, enabling recording and mixing engineers to separate the audio so that different sounds appear to be coming from different places. For example, the engineer can make one guitar sound as though it's positioned on the left and another guitar sound as though it's positioned on the right. Or the engineer might pan a sound from left to right so it seems to go across the listener.

Normal stereo (sometimes called *plain stereo*) uses two tracks: one for the left stereo channel and another for the right stereo channel. As its name suggests, normal stereo is the form of stereo that's usually used. For example, if you buy a CD that's recorded in stereo and play it back through your boom box, you're using normal stereo.

Joint stereo (sometimes called *mid/side stereo*) divides the channel data differently to make better use of a small amount of data storage. The encoder averages out the two original channels (assuming the sound source is normal stereo) to a mid channel. It then encodes this channel, devoting to it the bulk of the available space assigned by the bitrate. One channel contains the data that's the same on both channels. The second channel contains the data that's different on one of the channels. By reducing the channel data to the common data (which takes the bulk of the available space) and the data that's different on one of the channels (which takes much less space), joint stereo can deliver higher audio quality at the same bitrate as normal stereo.

Use joint stereo to produce better-sounding audio when encoding at lower bitrates, and use normal stereo for all your recordings at your preferred bitrate. Where the threshold for lower-bitrate recording falls depends on you. Many people recommend using normal stereo for encoding at bitrates of 160 Kbps and above, and using joint stereo for lower bitrates (128 Kbps and below). Others recommend not using normal stereo below 192 Kbps. Experiment to establish what works for you.

The results you get with joint stereo depend on the quality of the MP3 encoder you use. Some of the less-capable MP3 encoders produce joint-stereo tracks that sound more like mono tracks than like normal-stereo tracks. Better encoders produce joint-stereo tracks that sound very close to normal-stereo tracks. iTunes produces pretty good joint-stereo tracks.

Using the same MP3 encoder, normal stereo delivers better sound quality than joint stereo—at high bitrates. At lower bitrates, joint stereo delivers better sound quality than normal stereo, because joint stereo can retain more data about the basic sound (in the mid channel) than normal stereo can retain about the sound in its two separate channels. But joint stereo provides less separation between the left and right channels than normal stereo provides. (The lack of separation is what produces the mono-like effect.)

FIGURE 7-3   If you choose to encode to AIFF or WAV files, you can set encoding options
in the AIFF Encoder dialog box (left) or the WAV Encoder dialog box (right).

Choose Custom AIFF and WAV Encoding Settings

The AIFF Encoder dialog box (shown on the left in Figure 7-3) and the WAV Encoder
dialog box (shown on the right in Figure 7-3) offer similar settings. AIFFs and WAVs are
essentially the same apart from the file header, which distinguishes the file formats
from each other.

In either of these dialog boxes, you can choose the following settings:

- **Sample Rate**   Choose Auto (the default setting) to encode at the same sample
  rate as the original you're ripping. Otherwise, choose a value from the range
  available (8 KHz to 48 KHz).
- **Sample Size**   Select Auto to have iTunes automatically match the sample size
  to that of the source. Otherwise, select 8 Bit or 16 Bit, as appropriate. PCM audio
  uses 16 bits, so if you're encoding files from CDs, iTunes automatically uses a
  16-bit sample size.
- **Channels**   Select Auto (the default setting) to encode mono files from mono
  sources and stereo files from stereo sources. Otherwise, select Mono or Stereo,
  as appropriate.

Deal with CDs That Your Computer Can't Rip

iTunes and your computer should be able to rip songs from any CD that uses the
regular audio CD format. This standard is called Red Book, because it was published in
a red binder. But you may run into audio discs that look like CDs but that use different
formats and content-protection technologies to prevent you ripping them.

Until several years ago, it looked as though CD protection would become widespread,
with record companies deploying content-protection technologies such as Macrovision's

CDS-300 and SunnComm's MediaMax on ever more CDs. But then Sony BMG used a copy-protection system named Extended Copy Protection (XCP) on some audio discs in 2005 that installed what computer hackers call a *rootkit* on Windows computers that tried to play the discs. The rootkit severely compromised the computers' security, and caused a storm of protest. Sony BMG eventually withdrew the XCP-protected discs and offered to exchange those that had been bought.

Watch Out for Copy-Protected Discs

If you're unlucky, you may still run into copy-protected discs. These are bad news because they can

- Cause your computer to freeze, or make it unable to eject the disc.
- Install files on your PC (not on a Mac) without your permission.
- Restrict you to playing back low-quality audio.

Use these three indicators to spot copy-protected discs:

- **Look for the Compact Disc Digital Audio (CDDA) logo**   This isn't a reliable indicator, because some Red Book CDs don't have the logo, and some non–Red Book discs do. But if the disc doesn't have the logo, examine it carefully.
- **Look for a disclaimer, warning, or notice**   This will say something like "Will not play on PC or Mac," "This CD cannot be played on a PC/Mac," "Copy Control," or "Copy Protected."
- **Watch out for odd behavior**   If the disc attempts to install software that you must use to access the music on the disc, it's protected. Or if the disc won't play on your computer, or it will play but won't rip, it's most likely protected (it could also be scratched or damaged).

Deal with Copy-Protected Discs

Here are tricks you can try for dealing with copy-protected discs:

- **Turn off AutoPlay in Windows**   Most of the copy-protection technologies use Windows' AutoPlay feature to run and install software automatically. Turning AutoPlay off in the Control Panel gives you some protection.
- **Use a different optical drive**   Some optical drives are more tolerant than others of the faults deliberately introduced on the CD by some copy-protection systems.
- **Use a heavy-duty ripper**   A heavy-duty ripper such as Exact Audio Copy (www.exactaudiocopy.de; free) can extract audio from CDs that are corrupted or scratched badly enough to defeat other rippers. Technically, using a program such as this to defeat copy-protection is illegal, but using such a program on a scratched or damaged CD is fine.

Eject Stuck Audio Discs from a Mac

If you get an audio disc stuck in your Mac, follow as many of these steps as necessary to eject it:

1. Restart your Mac. If it's too hung to restart by conventional means, press the Reset button (if it has one) or press ⌘-CTRL-POWER. At the system startup sound, hold down the mouse button until your Mac finishes booting. This action may eject the disc.
2. Restart your Mac again. As before, if the Mac is too hung to restart by conventional means, press the Reset button or press ⌘-CTRL-POWER. At the system startup sound, hold down ⌘-OPTION-O-F to boot to the Open Firmware mode.
3. Type **eject cd** and press RETURN. If all is well, the CD drive will open. If not, you may see the message "read of block0 failed. can't OPEN the EJECT device." Either way, type **mac-boot** and press RETURN to reboot your Mac.

If Open Firmware mode won't fix the problem, you'll need to take your Mac to a service shop.

Convert Other File Types to Formats an iPod Can Play

Most iPods can play AAC files, MP3 files (including files in the Audible audiobook format), Apple Lossless Encoding files, AIFF files, and WAV files. The second-generation iPod shuffle can play all these file types except Apple Lossless Encoding. These common formats should take care of all your regular listening in iTunes and on the iPod.

But if you receive files from other people, or download audio from the Internet (as described in Chapter 8), you'll encounter many other digital audio formats. This section describes a couple of utilities for converting files from other formats to ones the iPod can use.

Convert a Song from AAC to MP3 (or Vice Versa)

Sometimes, you may need to convert a song from the format in which you imported it, or (more likely) in which you bought it, to a different format. For example, you may need to convert a song in AAC format to MP3 so that you can use it on an MP3 player that can't play AAC files.

If the AAC file is a protected song you bought from the iTunes Store, you cannot convert it directly. Instead, you must burn it to a CD, and then rip that CD to the format you need.

Did You Know?

What Happens When You Convert a File from One Compressed Format to Another

Don't convert a song from one compressed format to another compressed format unless you absolutely must, because such a conversion loses audio quality.

For example, say you have a WMA file. The audio is already compressed with lossy compression, so some parts of the audio have been lost. When you convert this file to an MP3 file, the conversion utility expands the compressed WMA audio to uncompressed audio, and then recompresses it to the MP3 format, again using lossy compression.

The uncompressed audio contains a faithful rendering of all the defects in the WMA file. So the MP3 file contains as faithful a rendering of this defective audio as the MP3 encoder can provide at that compression rate, plus any defects the MP3 encoding introduces. But you'll be able to play the file on the iPod—which may be your main concern.

So if you still have the CD from which you imported the song, import the song again using the other compressed format rather than converting the song from one compressed format to another. Doing so will give you significantly higher quality. But if you don't have the CD—for example, because you bought the song in the compressed format—converting to the other format will produce usable results.

To convert a song from one compressed format to another, follow these steps:

1. In iTunes, display the Advanced menu and see which format is listed in the Create Version command (for example, Create AAC Version or Create MP3 Version). If this is the format you want, you're all set, but you might want to double-check the settings used for the format.

You can also right-click a file (or CTRL-click on the Mac) and look at the Create Version item on the shortcut menu.

2. Display the iTunes dialog box or the Preferences dialog box:
   - In Windows, choose Edit | Preferences or press CTRL-COMMA or CTRL-Y to display the iTunes dialog box.
   - On the Mac, choose iTunes | Preferences or press ⌘-COMMA or ⌘-Y to display the Preferences dialog box.
3. Click the General tab to display its contents.
4. Click the Import Settings button to display the Import Settings dialog box.
5. In the Import Using drop-down list, select the encoder you want to use. For example, choose MP3 Encoder if you want to convert an existing file to an MP3 file; choose AAC Encoder if you want to create an AAC file; or choose Apple Lossless Encoder if you want to create an Apple Lossless Encoding file.

Unless the song file is currently in WAV or AIFF format, it's usually not worth converting it to Apple Lossless Encoding, because the source file is not high enough quality to benefit from Apple Lossless Encoding's advantages over AAC or MP3.

6. If necessary, use the Setting drop-down list to specify the details of the format. (See "Check or Change Your Importing Settings" earlier in this chapter for details.)
7. Click the OK button to close the Import Settings dialog box.
8. Click the OK button to close the iTunes dialog box or the Preferences dialog box.
9. In your library, select the song or songs you want to convert.
10. Choose Advanced | Create *Format* Version. (The Create Version item on the Advanced menu changes to reflect the encoder you chose in Step 5.) iTunes converts the file or files, saves it or them in the folder that contains the original file or files, and adds it or them to your library.

Because iTunes automatically applies tag information to converted files, you may find it hard to tell in iTunes which file is in AAC format and which is in MP3 format. The easiest way to find out is to issue a Get Info command for the song (for example, right-click or CTRL-click the song and choose Get Info from the shortcut menu) and check the Kind readout on the Summary tab of the Item Information dialog box.

After converting the song or songs to the other format, remember to restore your normal import setting in the Import Settings dialog box before you import any more songs from CD.

Convert WMA Files to MP3 or AAC

If you buy music from any of the online music stores that focus on Windows rather than on the Mac, the songs may be in WMA format. WMA is the stores' preferred format for selling online music because it offers DRM features for protecting the music against being stolen.

In iTunes for Windows, you can convert a WMA file to your current importing format (as set in the Import Settings dialog box) by dragging the file to your library or by using either the File | Add File To Library or the File | Add Folder To Library command. iTunes for the Mac doesn't have this capability—but if you have access to a PC running Windows, you can then copy or transfer the converted files to the Mac.

To convert WMA files on Mac OS X, you need to use a third-party converter. At this writing, the best free choice is the free version of Switch (www.nch.com.au/switch/). There's also a paid version of Switch that has more features.

If you buy WMA files protected with DRM, you'll be limited in what you can do with them. In most cases, you'll be restricted to playing the songs with Windows Media Player (which is one of the underpinnings of the WMA DRM scheme), which won't let you convert the songs directly to another format. But most online music stores allow you to burn the songs you buy to CD. In this case, you can convert the WMA files to MP3 files or AAC files by burning them to CD and then use iTunes to rip and encode the CD as usual.

Create Audio Files from Cassettes or Vinyl Records

If you have audio on analog media such as cassette tapes, vinyl records, or other waning technologies, you may want to transfer that audio to your computer so you can listen to it using iTunes or an iPod. Dust off your gramophone, cassette deck, or other audio source, and then work your way through the following sections.

 You may need permission to create audio files that contain copyrighted content. If you hold the copyright to the audio, you can copy it as much as you want. If not, you need specific permission to copy it, unless it falls under a specific copyright exemption. For example, the Audio Home Recording Act (AHRA) personal use provision lets you copy a copyrighted work (for example, an LP) onto a different medium so you can listen to it—but only provided that you use a "digital audio recording device," a term that doesn't cover computers.

Connect the Audio Source to Your Computer

Start by connecting the audio source to your computer with a cable that has the right kinds of connectors for the audio source and your sound card. For example, to connect a typical cassette player to a typical sound card, you'll need a cable with two RCA plugs at the cassette player's end (or at the receiver's end) and a male-end stereo miniplug at the other end to plug into your sound card. If the audio source has only a headphone socket or line-out socket for output, you'll need a miniplug at the source end too.

 Because record players produce a low volume of sound, you'll almost always need to put a record player's output through the Phono input of an amplifier before you can record it on your computer.

If your computer's sound card has a line-in port and a mic port, use the line-in port. If your computer's sound card has only a mic port, turn the source volume down to a minimum for the initial connection, because mic ports tend to be sensitive.

 If you have a Mac that doesn't have an audio input, consider an external audio interface such as the Griffin iMic (www.griffintechnology.com), which lets you record via USB.

Get a Suitable Program for Recording Audio

Both Windows and Mac OS X include programs that can record audio:

- **Windows**   You'll find Sound Recorder in the Accessories folder.
- **Mac OS X**   You'll find QuickTime Player in the Applications folder. And if you have iLife, you can also use GarageBand to record audio.

You can use Sound Recorder or QuickTime Player in a pinch, but neither has the features you'll normally want. GarageBand, on the other hand, is effective for recording existing audio from other sources, but is really more geared to composing and recording your own musical creations.

So usually you're better off getting a third-party program for recording your existing audio to create files for iTunes and your iPod. Many audio-recording programs are available, but I recommend Audacity, which you can download for free from the Audacity web page on SourceForge (http://audacity.sourceforge.net/). Audacity runs on both Windows and Mac OS X (and on Linux, if you use that too).

If you want to try recording audio with Sound Recorder or QuickTime Player, visit this book's page on my website (www.ghdbooks.com) for instructions.

Download and Install Audacity

Go to SourceForge (http://audacity.sourceforge.net) and download Audacity by following the link for the latest stable version and your operating system (for example, Windows or Mac OS X). At this writing, you download the file itself from one of various software-distribution sites by following a link from the Audacity page on SourceForge.

Once you've downloaded the Audacity distribution file, install it like this:

- **Windows** Double-click the distribution file, and then follow through the installation wizard that runs.
- **Mac OS X** Expand the downloaded file, and then drag the resulting Audacity folder to your Applications folder.

Run Audacity and Choose Your Language

The first time you run Audacity, you may need to choose the language you want to use—for example, English. You then see Audacity. Figure 7-4 shows the opening Audacity screen on the Mac. The Windows version is almost identical.

Install the LAME MP3 Encoder

After you install Audacity, you'll need to add an MP3 encoder if you want to be able to create MP3 files with Audacity. (Instead of adding the MP3 encoder, you can create WAV files with Audacity and then use iTunes to create MP3 files or AAC files.)

Follow these steps to add an MP3 encoder to Audacity:

1. Open the Audacity Preferences dialog box in one of these ways:
   - **Windows** Press CTRL-P or choose Edit | Preferences.
   - **Mac OS X** Press ⌘-COMMA or choose Audacity | Preferences.
2. In the left pane, click the Libraries category to display its contents (see Figure 7-5).
3. Check the MP3 Export Library area. If the MP3 Library Version readout says "MP3 export library not found," you need to add an MP3 encoder.

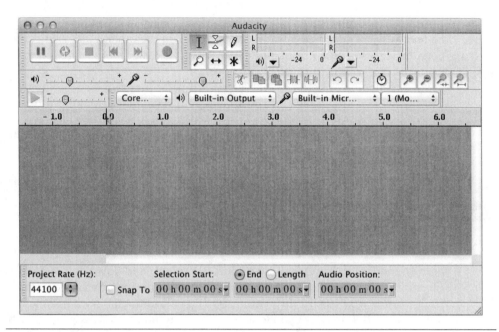

FIGURE 7-4 Audacity is a great freeware application for recording audio and fixing problems with it.

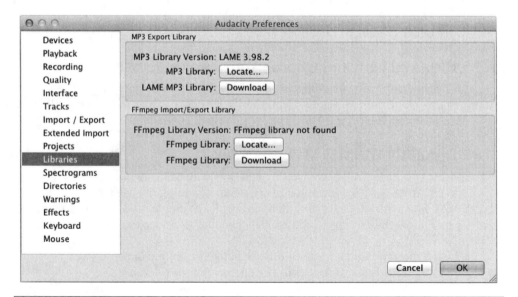

FIGURE 7-5 Use the File Formats tab of the Audacity Preferences dialog box to add an MP3 encoder to Audacity.

4. Click the Download button in the MP3 Export Library area. Audacity opens a web page in your default browser (for example, Internet Explorer on Windows or Safari on the Mac) giving instructions for downloading and installing the LAME MP3 encoder.
5. Follow the instructions to download the encoder and install it. When you have done so, its name and version appear next to the MP3 Library Version readout.

Leave the Audacity Preferences dialog box open so that you can set audio playback and recording settings, as discussed next.

Choose Audio Playback and Recording Settings

With the Audacity Preferences dialog box still open, choose your audio playback and recording settings. Follow these steps:

1. In the left pane, click the Devices category to display its contents (see Figure 7-6).
2. In the Device drop-down list in the Playback box, choose the output device—for example, Built-in Output.
3. In the Device drop-down list in the Recording box, choose the device from which to record—for example, Built-in Input or a third-party device you've connected.
4. In the Channels drop-down list, choose 2 (Stereo).
5. Click the OK button to close the Audio Preferences dialog box.

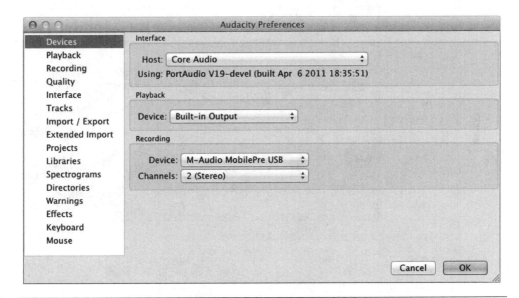

FIGURE 7-6 Choose your recording device and the number of channels in the Devices category of the Audacity Preferences dialog box.

Record Audio with Audacity

To record audio with Audacity, follow these steps:

1. Start Audacity if it's not already running.
2. If necessary, choose a different sound source in the Default Input Source drop-down list on the right side of the window.
3. Cue your audio source.
4. Click the Record button (the button with the red circle) to start the recording (see Figure 7-7).
5. If necessary, change the recording volume by dragging the Input Volume slider (the slider with the microphone at its left end). When you've got it right, stop the recording, create a new file, and then restart the recording.
6. Click the Record button again to stop recording.
7. Choose File | Save Project to open the Save Project As dialog box, specify a filename and folder, and then click the Save button.

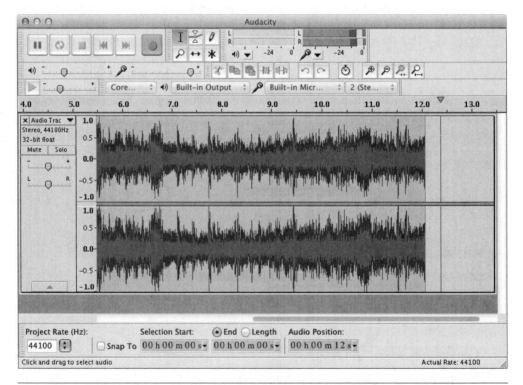

FIGURE 7-7   Adjust the input volume if the signal is too low or too high.

8. When you are ready to export the audio file, choose File | Export to display the Save As dialog box (shown here).

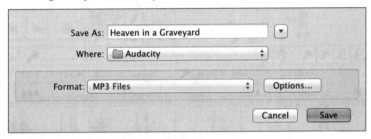

9. Choose MP3 Files in the Format drop-down list.
10. Click the Options button to display the Specify MP3 Options dialog box (shown here).

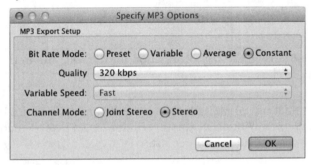

11. In the Bit Rate Mode area, choose the bitrate mode by selecting the Preset option button, the Variable option button, the Average option button, or the Constant option button. As discussed earlier in this chapter, a variable bitrate gives you the best quality for a given file size, but a constant bitrate is more compatible with older players.
12. In the Quality drop-down list, choose the bitrate you want to use—for example, 320 Kbps.
13. If you selected the Variable option button, choose the variable speed in the Variable Speed drop-down list.
14. In the Channel Mode area, select the Joint Stereo option button or the Stereo option button, as needed. As discussed earlier in this chapter, normal stereo (the Stereo option button here) gives better sound at higher bitrates.
15. Click the OK button. Audacity returns you to the Save As dialog box.
16. Click the Save button. Audacity displays the Edit Metadata dialog box (see Figure 7-8).
17. Enter the song's metadata—the artist name, song name, album title, and so on.
18. Click the OK button. Audacity exports the song to an MP3 file.

FIGURE 7-8　Type the tag information for the song file in the Edit Metadata dialog box.

After creating the MP3 file, you can add it to your iTunes library. For example, click the file in a Windows Explorer window or a Finder window and then drag it to the Library section of the Source list.

How to... Remove Scratches and Hiss from Audio Files

If you record tracks from vinyl records, audio cassettes, or other analog sources, you may well get some clicks or pops, hiss, or background hum in the file. Scratches on a record can cause clicks and pops, audio cassettes tend to hiss (even with noise-reduction such as Dolby), and record players or other machinery can add hum.

All these noises—very much part of the analog audio experience, and actually appreciated as such by some enthusiasts—tend to annoy people accustomed to digital audio. The good news is that you can remove many such noises by using the right software.

Unless you already have an audio editor that has noise-removal features, your best choice is probably Audacity. To remove noise from a recording using Audacity, follow these steps:

1. In Audacity, open the project containing the song.
2. Select a part of the recording with just noise—for example, the opening few seconds of silence (except for the stylus clicking and popping along).

3. Choose Effect | Noise Removal to open the Noise Removal dialog box (shown here ready for the second stage of the noise-removal process).

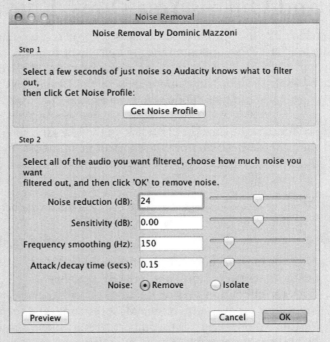

4. Click the Get Noise Profile button. The Noise Removal system analyzes your sample and applies the corresponding noise profile.
5. Select the part of the recording that you want to affect:
   - To affect the entire recording, choose Edit | Select | All. This is usually the easiest approach.
   - To affect only part of the recording, drag through it. For example, you might want to affect only the end of the recording if this is where all the scratches occur.
6. Choose Effect | Noise Removal to open the Noise Removal dialog box again.
7. Drag the sliders in the Step 2 box to specify how much noise you want to remove, the sensitivity, the frequency smoothing, and the attack and decay time.
8. In the Noise area, make sure the Remove option button is selected rather than the Isolate option button.
9. Click the Preview button to get a preview of the effect this will have, and adjust the sliders as needed.
10. When you're satisfied with the effect, click the OK button to remove the noise.
11. Choose File | Save to save your project.

Trim Audio Files to Get Rid of Intros and Outros You Don't Like

If you don't like the intro of a particular song, you can tell iTunes to suppress it by setting the Start Time option on the Options tab of the Item Information dialog box to the point where you want the song to start playing. Similarly, you can suppress an outro by using the Stop Time option, also on the Options tab.

You can also use these options to trim an audio file. Follow these steps:

1. In iTunes, right-click (or CTRL-click on the Mac) the song you want to shorten, and then choose Get Info from the shortcut menu to display the Item Information dialog box. (This dialog box's title bar shows the song name, not the words "Item Information.")

 If you've recorded songs that have empty audio at the beginning or end (or both), use this technique to remove the empty audio.

2. Click the Options tab to display its contents.
3. Set the Start Time, Stop Time, or both, as needed.
4. Click the OK button to close the Item Information dialog box.
5. Right-click (or CTRL-click on the Mac) the song, and then choose Create *Format* Version, where *Format* is the import format you've chosen in the Import Settings dialog box—for example, Create AAC Version.
6. iTunes creates a shorter version of the song. It's a good idea to rename the song immediately to avoid confusing it with the source file. Alternatively, delete the source file if you no longer want to keep it.

 You can even use this trick to split a song file into two or more different files. For example, to create two files, work out where the division needs to fall. Create the first file by setting the Stop Time to this time and then performing the conversion. Return to the source file, set the Start Time to the dividing time, and then perform the conversion again.

Tag Your Compressed Files with the Correct Information for Sorting

The best thing about compressed audio formats such as AAC, MP3, and Apple Lossless Encoding—apart from their being compressed and still giving high-quality audio—is that each file format can store a full set of tag information about the song the file contains. The tag information lets you sort, organize, and search for songs on iTunes. The iPod needs correct artist, album, and track name information in tags to be able to organize your AAC files and MP3 files correctly. If a song lacks this minimum of information, iTunes doesn't transfer it to the iPod.

You can force iTunes to load untagged songs on an iPod by assigning them to a playlist and loading the playlist. But in most cases it's best to tag all the songs in your library—or at least tag as many as is practicable.

You can tag your song files using any tool you choose, but you'll probably want to use iTunes much of the time, because it provides solid if basic features for tagging one or more files at once manually. But if your library contains many untagged or mistagged files, you may need a heavier-duty application. This section shows you how to tag most effectively in iTunes.

 If you need more powerful tagging features than what iTunes offers, try Tag&Rename ($29.95; www.softpointer.com/tr.htm; trial version available) for Windows or Media Rage ($29.95; www.chaoticsoftware.com; trial version available) for Mac OS X.

The easiest way to add tag information to an AAC file or MP3 file is by downloading the information from CDDB (the CD Database) when you rip the CD. But sometimes you'll need to enter (or change) tag information manually to make iTunes sort the files correctly—for example, when the CDDB data is wrong or not available, or for existing song files created with software other than iTunes, such as song files you've created yourself.

How to... Tag Song Files After Encoding When Offline

Even if you rip CDs when your computer has no Internet connection, you can usually apply the CD information to the song files once you've reestablished an Internet connection. To do so, select the album or the songs in your library and then choose Advanced | Get Track Names. If the CD's details are in CDDB, iTunes should then be able to download the information.

If you imported the songs by using software other than iTunes, or if you imported the songs using iTunes on another computer and then copied them to this computer, iTunes objects with the "iTunes cannot get CD track names" dialog box shown here. In this case, you'll need to either reimport the songs on this computer or tag the songs manually.

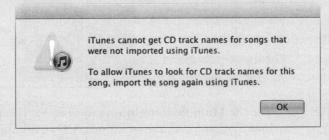

Often, MP3 files distributed illegally on the Internet lack tag information or include incorrect tags. That said, officially tagged files aren't always as accurate as they might be—so if you want your files to be as easy to find and manipulate as possible, it's worth spending some time checking the tags and improving them as necessary.

If you need to change the tag information for a whole CD's worth of songs, proceed as follows:

1. In iTunes, select all the song files you want to affect.
2. Right-click (or CTRL-click on the Mac) the selection and choose Get Info from the shortcut menu to display the Multiple Item Information dialog box. Alternatively, choose File | Get Info or press CTRL-I (Windows) or ⌘-I (Mac). Figure 7-9 shows the Windows version of the Multiple Item Information dialog box with the Info tab at the front.

 By default, when you issue a Get Info command with multiple songs selected, iTunes displays a dialog box to check that you want to edit the information for multiple songs. Click the Yes button to proceed; click the Cancel button to cancel. If you frequently want to edit tag information for multiple songs, select the Do Not Ask Me Again check box in the confirmation dialog box to turn off confirmations in the future.

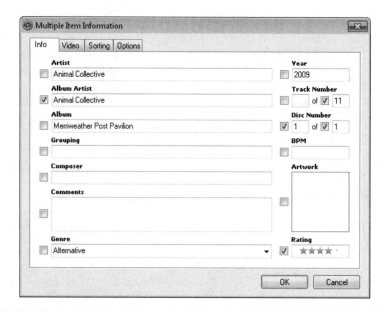

FIGURE 7-9 Use the Multiple Item Information dialog box to enter common tag information for all the songs on a CD or album at once.

3. Enter as much common information as you can: the artist, year, album, total number of tracks, disc number, composer, comments, and so on. If you have the artwork for the CD available, drag it to the Artwork well on the Info tab.

4. Click the OK button to close the dialog box and apply the information to the songs.

5. Click the first song to clear the current selection. Right-click (or CTRL-click on the Mac) the song and choose Get Info from the shortcut menu to display the Item Information dialog box for the song. Click the Info tab to display it if iTunes doesn't display it automatically. Figure 7-10 shows the Windows version of the Item Information dialog box for the song "My Girls." The song's title appears in the title bar of the dialog box.

6. Add any song-specific information here: the song name, the track number, and so on.

7. If you need to change the song's relative volume, equalizer preset, rating, start time, or stop time, work on the Options tab.

8. If you want to add lyrics to the song (either by typing them in or by pasting them from a lyrics site), work on the Lyrics tab.

9. Click the Previous button or the Next button to display the information for the previous song or next song.

10. Click the OK button to close the Item Information dialog box when you've finished adding song information.

FIGURE 7-10   Use the Item Information dialog box (whose title bar shows the song's name) to add song-specific information.

How to... **Submit CD Information to CDDB Using iTunes**

If iTunes tells you a CD you want to rip doesn't have an entry in CDDB, you can submit an entry yourself. Users submitting entries like this have added many of the entries in CDDB for older or less widely known CDs. Mainstream entries are submitted by the record companies themselves when they release a new CD.

CDDB contains entries for an enormous number of CDs—so unless you have an unusual CD, chances are any CD you want to rip already has an entry in CDDB. You may find that your CD is listed under a slightly different title or artist name than you're expecting—for example, the artist might be listed as "Sixpack, Joe" rather than "Joe Sixpack." Check carefully for any close matches before submitting an entry so you don't waste your time. You may also find CDDB contains two or more entries for the same CD.

When submitting an entry to CDDB, type the CD title, artist name, and song titles carefully using standard capitalization, and double-check all the information before you submit it. Otherwise, if your entry is accepted and entered in CDDB, anyone who looks up that CD will get the misspellings or wrong information you entered.

Here's how to submit an entry to CDDB:

1. Enter the tag information for the CD.
2. Choose Advanced | Submit CD Track Names to display the CD Info dialog box, and then check the information in the Artist, Composer, Album, Disc Number, Genre, and Year fields. Select the Compilation CD check box if the CD is a compilation rather than a work by an individual artist.
3. Establish an Internet connection if you need to do so manually.
4. Click the OK button. iTunes connects to CDDB and submits the information.

Save Audio Streams to Disk So You Can Listen to Them Later

If you enjoy listening to Internet radio, you may want to record it so that you can play it back later. iTunes doesn't let you save streaming audio to disk because recording streaming audio without specific permission typically violates copyright. So you need to use either a hardware solution or a third-party application to record streams.

Save Audio Streams to Disk Using Hardware

To solve the problem via hardware, use a standard audio cable to pipe the output from your computer's sound card to its line-in socket. You can then record the audio stream as you would any other external input by using an audio-recording application such as Audacity, discussed earlier in this chapter.

The only problem with using a standard audio cable is that you won't be able to hear via external speakers the audio stream you're recording. To solve this problem, get a stereo Y-connector. Connect one of the outputs to your external speakers and the other to your line-in socket. Converting the audio from digital to analog and then back to digital like this degrades its quality, but unless you're listening to the highest-bitrate Internet radio stations around, you'll most likely find the quality you lose to be a fair trade-off for the convenience you gain.

Save Audio Streams to Disk Using Software

To solve the problem via software, get an application that can record the audio stream directly.

At this writing, the best program for Windows is Total Recorder (www.highcriteria .com). Total Recorder comes in three editions: Standard, Professional, and Developer. Start by downloading the evaluation version to make sure that Total Recorder works with your PC and provides the features you need.

Here are three applications for the Mac:

- **RadioLover (www.bitcartel.com/radiolover)** RadioLover lets you record one or more radio streams at once.
- **Audio Hijack Pro (www.rogueamoeba.com/audiohijackpro)** Audio Hijack Pro lets you record the audio output from any application. You can set timers to record the items you want.
- **Radioshift (www.rogueamoeba.com/radioshift)** Radioshift lets you record Internet radio streams.

8

Buy and Download Songs, Videos, and More Online

HOW TO...

- Understand digital rights management (DRM) and what it's for
- Understand what the iTunes Store is
- Set up an account with the iTunes Store
- Configure iTunes Store settings
- Access the iTunes Store
- Buy songs, videos, and movies from the iTunes Store
- Listen to songs and watch videos and movies you've purchased
- Authorize and deauthorize computers for the iTunes Store
- Buy and download music from other online music stores
- Download music from other online sources

Instead of creating song files by ripping your own CDs, tapes, and records, you can buy songs online. You can also buy videos, movies, audio books, and other content.

If iTunes has its way, your first stop for buying content will be the iTunes Store, Apple's online service for songs, videos, movies, and more. This chapter discusses what the iTunes Store is, how it works, and how to use it. Because the iTunes Store works in almost exactly the same way on Mac OS X and Windows, this chapter discusses both operating systems together and, for balance, shows some screens from each.

The beginning of this chapter discusses digital rights management (DRM), because you'll benefit from understanding the essentials of DRM before buying content online. The end of the chapter discusses other online sources of songs, from online music stores other than the iTunes Store to free sources.

What Digital Rights Management (DRM) Is and What It's For

Digital rights management (DRM) is a type of technology used to protect digital content, such as songs and movies, against unauthorized copying or use. For the past ten or so years, the movie and music industry bodies have been struggling with consumers over how music and videos are sold (or stolen) and distributed.

Here's a quick summary:

- The record companies have applied copy-protection mechanisms to some audio discs to prevent their customers from making unauthorized pure-digital copies of music.
- Most video content is sold with copy-protection applied. For example, regular DVDs use the Content Scramble System (CSS) to protect their content. High-definition DVDs use the Advanced Access Content System (AACS) for protection.
- Some consumers are trying to protect their freedom to enjoy the music and video they buy in the variety of ways that law and case law have established to be either definitely legal or sort-of legal. For example, legal precedents that permit the use of VCRs, personal video recorders (PVRs), and home audio taping suggest that it's probably legal to create compressed audio files from a CD, record, or cassette, as long as they're for your personal use.
- Other people are deliberately infringing the media companies' copyrights by copying, distributing, and stealing music and video via peer-to-peer (P2P) networks, recordable CDs and DVDs, and other means.

Understand That DRM Is Neither "Good" nor "Bad"

DRM is often portrayed by consumer activists as being the quintessence of the Recording Industry Association of America's and Motion Picture Association of America's dreams and of consumers' nightmares. The publisher of a work can use DRM to impose a wide variety of restrictions on the ways in which a consumer can use the work. For example, a publisher could provide a music file that you could play only on your computer and that required you to pay for each extra play. As you'd imagine, such restrictions aren't popular, and early DRM quickly got a bad reputation.

But how good or bad DRM is in practice depends on the implementation. DRM can also be a compromise—for example, when Apple launched the iTunes Store, the only way it could persuade the record companies to make the songs available was by agreeing to apply DRM to the songs to limit what buyers could do with them.

The compromise worked adequately for both the record companies and the consumers. In May 2007, however, Apple convinced EMI to make songs available without DRM and at a higher quality. Following this move, other record companies have begun to make songs available without DRM. In January 2009, Apple announced that it would phase out DRM from the iTunes Store completely.

Music is almost ideal for digital distribution, and the record companies are sitting on colossal archives of songs that are out of print but still well within copyright. It's not economically viable for the record companies to sell pressed CDs of these songs, because demand for any given CD is likely to be relatively low. But demand is there, as has been demonstrated by the millions of illegal copies of such songs that have been downloaded from P2P services. If the record companies can make these songs available online with acceptable DRM (or without DRM), they'll almost certainly find buyers.

Some enterprising smaller operators *have* managed to make an economic proposition out of selling pressed CDs or recorded CDs of out-of-print music to which they've acquired the rights. By cutting out middlemen and selling directly via websites and mail order, and in some cases by charging a premium price for a hard-to-get product, such operators have proved that making such music available isn't impossible. Many independent musicians are also selling directly to the public, either on CD or over the Internet, which gives them creative control over their music as well as direct feedback from their fans.

Historically, video has not been a good candidate for digital distribution, because the files have been too big to transfer easily across the Internet. But now that faster broadband connections are becoming increasingly widespread, and YouTube is used for everything from promoting music to promoting presidential candidates, distributing even full-quality video files is workable. At this writing, the Netflix movie-rental company is trying to move its customers from receiving and returning DVDs by mail to downloading them via the Internet.

Know a Store's DRM Terms Before You Buy Any Protected Songs or Videos

Before you buy any song (or video, or movie) that is protected by DRM, make sure you understand what the DRM involves, what restrictions it places on you, and what changes the implementer of the DRM is allowed to make.

In most cases, when you "buy" a song that is protected by DRM, you buy not the song but a license to play the song in limited circumstances—for example, on a single computer or several computers, or for a limited length of time or a limited number of plays. You may or may not be permitted to burn the song to disc for storage or so that you can play it in conventional audio players (rather than on computers). In most cases, you are not permitted to give or sell the song to anyone else, nor can you return the song to the store for a refund or exchange. This may all seem too obvious to state—but it's completely different from most other things you buy, from a CD to a car.

The store that sells you the license to the song usually retains the right to change the limitations on how you can use the song. For example, the store can change the number of computers on which you can play the song, prevent you from burning it to disc, or even prevent you from playing it anymore. Any restrictions added may not take place immediately if your computer isn't connected to the Internet, but most online music stores require periodic authentication checks to make sure the music is still licensed for playing.

In general, "buying" DRM-protected songs online compares poorly to buying a physical CD, even though you have the option of buying individual songs rather than having to buy the entire contents of the CD. While you don't own the music on the CD, you own the CD itself, and can dispose of it as you want. For example, you can create digital copies of its contents (assuming that the CD is not copy-protected), lend the CD to a friend, or sell the CD to an individual or a store. But you can't distribute the digital copies freely without specific permission.

Before buying from an online store such as the iTunes Store, check the terms and conditions to make sure you know what you're getting and what you're not. For example, most video and movie files you buy from the iTunes Store are encumbered with DRM. In most cases, if the same content is available on a conventional medium (such as a DVD or a video cassette), buying it on that medium gives you more flexibility than buying a digital file.

Buy Songs, Videos, and Movies from the iTunes Store

So far, the iTunes Store is one of the largest and most successful attempts to sell music online. (The latter part of this chapter discusses other online music services, including Amazon.com, the second-generation Napster, and eMusic.) The iTunes Store is far from perfect, and its selection is still very limited compared to what many users would like to be able to buy, but it's an extremely promising start. At this writing, the iTunes Store is available to iTunes users on Windows and the Mac.

Here's the deal with the iTunes Store:

- Until January 2009, most songs cost $0.99 each for a DRM-protected version and $1.29 for a DRM-free version (if there was one). But in January 2009, Apple announced it would start phasing out DRM completely—and pricing songs at different levels ($0.69, $0.99, and $1.29).
- The cost of albums varies, but costs tend to be around what you'd pay for a discounted CD in many stores. Some CDs are available only as "partial CDs," which typically means that you can't buy the songs you're most likely to want. Extra-long songs (for example, those 13-minute jam sessions that used to max out a CD) are sometimes available for purchase only with an entire CD.
- Most video items cost $1.99 or more, but you can also buy them in bulk and save. For example, you might buy a whole season of *Desperate Housewives*.
- You can listen to a preview of any song to make sure it's what you want. Most previews are 90 seconds, unless the song is shorter than that or the record company has dug in its heels and insisted on 30 seconds. After you buy a song, you download it to your music library.

- You can burn songs to CD an unlimited number of times, although you can burn any given playlist only seven times without changing it or re-creating it under another name.
- The songs you buy are encoded in the AAC format (discussed in the section "AAC" in Chapter 7). Most videos and movies you buy are in the MPEG-4 video format and are protected with DRM.
- You can play the songs you buy on any number of iPods (or iPhones, or iPads) that you synchronize with your PC or Mac. You may also be able to play the songs on other music players that can use the AAC format (for example, some mobile phones other than iPhones can play AAC files).
- You can play the DRM-protected items you buy on up to five computers at once. These computers are said to be "authorized." You can change which computers are authorized for the items bought on a particular iTunes Store account.
- You can download any item you buy from the iTunes Store again if necessary, and you can share the items among all the devices linked to your iTunes Store account. For example, if you buy a song on your computer, you can download it to your iPad and iPhone as well.
- You can rent a movie and watch it on your computer, iPod, iPhone, iPad, or Apple TV. You can watch a rented movie on only one device at a time. So when you transfer a rented movie from your computer to one of the other devices mentioned above, it disappears from the iTunes library on your computer.

Know the Disadvantages of Buying from the iTunes Store

As of summer 2011, the iTunes Store offered more than 18 million songs and had sold more than 10 billion songs altogether.

For customers, it's great to be able to find songs easily, buy them almost instantly for reasonable prices, and use them in enough of the ways they're used to (play the songs on their computer; play them on their iPod, iPhone, or iPad; or burn them to disc). For the record companies, the appeal is a market that can provide a revenue stream at minimal cost (no physical media are involved) and with an acceptably small potential for abuse. (For example, most people who buy songs from the iTunes Store won't share them with others.)

Before you buy from the iTunes Store, though, make sure you know the disadvantages:

- Even though the AAC format provides relatively high audio quality, the songs sold by the iTunes Store are significantly lower quality than CD-quality audio. Test a few songs through headphones or high-end speakers to make sure you're happy with the quality you're getting.
- When you buy a CD, you own it. You can't necessarily do what you want with the music—not legally, anyway. But you can play it as often as you want on whichever player, lend it to a friend, sell it to someone else, and so on. By contrast, when you buy a song from the iTunes Store, you're not allowed to lend it to other people, or to sell it.

As well as songs, the iTunes Store sells video files and movies. As with songs, the convenience of buying via download is wonderful, but there are still disadvantages:

- Even the high-definition format provides lower quality than a high-definition DVD.
- You buy not a tangible object but a license to use the file. You can't resell the file—in fact, you can't even give it to someone else.
- If the video or movie file is protected by DRM (as most are), Apple can change your rights to use it, or simply stop you from playing it.

Set Up an Account with the iTunes Store

To use the iTunes Store, you need a PC or a Mac running iTunes as well as an Apple ID or an AOL screen name. You can get an Apple ID by setting up an account with Apple's iCloud service or an account on the iTunes Store.

 If you already have an account with Apple's MobileMe service, you already have an Apple ID. But Apple has announced that it will close MobileMe on June 30, 2012, so it is no longer selling MobileMe accounts. By that date, all MobileMe users will need to migrate to the iCloud service or lose access to their MobileMe content.

To get started with the iTunes Store, open it in iTunes. If you want to be able to keep your music playing while you browse the iTunes Store, double-click the iTunes Store item in the Source list to open a separate window showing the iTunes Store. If you prefer to work in the main iTunes window, simply click the iTunes Store item in the Source list in iTunes.

iTunes accesses the iTunes Store and displays its home page. Figure 8-1 shows an example on the Mac, using a separate window.

To sign in or to create an account, click the Sign In button. iTunes displays the Sign In To Download From The iTunes Store dialog box (see Figure 8-2).

If you have an Apple ID, type it in the Apple ID text box, type your password in the Password text box, and click the Sign In button. Likewise, if you have an AOL screen name, select the AOL option button, type your screen name and password, and click the Sign In button.

 Remember that your Apple ID is the full e-mail address, including the domain—not just the first part of the address. For example, if your Apple ID is an iCloud address, enter **yourname@me.com** rather than just **yourname.**

The first time you sign in to the iTunes Store, iTunes displays a dialog box pointing out that your Apple ID or AOL screen name hasn't been used with the iTunes Store and suggesting that you review your account information:

FIGURE 8-1 The iTunes Store home page provides quick access to the songs, videos, and other items available. You can display the iTunes Store either in a separate window, as shown here, or in the main iTunes window.

Click the Review button to review your account information. (This is a compulsory step. Clicking the Cancel button doesn't skip the review process, as you might hope—instead, it cancels the creation of your account.)

To create a new account, click the Create New Account button and then click the Continue button on the Welcome To The iTunes Store page. The subsequent screens then walk you through the process of creating an account. You have to provide your credit card details and billing address. Beyond this, you get a little homily on what you

FIGURE 8-2 From the Sign In dialog box, you can sign in to an existing account or create a new account.

may and may not legally do with the items you download, and you must agree to the terms of service of the iTunes Store.

Understand the Terms of Service

Almost no one ever reads the details of software licenses, which is why the software companies have been able to establish as normal the sales model in which you buy not software itself but a limited license to use it, and you have no recourse if it corrupts your data or reduces your computer to a pitiful puddle of silicon and steel. But you'd do well to read the terms and conditions of the iTunes Store before you buy music from it, because you should understand what you're getting into.

 The iTunes window doesn't give you the greatest view of the terms of service. To get a better view, click the Printable Version link at the very bottom of the scroll box or direct your browser to www.apple.com/legal/itunes/us/service.html.

The following are the key points of the terms of service:

- You can play DRM-protected items that you download on five Apple-authorized devices—computers, iPods, iPads, or iPhones—at any time. You can authorize and deauthorize computers, so you can (for example) transfer your DRM-protected items from your old computer to a new computer you buy.
- You can use, export, copy, and burn songs for "personal, noncommercial use." Burning and exporting are an "accommodation" to you and don't "constitute a

grant, waiver, or other limitation of any rights of the copyright owners." If you think that your being allowed to burn what would otherwise be illegal copies must limit the copyright owners' rights, I'd say you're right logically but wrong legally.

- You're not allowed to burn videos. Period.
- You agree not to violate the Usage Rules imposed by the agreement.
- You agree that Apple may disclose your registration data and account information to "law enforcement authorities, government officials, and/or a third party, as Apple believes is reasonably necessary or appropriate to enforce and/or verify compliance with any part of this Agreement." The implication is that if a copyright holder claims that you're infringing their copyright, Apple may disclose your details without your knowledge, let alone your agreement. This seems to mean that, say, Sony Music or the RIAA can get the details of your e-mail address, physical address, credit card, and listening habits by claiming a suspicion of copyright violation.
- Apple and its licensors can remove or prevent you from accessing "products, content, or other materials."
- Apple reserves the right to modify the Agreement at any time. If you continue using the iTunes Store, you're deemed to have accepted whatever additional terms Apple imposes.
- Apple can terminate your account for your failing to "comply with any of the provisions" in the Agreement—or for your being suspected of such failure. Terminating your account prevents you from buying any more songs and videos immediately, but you might be able to set up another account. More seriously, termination may prevent you from playing songs and videos you've already bought—for example, if you need to authorize a computer to play them.

Configure iTunes Store Settings

By default, iTunes displays a Store category in the Source list with an iTunes Store item and the Ping social-networking item. After you buy one or more items from the iTunes store, the Purchased item appears as well. If you buy items on an iPhone, iPad, or iPod touch, a Purchased On *Device* appears too—for example, Purchased On Jane's iPhone.

iTunes also uses 1-Click buying and downloading. You may want to remove the iTunes Store category or use the shopping basket. To change your preferences, follow these steps:

1. Display the iTunes dialog box or the Preferences dialog box:
   - In Windows, choose Edit | Preferences or press CTRL-COMMA or CTRL-Y to display the iTunes dialog box.
   - On the Mac, choose iTunes | Preferences or press ⌘-COMMA or ⌘-Y to display the Preferences dialog box.
2. Click the Parental tab to display the Parental preferences. Figure 8-3 shows the Parental tab on the Mac.

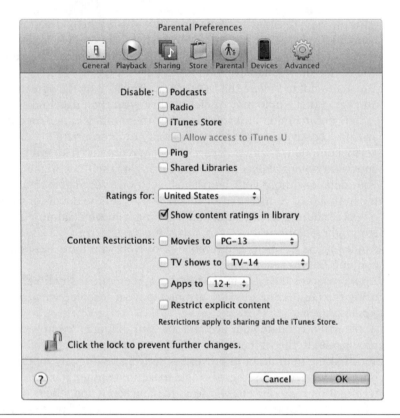

FIGURE 8-3 The Parental tab of the iTunes dialog box or Preferences dialog box lets you disable the iTunes Store or restrict the content it displays.

3. In the Disable area, select the iTunes Store check box if you want to remove the iTunes Store item from the Store category in the Source list. Select the Allow Access To iTunes U check box if you want to leave iTunes U's educational content enabled.

 If you want to prevent anyone else from reenabling the iTunes Store, click the lock icon and then go through User Account Control for the iTunes Parental Controls Operation (on Windows 7 or Windows Vista) or authenticate yourself (on the Mac).

4. Also in the Disable area, select the Ping check box if you want to turn off the Ping social-networking feature.
5. If you didn't disable the iTunes Store, choose content ratings and restrictions:
   - Select your country in the Ratings For drop-down list.
   - Select the Show Content Ratings In Library check box if you want iTunes to display content ratings.
6. In the Content Restrictions area, choose whether to restrict movies, TV shows, apps, and explicit content. For example, to restrict movies to the PG rating, select

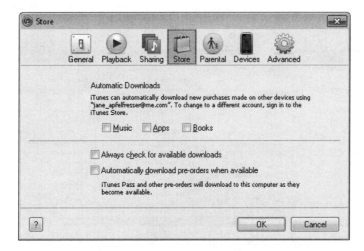

FIGURE 8-4 Configure the settings on the Store tab of the iTunes dialog box or the Preferences dialog box to make sure you don't buy any songs unexpectedly.

the Movies To check box, and then choose PG in the drop-down list. Click the Store tab (Windows) or Store button (Mac) to display the Store tab. Figure 8-4 shows the Store tab on Windows. The Store tab on the Mac has the same controls.

7. In the Automatic Downloads area, select the check box for each item—the Music check box, the Apps check box, and the Books check box—you want iTunes to download automatically to this computer when you've purchased it from another computer, or iPhone, iPod, or iPad.

8. Select the Always Check For Available Downloads check box if you want iTunes to look for new items you've purchased but not yet downloaded. Clear this check box if you prefer to check for new items manually—for example, because you need to run your downloads when your Internet connection isn't busy.

9. Select the Automatically Download Pre-Orders When Available check box if you want iTunes to automatically download content you've bought using prepurchase features such as iTunes Pass (a kind of season ticket for items that come in episodes).

10. Click the OK button to apply your choices and close the dialog box.

Find the Songs, Videos, and Movies You Want

You can find songs, videos, and movies in the iTunes Store in several ways that will seem familiar if you've used other online stores:

- You can meander through the interface looking for items by clicking links from the home page.

FIGURE 8-5 Use the column browser to browse through the iTunes Store's offerings.

- You can browse by genre, subgenre, artist, and album. Click the Browse button, click the Browse link in the Quick Links area on the home page, choose View | Column Browser | Show Column Browser, or press CTRL-B (Windows) or ⌘-B (Mac) to display the column browser at the top of the iTunes Store (see Figure 8-5).
- You can search for specific items either by using the Search Store box or by clicking the Power Search link (in the Quick Links box on the right of the home page) and using the Power Search page to specify multiple criteria. Figure 8-6 shows the Power Search page with some results found. You can sort the search results by a column heading by clicking it. Click the column heading again to reverse the sort order.

Preview Songs, Videos, and Movies

One of the most attractive features of the iTunes Store is that it lets you preview a song, video, or movie before you buy it. This feature helps you ensure both that you've found the right song, video, or movie and that you like it.

For most songs, the previews are 90 seconds long—either the first part of the song or the most distinctive part (for example, the chorus or a catchy line). For videos and movies, the previews are 20 seconds of the most identifiable highlights.

Double-click a song's or video's listing to start the preview playing. To view the trailer for a movie, click the View Trailer button.

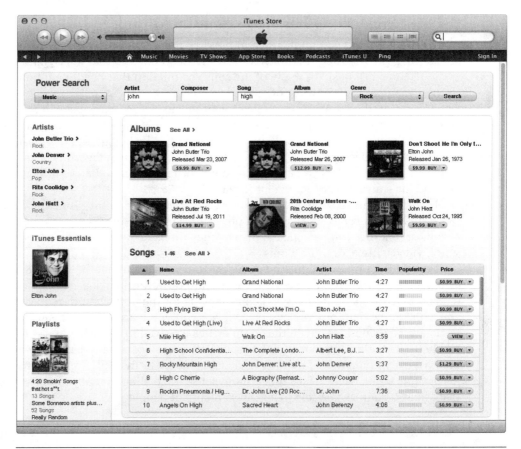

FIGURE 8-6   Use the Power Search feature to search for songs by song title, artist, album, genre, and composer.

Understand A*******s, "Explicit," and "Clean"

The iTunes Store censors supposedly offensive words to help minimize offense:

- Songs, videos, or movies deemed to have potentially offensive lyrics are marked EXPLICIT in the Name column. Where a sanitized version is available, it's marked CLEAN in the Name column. Some of the supposedly explicit items contain words no more offensive than "love." Some supposedly explicit songs are instrumentals.
- Strangely, other songs, videos, and movies that contain words that are offensive to most people aren't flagged as being explicit. So if you worry about what you and yours hear, don't trust the iTunes Store ratings too far.
- Any word deemed offensive is censored with asterisks (**), at least in theory. (In practice, some words sneak through.) When searching, use the real word rather than censoring it yourself.

Request Songs or Other Items You Can't Find

Eighteen million songs sound like an impressive number, but it's a mere jugful in the bucket of all the songs that have ever been recorded (and that music enthusiasts would like to buy). Besides, many of the songs counted in that headline number are alternative versions or remixes of others.

As a result, the iTunes Store's selection of music pleases some users more than others. Not surprisingly, Apple and the record companies seem to be concentrating first on the songs that are most likely to please (and to be bought by) the most people. If you want the biggest hits—either the latest ones or longtime favorites—chances are that the iTunes Store has you covered. But if your tastes run to the esoteric, you may not find the songs you're looking for in the iTunes Store.

If you can't find a song or other item you're looking for in the iTunes Store, you can submit a request for it. If a search produces no results, the iTunes Store offers you a Request link that you can click to display the iTunes Request form for requesting songs, videos, films, or other items.

Beyond the immediate thank-you-for-your-input screen that the iTunes Store displays, requesting items feels unrewarding at present. Apple doesn't respond directly to requests, so unless you keep checking for the items you've requested, you won't know that they've been posted. Nor will you learn if the items will ever be made available. Besides, given the complexities involved in licensing items, it seems highly unlikely that Apple will make special efforts to license any particular item unless a truly phenomenal number of people request it. Instead, Apple seems likely to continue doing what makes much more sense—licensing as many items as possible that are as certain as possible to appeal to plenty of people.

Navigate the iTunes Store

To navigate from page to page in the iTunes Store, click the buttons in the toolbar. Alternatively, use these keyboard shortcuts:

- In Windows, press CTRL-[to return to the previous page and CTRL-] to go to the next page.
- On the Mac, press ⌘-[to return to the previous page and ⌘-] to go to the next page.

Buy an Item from the iTunes Store

To buy an item from the iTunes Store, simply click its Buy button.

If you're not currently signed in, iTunes displays the Sign In To Download From The iTunes Store dialog box, as shown here.

Type your ID and password. Select the Remember Password For Purchasing check box if you want iTunes to remember your password so that you don't need to enter it in the future. Then click the Buy button. iTunes then displays a confirmation message box like this:

Click the Buy button to make the purchase. Select the Please Don't Ask Me About Buying Songs Again check box if you don't want to have to confirm your purchases in the future. Leave this check box cleared if you're feeling the credit crunch and want to rein in your impulse buying.

iTunes then downloads the song, video, or movie to your library and adds an entry for it to your Purchased playlist.

Listen to Songs or Watch Videos and Movies You've Purchased

When you download a song, video, or movie from the iTunes Store, iTunes adds it to the playlist named Purchased in the Source list. When you click the Purchased playlist, iTunes automatically displays a message box to explain what the playlist is. Select the Do Not Show This Message Again check box before dismissing this message box, because otherwise it will soon endanger your sanity.

The Purchased playlist is there to provide a quick-and-easy way to get to all the items you buy. Otherwise, if you purchase items on impulse without keeping a list, they might vanish into your huge media library.

To delete the entry for an item in the Purchased playlist, right-click it (or CTRL-click it on the Mac), choose Clear from the shortcut menu, and click the Yes button in the confirmation dialog box. But, unlike for regular files, iTunes doesn't offer you the opportunity to delete the file itself—the file remains in your library on the basis that, having paid for it, you don't actually want to delete it.

 You can drag items that you haven't purchased to the Purchased playlist as well.

Restart a Failed Download

If a download fails, you may see an error message that invites you to try again later. If this happens, iTunes terminates the download but doesn't roll back the purchase.

To restart a failed download, choose Store | Check For Available Downloads. If you're not currently signed in, type your password in the Enter Account Name And Password dialog box, and then click the Check button. iTunes attempts to restart the failed download and also checks for any other items (such as new podcast episodes or items you've preordered) that are lined up for downloading to your computer.

Review What You've Purchased from the iTunes Store

To see what you've purchased from the iTunes Store, follow these steps:

1. Click the Account button (the button that displays your account name) and enter your password to display the Account Information screen.
2. In the Purchase History area, click the See All button to display details of all the items you've purchased.
3. Click the arrow to the left of an order date to display details of the purchases on that date.
4. Click the Done button when you've finished examining your purchases. iTunes returns you to your Account Information page.

Authorize and Deauthorize Computers for the iTunes Store

As mentioned earlier in this chapter, when you buy a DRM-protected item from the iTunes Store, you're allowed to play it on up to five different computers or devices at a time. iTunes implements this limitation through a form of license that Apple calls *authorization*. iTunes tracks which computers are authorized to play items you've purchased and stops you from playing the items when you're out of authorizations.

iTunes also uses authorization for its Home Sharing feature, to make sure you're not sharing items with other people. (The reason for this limitation is that most songs, videos, and other media items are protected by copyright.)

If you then want to play items you've purchased on another computer, you need to *deauthorize* one of the authorized computers so as to free up an authorization for use on the extra computer. You may also need to specifically deauthorize a computer to prevent it from playing the items you've bought. For example, if you sell or give away your Mac, you'd probably want to deauthorize it. You might also need to deauthorize a computer if you're planning to rebuild it and reinstall the operating system.

 Your computer must be connected to the Internet to authorize and deauthorize computers.

Authorize a Computer to Use the iTunes Store

To authorize a computer to use the iTunes Store, follow these steps:

1. Choose Store | Authorize This Computer to display the Authorize This Computer dialog box (shown here).

 You can also trigger an authorization request by setting up Home Sharing on an unauthorized computer or by trying to play a DRM-protected item purchased from the iTunes Store and stored on another computer—for example, when you access a purchased item in a shared library.

2. Type your Apple ID and password.
3. Click the Authorize button. iTunes checks in with the servers, and then displays the Computer Authorization Was Successful dialog box (shown here) if all is well. The dialog box shows how many of your available authorizations you've used so far.

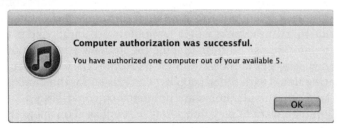

Deauthorize a Computer from Using the iTunes Store

To deauthorize a computer so that it can no longer play the items you've purchased from the iTunes Store, follow these steps:

1. Choose Store | Deauthorize This Computer to display the Deauthorize This Computer dialog box, shown here.

2. Type your Apple ID and password, and then click the Deauthorize button. iTunes deauthorizes the computer and displays a message box to tell you it has done so, as shown here.

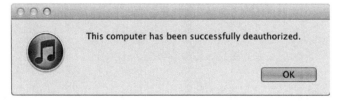

How to... **Deauthorize a Computer You Can't Currently Access**

The procedure you've just seen for deauthorizing a computer is easy—but you must be able to access the computer. If you've already parted with the computer, or if the computer has stopped working, this gives you a problem.

The solution is to deauthorize *all* your computers at once, and then reauthorize those you want to be able to use. You're allowed to do this only once.

To deauthorize all your computers, follow these steps:

1. Click the Account button (the button that displays your account name) and then enter your password to display the Account Information window.
2. Click the Deauthorize All button. iTunes displays a confirmation dialog box, as shown here.

3. Click the Deauthorize All Computers button. iTunes deauthorizes all the computers, and then displays a message box to let you know it has done so.

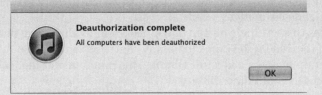

4. Click the OK button, and then click the Home button to return to the iTunes Store home screen.

Buy Music from Other Online Music Stores

Given that you have an iPod, the iTunes Store is the best of the large online music stores, because it sells songs in a format that your iPod can play, whereas most other online music stores use incompatible formats (such as WMA). But you may want to use other online music stores for a couple of reasons:

- Some sell songs that the iTunes Store doesn't have.
- Some offer subscription pricing that lets you download and listen to as much music as you want for a monthly fee.

Most Other Online Music Stores Work Only with Windows

Most of the online music services work only with Windows at the time of writing. To complicate things still more for anyone using an iPod, most of the online music services use WMA files protected with DRM for their songs. Some services are also tied to specific hardware players, some to their own software players, and some to Windows Media Player.

To use protected WMA files with your iPod, you must burn them to CD, and then rip and encode the CD to AAC files or MP3 files. You could also use Apple Lossless Encoding, but because the WMA files are lower quality than Apple Lossless Encoding, doing so makes little sense.

Most of the online music services permit you to burn songs to CD, but creating further copies of the songs could be interpreted to be against the terms and conditions of some services.

This section discusses some of the main online music stores at this writing, starting with the one that is most likely to be of interest to you as an iPod owner—Amazon.com.

Amazon.com

Amazon.com (www.amazon.com) sells songs in the MP3 format, with most encoded at the 256-Kbps bitrate. Most songs cost $0.69, $0.99, or $1.29 apiece, but there are special deals on many whole albums.

At this writing, you can download an individual song directly to your computer (and then add it to iTunes manually), but you need to use Amazon's custom download program to download a full album. This program automatically adds the songs you've bought to your iTunes library.

eMusic

eMusic (www.emusic.com) offers more than 8 million songs for download—and the songs are in the unprotected MP3 format, so you can use them freely in iTunes, on an iPod or iPhone, or on almost any other music player.

eMusic offers various pricing plans, including yearly subscriptions. Each plan has a free 14-day trial, but you must provide valid credit card details. You download the songs using eMusic's software.

Napster 2.0

Napster 2.0 (www.napster.com) offers more than 15 million songs at this writing. Napster 2.0 has nothing to do with the pioneering file-sharing application Napster except·the name and logo. Napster sells songs in MP3 format and provides an iPhone app that enables iPhone users to play music straight from the iPhone.

Real Rhapsody

Real Rhapsody (http://mp3.rhapsody.com) is a service that provides unlimited streaming access to over 9 million songs. You can buy songs and put them on a variety of devices, including the iPod. Like Napster, Rhapsody provides a good way to listen to a wide variety of music for a fixed fee.

Russian MP3 Download Sites

You can also find high-quality MP3 files—without DRM—for download on sites hosted in Russia and other former Eastern Bloc countries. These sites typically offer a wide selection of music at very low prices.

At this writing, the legal position of these sites is not clear. While these sites insist they are operating legally, most Western legal experts disagree. Music industry bodies, such as the RIAA, are actively trying to close these sites down.

Find Free Songs Online

Beyond the iTunes Store and the other online music stores discussed so far in this chapter, you'll find many sources of free music online. Some of this free music is legal, but much of it is illegal.

Find Free Songs on the Online Music Stores

Most of the major online music stores provide some free songs, usually to promote either up-and-coming artists or major releases from established artists. For example, the iTunes Store provides a single for free download each week, and Amazon.com has an Artists on the Rise section that offers ten free songs each month. The stores typically make you create an account before you can download such free songs as they're offering.

Find Free Songs for Legal Download

Sadly, many of the sites that provided free songs in the early days of the Internet have closed down. But the Internet still contains some sources of songs that are distributed for free by the artists who created them. Usually, the best way to discover these sites is to visit an artist's own website, Facebook presence, or MySpace page.

 Tip Sites such as Pandora (www.pandora.com), Spotify (www.spotify.com), and Musicovery (www.musicovery.com) can be a great way of finding interesting music.

Find Free Songs for Illegal Download

Beyond the legal offerings of the online music stores and the free (and legal) sites, you can find pretty much any song for illegal download on the Internet. Finding a song that you can't find anywhere else can be wonderful, and getting the song for free is even more so. But before you download music illegally, you should be aware of possible repercussions to your computer, your wallet, and even your future.

Threats to Your Computer

Downloading files illegally may pose several threats to your computer:

- Many companies that produce P2P software include other applications with their products. Some of these applications are shareware and can be tolerably useful; others are adware that are useless and an irritant; still others are spyware that report users' sharing and downloading habits.

 To detect and remove spyware from your computer, use an application such as the free Ad-Aware from LavaSoft (www.lavasoft.com) or Spybot–Search & Destroy (www.safer-networking.org; make sure you use the hyphen in the name, as there is also a www.safernetworking.org site).

- Many of the files shared on P2P networks contain only the songs they claim to contain. Others are fake files provided by companies working for the RIAA and the record companies to "poison" the P2P networks and discourage people from downloading files by wasting their time.
- Other files *are* songs but also harbor a virus, worm, or Trojan horse. Even apparently harmless files can have a sting in the tail. For example, the tags in music files can contain URLs to which your player's browser component automatically connects. The site can then run a script on your computer, doing anything from opening some irritating advertisement windows, to harvesting any sensitive information it can locate, to deleting vital files or damaging the firmware on your computer.

 Whether you're downloading songs illegally or not, use virus-checking software to scan all incoming files to your computer, no matter whom they come from— friends, family, coworkers, or the Internet.

Threats to Your Wallet, Your ID, and Your Future

Even if your computer remains in rude health, downloading files illegally poses several threats. Unless you use a service (such as Anonymizer, www.anonymizer.com) that masks your computer's IP address, any action that you take on the Internet can be tracked back to your computer.

Sharing digital files of other people's copyrighted content without permission is illegal. So is receiving such illegal files. The No Electronic Theft Act (NET Act) of 1997 and the Digital Millennium Copyright Act (DMCA) of 1998 provide savage penalties for people caught distributing copyrighted materials illegally. Under the DMCA, you can face fines of up to $500,000 and five years' imprisonment for a first offense, and double those for a second offense.

P2P networks also expose users to social-engineering attacks through the chat features that most P2P tools include. However friendly other users are, and however attractive the files they provide, it can be a severe mistake to divulge personal information. A favored gambit of malefactors is to provide a quantity of "good" (malware-free) files followed by one or more files that include a Trojan horse or keystroke logger to capture sensitive information from your computer.

Find P2P Software

At this writing, there are various P2P networks, some of which interoperate with each other. But for legal reasons, P2P networks frequently change their nature or close.

To find up-to-date information on P2P software, consult a resource such as Wikipedia (http://en.wikipedia.org/wiki/Main_Page; see the "peer-to-peer file sharing" entry) or a search engine.

9

Create Video Files That Work with the iPod classic

HOW TO...

- Create iPod-friendly video files from your digital video camera
- Create iPod-friendly video files from your existing video files
- Create video files from your DVDs

The iPod classic is great for playing various kinds of video files—anything from music videos to TV shows or entire movies. You can play a movie either on the iPod's built-in screen or on a TV to which you connect the iPod via a cable.

Apple's iTunes Store provides a wide selection of video content, including TV series and full-length movies, and you can buy or download video in iPod-compatible formats from various other sites online. But if you enjoy watching video on the iPod, you'll almost certainly want to put your own video content on it. You may also want to rip files from your own DVDs so that you can watch them on the iPod.

Create iPod-Friendly Video Files from Your Digital Video Camera

If you make your own movies with a digital video camera, you can easily put them on the iPod. Use an application such as Windows Movie Maker (Windows) or iMovie (Mac) to capture the video from your digital video camera and turn it into a home movie.

 Video formats are confusing at best—but the iPod and iTunes make the process of getting suitable video files as easy as possible. The iPod classic can play videos in the MP4 format up to 2.5 Mbps (megabits per second) or the H.264 format up to 1.5 Mbps. Programs designed to create video files suitable for the iPod typically give you a choice between the MP4 format and the H.264 format. As a point of reference, VHS video quality is around 2 Mbps, while DVD is about 8 Mbps.

157

Did You Know?

What You Can and Can't Legally Do with Other People's Video Content

Before you start putting your videos and DVDs on the iPod, it's a good idea to know the bare essentials about copyright and decryption:

- If you created the video (for example, it's a home video or DVD), you hold the copyright to it, and you can do what you want with it—put it on the iPod, release it worldwide, or whatever. The only exceptions are if what you recorded is subject to someone else's copyright or if you're infringing on your subjects' rights (for example, to privacy).
- If someone has supplied you with a legally created video file that you can put on the iPod, you're fine doing so. For example, if you download a video from the iTunes Store, you don't need to worry about legalities.
- If you own a copy of a commercial DVD, you need permission to rip (extract) it from the DVD and convert it to a format the iPod can play. Even decrypting the DVD in an unauthorized way (such as creating a file rather than simply playing the DVD) is technically illegal.

Create iPod-Friendly Video Files Using Windows Live Movie Maker or Windows Movie Maker

Unlike the last few versions of Windows, Windows 7 doesn't include Windows Movie Maker, the Windows program for editing videos. But you can download the nearest equivalent, Windows Live Movie Maker, from the Windows Live website (http://explore.live.com/windows-live-movie-maker).

 When you install Windows Live Movie Maker, the Windows Live Essentials installer encourages you to install all the Windows Live Essentials programs—Messenger, Photo Gallery, Mail, Writer, Family Safety, and several others. If you don't want the full set, click the Choose The Programs You Want To Install button on the What Do You Want To Install? screen, and then select only the programs you actually want.

Windows Live Movie Maker can't export video files in an iPod-friendly format, so what you need to do is export the video file in the WMV format, and then convert it using another application, such as Full Video Converter Free (discussed later in this chapter).

Similarly, the versions of Windows Movie Maker included with Windows Vista and Windows XP can't export video files in an iPod-friendly format, so what you need to do is export the video file in a standard format (such as AVI) that you can then convert using another application.

Create a WMV File from Windows Live Movie Maker

To create a WMV file from Windows Live Movie Maker, open the project and follow these steps:

1. Choose File | Save Movie to display the Save Movie panel. The tab I'm calling "File" here is the unnamed tab at the left end of the Ribbon.
2. In the Common Settings section, click For Computer. The Save Movie dialog box opens.
3. Type the name for the movie, choose the folder, and then click the Save button.

Now that you've created a WMV file, use a converter program such as Full Video Converter Free (discussed later in this chapter) to convert it to a format that the iPod can play.

Create an AVI File from Windows Movie Maker on Windows Vista

To save a movie as an AVI file from Windows Movie Maker on Windows Vista, follow these steps:

1. With your movie open in Windows Movie Maker, choose File | Publish Movie (or press CTRL-P) to launch the Publish Movie Wizard. The Wizard displays the Where Do You Want To Publish Your Movie? screen.
2. Select the This Computer item in the list box, and then click the Next button. The Wizard displays the Name The Movie You Are Publishing screen.
3. Type the name for the movie, choose the folder in which to store it, and then click the Next button. The Wizard displays the Choose The Settings For Your Movie screen (see Figure 9-1).
4. Select the More Settings option button, and then select the DV-AVI item in the drop-down list.

 The DV-AVI item appears as DV-AVI (NTSC) or DV-AVI (PAL), depending on whether you've chosen the NTSC option button or the PAL option button on the Advanced tab of the Options dialog box. NTSC is the video format used in most of North America; PAL's stronghold is Europe.

5. Click the Publish button to export the movie in this format. When Windows Movie Maker finishes exporting the file, it displays the Your Movie Has Been Published screen.
6. Clear the Play Movie When I Click Finish check box if you don't want to watch the movie immediately in Windows Media Player. Often, it's a good idea to check that the movie has come out okay.
7. Click the Finish button.

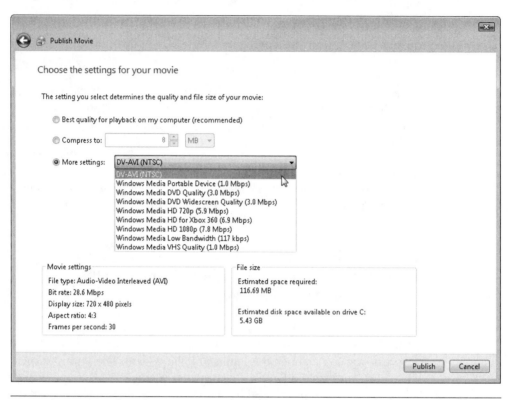

FIGURE 9-1   On the Choose The Settings For Your Movie screen, select the More Settings option button, and then pick the DV-AVI item in the drop-down list.

Now that you've created an AVI file, use a converter program such as Full Video Converter Free (discussed later in this chapter) to convert it to a format that works on the iPod.

Create an AVI File from Windows Movie Maker on Windows XP

To save a movie as an AVI file from Windows Movie Maker on Windows XP, follow these steps:

1. Choose File | Save Movie File to launch the Save Movie Wizard. The Wizard displays its Movie Location screen.
2. Select the My Computer item, and then click the Next button. The Wizard displays the Saved Movie File screen.
3. Enter the name and choose the folder for the movie, and then click the Next button. The Wizard displays the Movie Setting screen (shown in Figure 9-2 with options selected).

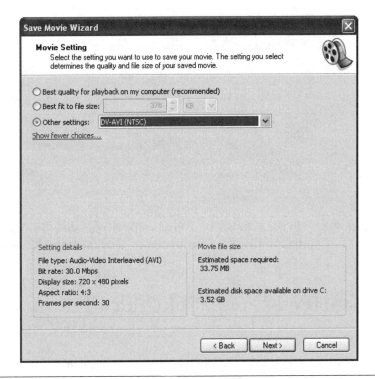

FIGURE 9-2   Click the Show More Choices link to make the Other Settings option button available, then select the Other Settings option button and pick the DV-AVI item from the drop-down list.

4. Click the Show More Choices link to display the Best Fit To File Size option button and the Other Settings option button.
5. Select the Other Settings option button, and then select the DV-AVI item in the drop-down list.

The DV-AVI item appears as DV-AVI (NTSC) or DV-AVI (PAL), depending on whether you've chosen the NTSC option button or the PAL option button on the Advanced tab of the Options dialog box.

6. Click the Next button to save the movie in this format. The Wizard displays the Completing The Save Movie Wizard screen.
7. Clear the Play Movie When I Click Finish check box if you don't want to test the movie immediately in Windows Media Player. Usually, it's a good idea to make sure the movie has come out right.
8. Click the Finish button.

Now that you've created an AVI file, use a converter program such as Full Video Converter Free (discussed later in this chapter) to convert it to a format that works on the iPod.

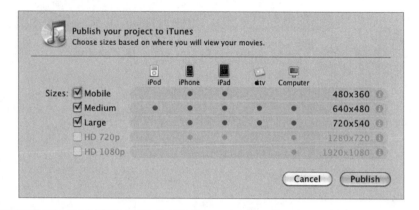

FIGURE 9-3   On the Publish Your Project To iTunes sheet in iMovie, choose which sizes of file you want to create—for example, Medium for the iPod.

Create iPod-Compatible Video Files Using iMovie

To use iMovie to create video files that will play on the iPod, follow these steps:

1. With the movie open in iMovie, choose Share | iTunes to display the Publish Your Project To iTunes sheet (see Figure 9-3).
2. In the Sizes area, select the check box for each size you want to create. The dots show the devices for which that size is suitable. For example, if you want to play the video files on an iPod classic, select the Medium check box.
3. Click the Publish button, and then wait while iMovie creates the compressed file or files and adds it or them to iTunes. iMovie then automatically displays iTunes.
4. Click the Movies item in the Source list, and you'll see the movies you just created. Double-click a file to play it, or simply drag it to the iPod to load it immediately.

Create iPod-Friendly Video Files from Your Existing Video Files

If you have existing video files (for example, files in the AVI format or QuickTime movies), you can convert them to iPod format in a couple of ways. The easiest way is by using the capabilities built into iTunes—but unfortunately, these work only for some video files. The harder way is by using QuickTime Pro, which can convert files from most known formats but which costs $30.

On Windows, you can also use third-party converter programs, such as Full Video Converter Free, discussed later in this chapter.

Create iPod Video Files Using iTunes

To create a video file for the iPod using iTunes, follow these steps:

1. Add the video file to your iTunes library in either of these ways:
   - Open iTunes if it's not running. Open a Windows Explorer window (Windows) or a Finder window (Mac) to the folder that contains the video file. Arrange the windows so that you can see both the file and iTunes. Drag the file to the Library item in iTunes.
   - In iTunes, choose File | Add To Library, use the Add To Library dialog box to select the file, and then click the Open button (Windows) or the Choose button (Mac).
2. Select the movie in the iTunes window, and then choose Advanced | Create iPod Or iPhone Version.

If the Create iPod Or iPhone Version command isn't available for the file, or if iTunes gives you an error message, you'll know that iTunes can't convert the file.

Create iPod-Friendly Video Files Using QuickTime

QuickTime, Apple's multimedia software for Mac OS X and Windows, comes in two versions: QuickTime Player (the free version) and QuickTime Pro, which costs $29.99.

Create iPod-Friendly Video Files Using QuickTime Player on the Mac

On Mac OS X, QuickTime Player is included in a standard installation of the operating system; and if you've somehow managed to uninstall it, it'll automatically install itself again if you install iTunes. The Mac version of QuickTime Player includes file conversions, which you can access by using the Share menu. For example, follow these steps:

1. Open QuickTime Player from Launchpad, the Dock, or the Applications folder.
2. Choose File | Open File, select the file in the Open dialog box, and then click the Open button.
3. Choose Share | iTunes to display the Save Your Movie To iTunes dialog box (see Figure 9-4).
4. Select the iPod & iPhone option button.
5. Click the Share button. QuickTime converts the file.

Create iPod-Friendly Video Files Using QuickTime Pro on Windows

On Windows, you install QuickTime Player when you install iTunes, because QuickTime provides much of the multimedia functionality for iTunes. The "Player" name isn't entirely accurate, because QuickTime provides encoding services as well as decoding

FIGURE 9-4 On the Mac, you can use QuickTime Player to convert video files to formats suitable for the iPod.

services to iTunes—but QuickTime Player on the PC doesn't allow you to create most formats of video files until you buy QuickTime Pro.

 QuickTime Pro for Windows gets rave reviews from some users but wretched reviews from others. If you are thinking of buying QuickTime Pro for Windows, read the latest reviews for it at the Apple Store (http://store.apple.com) first.

QuickTime Player for Windows is a crippled version of QuickTime Pro, so when you buy QuickTime Pro from the Apple Store, all you get is a registration code to unlock the hidden functionality. To apply the registration code, choose Edit | Preferences | Register In Windows to display the Register tab of the QuickTime Settings dialog box. On the Mac, choose QuickTime Player | Registration to display the Register tab of the QuickTime dialog box.

 When you register QuickTime Pro, you must enter your registration name in the Registered To text box in exactly the same format as Apple has decided to use it. For example, if you've used the name John P. Smith to register QuickTime Pro, and Apple has decided to address the registration to *Mr. John P. Smith*, you must use **Mr. John P. Smith** as the registration name. If you try to use **John P. Smith**, registration fails, even if this is exactly the way you gave your name when registering.

To create an iPod-friendly video file from QuickTime Pro, follow these steps:

1. Open the file in QuickTime Pro, and then choose File | Export to display the Save Exported File As dialog box.
2. Specify the filename and folder as usual, and then choose Movie To iPod in the Export drop-down list. Leave the Default Settings item selected in the Use drop-down list.
3. Click the Save button to start exporting the video file.

Create iPod Video Files Using Full Video Converter Free

If you have video files that you can't convert with iTunes on Windows, use a file conversion program such as Full Video Converter Free (see Figure 9-5). You can download this program from the CNET Download.com site (http://download.cnet.com) and other sites. When you install the program, make sure you decline any extra options such as adding a toolbar, changing your default search engine, or changing your home page.

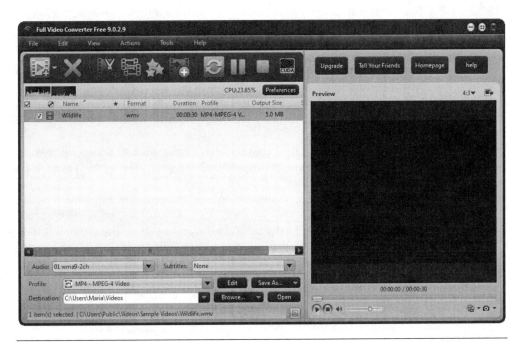

FIGURE 9-5 Full Video Converter Free lets you convert various types of videos to iPod-friendly formats.

You can find various other free programs online for converting video files. If you're looking for such programs, check carefully that what you're about to download is actually free rather than a crippled version that requires you to pay before you can convert files.

 Another way to convert video files from one format to another—on either Windows or the Mac—is to use an online file conversion tool such as Zamzar (www.zamzar .com). For low volumes of files, the conversion is free (though it may take a while), but you must provide a valid e-mail address. For higher volumes of files or higher priority, you can sign up for a paid account.

Create iPod Video Files Using HandBrake on the Mac

If you have video files that you can't convert with iTunes on the Mac, try using the free conversion program HandBrake (http://handbrake.fr). Download HandBrake, install it to your Applications folder, run it from there, and then follow these steps:

1. Click the Source button on the toolbar to display an Open dialog box.

 HandBrake can also rip DVDs, provided you have a third-party decryption utility installed. See the end of the chapter for details.

2. Click the file you want, and then click the Open button. HandBrake shows the details of the file.
3. In the Title drop-down list, choose which title—which of the recorded items in the file—you want. Most files have only one title, so the choice is easy; DVDs have various titles.
4. If the file is broken up into chapters (sections), choose which ones you want. Pick the first in the Chapters drop-down list and the last in the Through drop-down list—for example, Chapters 1 through 4.
5. In the Destination area, change the name and path for the converted file if necessary.
6. If the Presets pane isn't displayed on the right side of the window, click the Toggle Presets button on the toolbar to display it. Figure 9-6 shows the HandBrake window with the Presets pane displayed.
7. In the Presets pane, choose the iPod preset.
8. If necessary, change further settings. (Press ⌘-? to display the HandBrake User Guide for instructions.)
9. Click the Start button on the toolbar to start encoding the file.

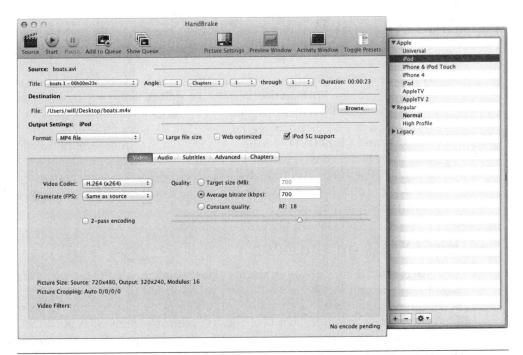

FIGURE 9-6   The Presets pane on the right side of the HandBrake window lets you instantly choose video settings for the iPod.

Create Video Files from Your DVDs

If you have DVDs, you'll probably want to put them on the iPod so that you can watch them without a DVD player. This section gives you an overview of how to create suitable files, first on Windows, and then on the Mac.

Because ripping commercial DVDs without specific permission is a violation of copyright law, there are no DVD ripping programs from major companies. You can find commercial programs, shareware programs, and freeware programs on the Internet—but keep your wits firmly about you, as some programs are a threat to your computer through being poorly programmed, while others include unwanted components such as adware or spyware. Always read reviews of any DVD ripper you're considering before you download and install it—and certainly before you pay for it. As usual on the Internet, if something seems too good to be true, it most likely *is* too good to be true.

Before you start ripping, make sure that your discs don't contain computer-friendly versions of their contents. At this writing, some Blu-Ray discs include such versions, which are licensed for you to load on your computer and your lifestyle devices (such as the iPod).

Rip DVDs on Windows

Here are two solutions for decrypting and ripping DVDs on Windows:

- **DVD43 and DVD Shrink**   DVD43 is a free DVD-decryption utility that you can download from the links on the DVD43 – Download Sites page (www.dvd43.com). DVD43 opens the DVD up for ripping but doesn't rip the content from the DVD. To rip, use a program such as DVD Shrink ($28.95; www.official-dvdshrink.org).
- **AnyDVD and CloneDVD Mobile**   AnyDVD from SlySoft (around $55 per year; www.slysoft.com) is a decryption utility that works with CloneDVD Mobile (around $45 per year; also from SlySoft). By using these two programs together, you can rip DVDs to formats that work on the iPod. SlySoft offers 21-day trial versions of these programs.

Rip DVDs on the Mac

The best tool for ripping DVDs on the Mac is HandBrake, which you met earlier in this chapter. To rip DVDs with HandBrake, you must install VLC, a DVD- and video-playing application (free; www.videolan.org). This is because HandBrake uses VLC's DVD-decryption capabilities; without VLC, HandBrake cannot decrypt DVDs.

Once you've installed VLC, simply run HandBrake, click the Source button, click the DVD in the Source list, and then click the Open button. HandBrake scans the DVD. You can then choose which "title" (which of the recorded tracks on the DVD) to rip, and which chapters from it. The chapters are the bookmarks on the DVD—for example, if you press the Next button on your remote, your DVD player skips to the start of the next chapter.

How to...

Prevent the Mac OS X DVD Player from Running Automatically When You Insert a DVD

When you insert a movie DVD, Mac OS X automatically launches DVD Player, switches it to full screen, and starts the movie playing. This behavior is great for when you want to watch a movie, but not so great when you want to rip it.

To prevent DVD Player from running automatically when you insert a DVD, follow these steps:

1. Choose Apple | System Preferences to open System Preferences.
2. In the Hardware section, click the CDs & DVDs item.
3. In the When You Insert A Video DVD drop-down list, you can choose Ignore if you want to be able to choose freely which application to use each time. If you always want to use the same application, choose Open Other Application, use the resulting Open dialog box to select the application, and then click the Choose button.
4. Choose System Preferences | Quit System Preferences or press ⌘-Q to close System Preferences.

10

Make Your Music Sound Great and Customize the iTunes Window

HOW TO...

- Play music with iTunes
- Make iTunes run automatically when you log on
- Improve the sound that iTunes produces
- Change the iTunes interface to meet your preferences
- Enjoy visualizations as you listen to music

In Chapter 3, you learned how to rip CDs and create playlists; in Chapter 7, you learned the ins and outs of creating high-quality audio files from both CDs and other sources, such as your records and tapes. This chapter shows you how to enjoy that music using iTunes and how to change the sound you get and the interface you see. But first, you may want to make iTunes run automatically when you log onto your PC or Mac.

Play Music with iTunes

By following the techniques described in Chapter 3 and Chapter 7, you've probably created a fair-sized library. Now it's time to enjoy your library, using as many of iTunes' features as you need.

How to... **Run iTunes Frequently—or Always on Startup**

Running iTunes from the iTunes icon on your desktop, from the Windows Start menu, or from the Dock in Mac OS X works well enough for frequent use. But if you intend to run iTunes frequently, or always, you can do better.

In Windows 7, you can pin iTunes either to the Taskbar or to the fixed part of the Start menu so that it always appears. To do so, navigate to the iTunes icon on the Start menu in Windows, right-click it, and then choose either Pin To Taskbar or Pin To Start Menu (as needed) from the shortcut menu.

To run iTunes even more quickly, configure a CTRL-ALT keyboard shortcut for it so that you can start iTunes by pressing the keyboard shortcut either from the Desktop or from within an application. Here's how to create the shortcut:

1. Right-click the iTunes icon on your Desktop or on your Start menu, and then choose Properties from the shortcut menu to display the iTunes Properties dialog box.
2. On the Shortcut tab, click in the Shortcut Key text box and then press the letter you want to use in the CTRL-ALT shortcut. For example, press I to create the shortcut CTRL-ALT-I.
3. Click the OK button to close the Properties dialog box.

In Windows 7 and Windows Vista, you'll need administrator privileges to create the keyboard shortcut for running iTunes. If your user account is an administrator account, you already have those privileges. If your user account is a standard account, you will need to provide an administrator name and password.

But if you use iTunes whenever you're using your computer, the best solution is to make iTunes start automatically whenever you log on. To do so, follow these steps in Windows:

1. Right-click the iTunes icon on your Desktop or on your Start menu, and then choose Copy from the shortcut menu to copy the shortcut to the Clipboard.
2. Open the Start menu's All Programs submenu, right-click the Startup folder, and choose Open to open a Windows Explorer window showing the folder's contents.
3. Right-click in the Startup folder and choose Paste from the shortcut menu to paste a copy of the iTunes shortcut into the folder.
4. Click the Close button (the × button), press ALT-F4, or choose Organize | Close to close the Windows Explorer window.

To make iTunes start automatically on the Mac when you log in, you need only CTRL-click or right-click the iTunes icon on the Dock, click Options, and then select the Open At Login item from the shortcut menu.

Play Back Music with iTunes

To play back music with iTunes, follow these general steps:

1. Navigate to the album, playlist, or song you want to play, select it, and then click the Play button.
2. Drag the diamond on the progress bar in the display to scroll forward or backward through the current track.
3. Use the Shuffle button to shuffle the order of the tracks in the current album or playlist. Click once to shuffle the songs; click again to restore the songs to their previous order.

 To reshuffle the current playlist on the Mac, OPTION-click the Shuffle button.

4. Click the Repeat button one or more times to repeat a playlist, album, or song:
   - **Repeat the current playlist or album**   Click the Repeat button once, so that iTunes turns the arrows on the button to blue.
   - **Repeat the current song**   Click the Repeat button again, so that iTunes adds to the blue arrows a blue circle bearing the number 1.
   - **Turn off repeat**   Click the Repeat button a third time, so that iTunes turns the arrows on the button black.
5. If you've scrolled the Song list so that the current song isn't visible, or switched to a different playlist or view, click the arrow button on the right side of the readout at the top of the iTunes window to go to the current song. Alternatively, press CTRL-L (Windows) or ⌘-L (Mac) to jump back to the current song. If you're still viewing the same playlist or category, you can also simply wait until the next song starts, at which point iTunes automatically scrolls back to it.
6. To open a Windows Explorer window (in Windows) or a Finder window (on the Mac) to the folder that contains the selected song file, press CTRL-SHIFT-R (Windows) or ⌘-SHIFT-R (Mac).

 On Windows, you can also right-click the song and click Show In Windows Explorer on the context menu to open a Windows Explorer window showing the song file. On the Mac, you can CTRL-click or right-click the file and then click Show In Finder on the context menu to open a Finder window showing the song file.

7. To toggle the display of the artwork viewer, click the Show Or Hide Item Artwork And Video Viewer button. To display the Artwork column in Album List view, choose View | Always Show Artwork.
8. On the Mac, you can also control iTunes by right-clicking or CTRL-clicking its Dock icon and making the appropriate choice from the shortcut menu, as

shown here. In Windows, if you've chosen to display an iTunes icon in the notification area, you can control iTunes from the icon.

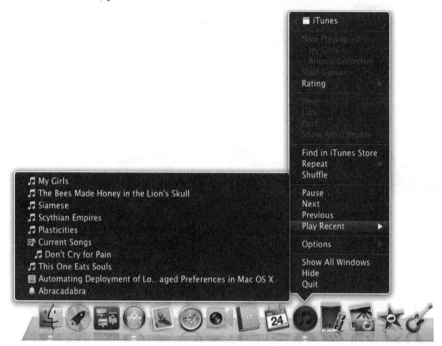

 You can change the information shown in the display window by clicking the items in it. Click the Play icon at the left of the display window to toggle between the track information and the equalization graph. Click the time readout at the right side of the playback bar to move between Remaining Time and Total Time.

How to... ## Create a Gapless Album or Join Tracks Together Without Gaps

iTunes' default settings are to create a separate file (AAC, MP3, Apple Lossless Encoding, AIFF, or WAV, depending on your preferences) from each song on CDs you rip.

For most CDs, this works well. But sometimes you'll want to rip a CD so that it plays back without any gaps between songs. For example, most live CDs have applause or banter rather than silence between songs, so having a break in the playback tends to be distracting.

To play back a CD without any gaps, you have two choices:

- **Create a gapless album** You can tell iTunes that an album shouldn't have a gap between songs. Creating a gapless album is a good idea when you will normally play the CD's songs in sequence rather than shuffle them.

- **Join two or more songs—or even the full CD—into a single file so that you can treat those songs (or CD) as a single unit**   The advantage of this approach is that you can prevent iTunes DJ and other Smart Playlists from playing individual songs from the CD (or from your selection of songs) out of context. The disadvantage is that the joined-together songs tend to be long and hard to navigate through, especially on the iPod.

You can create a gapless album either before or after you rip the CD:

- **Before you rip the CD**   Right-click (or CTRL-click on the Mac) the CD's entry in the Source list and choose Get Info. In the CD Info dialog box, shown here, select the Gapless Album check box and then click the OK button.

- **After you rip the CD**   Browse to the album, select it, and then choose File | Get Info. If iTunes asks whether you're sure you want to edit information for multiple tracks, click the Yes button. On the Options tab of the Multiple Item Information dialog box, choose Yes in the Gapless Album drop-down list, and then click the OK button. (Alternatively, right-click a song, choose Get Info, and then click the Options tab. Select the Part Of A Gapless Album check box, and then click the OK button.)

To rip two or more tracks from a CD into a single file, select the tracks and then choose Advanced | Join CD Tracks. iTunes brackets the tracks, as shown here. When you rip the tracks, iTunes creates a single file containing them.

If you made a mistake with the tracks you joined, select one or more of the joined tracks and then choose Advanced | Unjoin CD Tracks to separate the tracks again.

Listen to Audiobooks on Your iPod

Even if your iPod is almost full of songs, you may be able to cram on a good amount of spoken-word audio, such as audiobooks and podcasts. This is because spoken-word audio can sound great at much lower bitrates than music requires.

The iTunes Store provides a wide variety of content, including audiobooks, magazines, plays, and poems. You can also get audiobooks from other sources, such as from the Audible.com website (www.audible.com), which offers subscription plans for audio downloads. (Audible.com provides many of the audiobooks on the iTunes Store.)

 Most audiobooks contain chapter markers. When playing an audiobook, you can press CTRL-SHIFT–RIGHT ARROW (Windows) or ⌘-SHIFT–RIGHT ARROW (Mac) to go to the next chapter. Press CTRL-SHIFT–LEFT ARROW (Windows) or ⌘-SHIFT–LEFT ARROW (Mac) to go to the beginning of the chapter; press again to go back to the previous chapter.

Improve the Sound of Music

To make music sound as good as possible, you should apply suitable equalizations using iTunes' graphical equalizer. You can also crossfade one song into another, add automatic sound enhancement, and skip the beginning or end of a song.

Use the Graphical Equalizer to Make the Music Sound Great

iTunes includes a graphical equalizer that you can use to change the sound of the music (or other audio) you're playing. You can apply an equalization directly to the playlist you're currently playing, much as you would apply an equalization manually to a physical amplifier or receiver.

You can also apply a specific equalization to each song (or other item) in your iTunes library. Once you've done this, iTunes always uses that equalization when playing that song or item, no matter which equalization is currently applied to iTunes itself.

After playing an item that has an equalization specified, iTunes switches back to the equalization applied to iTunes itself for the next item that doesn't have an equalization specified.

Apply an Equalization to What's Currently Playing

To apply an equalization to what you're currently playing, follow these steps:

1. Display the Equalizer window (see Figure 10-1):
   - **Windows** Choose View | Show Equalizer or press CTRL-SHIFT-2.
   - **Mac** Choose Window | Equalizer or press ⌘-OPTION-2.
2. Select the equalization from the drop-down list. If you're playing an item, you'll hear the effect of the new equalization in a second or two.

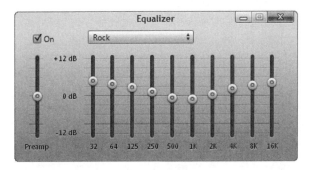

FIGURE 10-1 iTunes' Equalizer window offers preset equalizations, but you can also create custom equalizations.

Specify an Equalization for an Individual Item

To specify the equalization iTunes should use for a particular song or other item, follow these steps:

1. Select the item in your library or in a playlist.

 It doesn't matter whether you apply the equalization to the item in the library or in a playlist, because applying the equalization even in a playlist affects the item in the library as a whole. So if you can access an item more easily through a playlist than through your library, start from the playlist.

2. Press CTRL-I (Windows) or ⌘-I (Mac), or choose Get Info from the File menu or the shortcut menu, to display the Item Information dialog box. This dialog box's title bar shows "iTunes" or the item's name rather than the words "Item Information."
3. Click the Options tab to display its contents. Figure 10-2 shows the Options tab for iTunes for Windows. The Options tab for iTunes for the Mac has the same controls.
4. Select the equalization you want in the Equalizer Preset drop-down list.
5. Choose other options as necessary, and then click the OK button to close the Item Information dialog box. Alternatively, click the Previous button or the Next button to display the information for the previous item or next item in the Item Information dialog box so that you can continue applying equalizations.

 If the equalization you apply to an item is one of the equalizations built into your iPod, the iPod also automatically uses the equalization for playing back the item. But if the equalization is a custom one your iPod doesn't have, the player can't use it. The iPod doesn't pick up custom equalizations you create in iTunes. Equalizations don't apply to the iPod shuffle, because this player doesn't use equalizations.

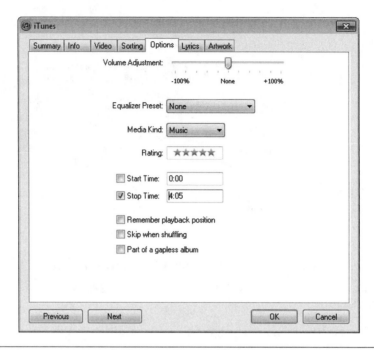

FIGURE 10-2   You can specify the equalization for a particular song or other item on the Options tab of the Item Information dialog box.

Create a Custom Equalization That Sounds Good to You

The preset equalizations in iTunes span a wide range of musical types—but even if there's one named after the type of music you're currently listening to, you may not like the effects it produces. When this happens, try all the other equalizations, however unsuitable their names may make them seem, to see if any of them just happens to sound great with this type of music. (For example, some people swear the Classical equalization is perfect for many Grateful Dead tracks.) If none of them suits you, create a custom equalization that gives the sound you want.

To create a new custom equalization, follow these steps:

1. Open the Equalizer window.
2. Drag the frequency sliders to the appropriate positions for the sound you want the equalization to deliver. When you change the first slider in the current preset, the drop-down list displays Manual.
3. If you need to change the overall volume of the song or item, drag the Preamp slider to a different level. For example, you might want to boost the preamp level on all the songs to which you apply a certain equalization.

4. Choose Make Preset from the drop-down list. iTunes displays the Make Preset dialog box:

5. Type the name for the equalization, and then click the OK button.

You can then apply your equalization from the drop-down list in the Item Information dialog box as you would any other preset equalization.

Delete and Rename Preset Equalizations

If you don't like a preset equalization, you can delete it. If you find an equalization's name unsuitable, you can rename it.

To delete or rename an equalization, start by following these steps:

1. Select the Edit List item from the drop-down list in the Equalizer window. iTunes displays the Edit Presets dialog box on Windows or the EQ Presets dialog box (shown here) on the Mac.
2. Select the preset equalization you want to affect.

To rename the equalization, follow these steps:

1. Click the Rename button to display the Rename dialog box, shown here.
2. Type the new name in the New Preset Name text box.
3. Click the OK button. iTunes displays a dialog box like the following, asking whether you want to change all songs currently set to use this equalization under its current name to use the equalization under the new name you've just specified.

4. Click the Yes button or the No button as appropriate.
5. Click the Done button if you want to close the Edit Presets (Windows) or EQ Presets (Mac) dialog box. If you want to work with other presets, leave it open.

To delete a preset equalization, follow these steps:

1. Click the Delete button.
2. iTunes displays a dialog box like the one shown here, asking you to confirm the deletion. Click the Delete button or the Cancel button, as appropriate.

3. To stop iTunes from confirming the deletion of preset equalizations, select the Do Not Warn Me Again check box before clicking the Delete button or the Cancel button. If you delete the preset, iTunes prompts you to choose whether to remove the equalization from all songs that are set to use it, as shown here. Click the Yes button or the No button as appropriate.

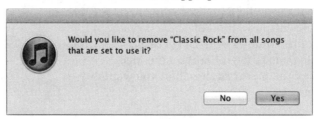

4. Click the Done button to close the Edit Presets (Windows) or EQ Presets (Mac) dialog box.

Choose Crossfading, Sound Enhancer, and Sound Check Settings

The Playback tab of the iTunes dialog box (Windows) or the Preferences dialog box (Mac) offers options for crossfading playback, changing the Sound Enhancer, and controlling whether iTunes uses its Sound Check feature to normalize the volume of songs. Figure 10-3 shows the Playback tab of iTunes for the Mac. The Playback tab for iTunes for Windows has the same controls.

- **Crossfade Songs** Makes iTunes fade in the start of the next song as the current song is about to end. This option lets you eliminate gaps between songs the way most DJs do. Drag the slider to increase or decrease the length of time that's crossfaded. Turn off crossfading if you prefer to have one song end before the next song begins.

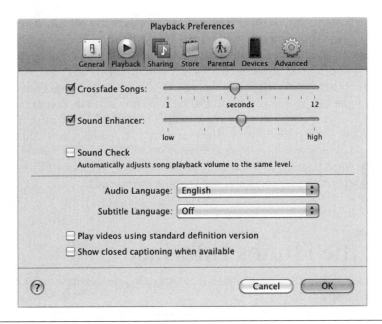

FIGURE 10-3 Choose crossfading, Sound Enhancer, and Sound Check options on the Playback tab of the iTunes dialog box or Preferences dialog box.

 Turning on crossfading prevents iTunes from using gapless playback for any song that does not have the gapless playback option explicitly turned on.

- **Sound Enhancer** Applies iTunes' sound enhancement to the audio you're playing. Experiment with different settings on the Low–High scale by dragging the slider to see which setting sounds best to you—or turn off sound enhancement if you don't like it. Sound enhancement can make treble sounds appear brighter and can add to the effect of stereo separation, but the results don't suit everybody. You may prefer to adjust the sound manually by using the graphical equalizer.
- **Sound Check** Controls whether iTunes uses its Sound Check feature to normalize the volume of different songs so that you don't experience widely varying audio levels in different songs. Many people find Sound Check useful. If you don't like Sound Check, or if you find that the extra processing power it requires makes your computer struggle to play music back satisfactorily, turn it off.

Skip the Boring Intro or Outro on a Song

If you disagree with the producer of a song about when the song should begin or end, use the Start Time and Stop Time controls on the Options tab of the Item Information dialog box (shown in Figure 10-2, earlier in this chapter) to specify how much of the track to lop off. This trimming works both in iTunes and on the iPod.

To trim the intro, enter in the Start Time text box the point at which you want the song to start. For example, enter **1:15** to skip the first minute and a quarter of a song. When you start typing in the Start Time text box, iTunes selects the Start Time check box for you, so you don't need to select it manually.

Similarly, you can change the value in the Stop Time text box to stop the song playing before its end. By default, the Stop Time text box contains a time showing when the song ends, down to thousandths of a second—for example, 4:56.769. When you reduce this time, iTunes selects the Stop Time check box automatically.

 When skipping an intro or outro isn't enough, you can edit a song file down to only that part you want. See Chapter 7 for details.

Tweak the iTunes Interface

You can change the iTunes interface by resizing the window and changing the columns of data displayed.

This section also shows you how to control iTunes by using keyboard shortcuts and how to use iTunes' visualizations.

Resize the iTunes Window to the Size You Need

iTunes offers various window sizes to suit the amount of space you're prepared to dedicate to it:

- In Windows, iTunes has four sizes: normal, maximized, small, and minute. The small and minute sizes are considered mini mode.
- On the Mac, iTunes has three sizes: normal, small, and minute. The small and minute sizes are considered mini mode.

 On Mac OS X versions before 10.7 (Lion), you can also use the iTunes widget to control iTunes from the Dashboard instead of using the main iTunes window. Lion doesn't include the iTunes widget.

By default, iTunes opens in a normal window that you can resize by dragging any of its borders or corners (on Windows) or by dragging the sizing handle in the lower-right corner (on the Mac).

In Windows, you can click the Maximize button to maximize the window so that it occupies all the space on your screen (apart from the taskbar, if you have it displayed), and you can click the Restore Down button to restore the maximized window to its previous size. You can also toggle the iTunes window between its maximized and normal states by double-clicking the title bar.

Once you've set the music playing, you'll often want to reduce the iTunes window to its essentials so that you can get on with your work (or play). To do so, in Windows, press CTRL-SHIFT-M or choose View | Switch To Mini Player to display iTunes in mini mode.

On the Mac, choose Window | Zoom or press ⌘-CTRL-Z to switch the window between its current size and maximizing it to fill the screen. You can click the Zoom button (the green button on the title bar), press ⌘-SHIFT-M, or choose View | Switch To Mini Player to toggle between normal mode and mini mode (shown here).

You can minimize the iTunes window by double-clicking the title bar, by clicking the Minimize button, or by pressing ⌘-M.

From here, you can drag the sizing handle in the lower-right corner to shrink iTunes down even further to its minute size. This can be handy when you're pushed for space, but it isn't very informative.

Here's how to restore iTunes to its normal size from mini mode:

- In Windows, press CTRL-SHIFT-M or click the Restore button.
- On the Mac, click the Zoom button, press ⌘-SHIFT-M, or choose View | Switch From Mini Player.

Change the Columns Displayed to Show the Information You Need

By default, iTunes displays the following columns in List view and in the lower part of Cover Flow view: Name, Time, Artist, Album, Genre, Rating, and Plays. In Album List view, iTunes displays the Name, Time, Artist, Genre, Rating, and Plays columns. You can change the columns displayed for the current item (for example, your music library or a playlist) by using either of two techniques.

To change the display of multiple columns in the same operation, press CTRL-J (Windows) or ⌘-J (Mac), or choose View | View Options, to display the View Options dialog box. Figure 10-4 shows the View Options dialog box for Windows; the View Options dialog box for the Mac has the same controls. The icon and label in the upper-left corner of the dialog box indicate which item's view you're customizing— for example, Music for your music library, or iTunes DJ for the iTunes DJ Smart playlist. Select the check boxes for the columns you want to display, and then click the OK button to close the dialog box and apply your choices.

To change the display of a single column in the current item, right-click (or CTRL-click on the Mac) the heading of one of the columns currently displayed. iTunes displays a menu of the available columns, showing a check mark next to those currently displayed. Select an unchecked column to display it. Select a checked column to remove it from the display.

The Plays item stores the number of times you've played each item in iTunes. iTunes uses this information to determine your favorite items—for example, to decide which songs Smart Playlist should add to a playlist. You can also use this information yourself if you so choose. For example, you can create a Never Played playlist (with the criterion Plays Is 0) to pick out all the items you've never played.

FIGURE 10-4 Use the View Options dialog box to specify which columns iTunes displays for the current item.

To change the order in which your selected columns appear, drag a column heading to the left or right. For example, if you want the Album column to appear before the Artist column, drag the Album column heading to the left until iTunes moves the column.

From the shortcut menu, you can also give the Auto Size Column command to automatically resize the column whose heading you clicked so that the column's width best fits its contents. Give the Auto Size All Columns command to automatically resize all columns like this.

 You can change the column width by dragging the bar at the right edge of a column heading to the left or right. Double-click this bar to set the column width to accommodate its widest entry.

Control iTunes via Keyboard Shortcuts

Controlling iTunes via the mouse is easy enough, but you can also control most of iTunes' features by using the keyboard. This can be useful both when your mouse is temporarily out of reach and when you've reduced the iTunes window to its small size or minute size, and thus hidden some of the controls.

Table 10-1 lists the keyboard shortcuts you can use to control iTunes. Most of these shortcuts work in any of iTunes' four display modes in Windows (normal, maximized, small, and mini) and iTunes' three display modes on the Mac (maximized, small, and mini), but the table notes the shortcuts that work only in some modes.

TABLE 10-1 Keyboard Shortcuts for iTunes

Action	Windows Keystroke	Mac Keystroke
Controlling Playback		
Play or pause the selected song.	SPACEBAR	SPACEBAR
Skip to the next song.	RIGHT ARROW CTRL–RIGHT ARROW	RIGHT ARROW ⌘–RIGHT ARROW
Skip to the previous song.	LEFT ARROW CTRL–LEFT ARROW	LEFT ARROW ⌘–LEFT ARROW
Rewind the song.	CTRL-ALT–LEFT ARROW	⌘-OPTION–LEFT ARROW
Fast-forward the song.	CTRL-ALT–RIGHT ARROW	⌘-OPTION–RIGHT ARROW
Skip to the next album in the list.	ALT–RIGHT ARROW	OPTION–RIGHT ARROW
Skip to the previous album in the list.	ALT–LEFT ARROW	OPTION–LEFT ARROW
Controlling the Volume		
Increase the volume.	CTRL–UP ARROW	⌘–UP ARROW
Decrease the volume.	CTRL–DOWN ARROW	⌘–DOWN ARROW
Toggle muting.	CTRL-ALT–UP ARROW CTRL-ALT–DOWN ARROW	⌘-OPTION–UP ARROW ⌘-OPTION–DOWN ARROW
Controlling the iTunes Windows		
Toggle the display of the iTunes main window.	n/a	⌘-OPTION-1
Show the Equalizer window (Windows).	CTRL-SHIFT-2	n/a
Toggle the display of the Equalizer window.	n/a	⌘-OPTION-2
Toggle between the mini player and full player.	CTRL-SHIFT-M	⌘-SHIFT-M
Minimize the iTunes window.	n/a	⌘-M
Move the focus to the Find box.	CTRL-ALT-F	⌘-OPTION-F
Display the Open Stream dialog box.	CTRL-U	⌘-U
Controlling the Visualizer		
Toggle the Visualizer on and off.	CTRL-T	⌘-T
Toggle full-screen mode on the Visualizer.	CTRL-F	⌘-F

Accompany Your Music with Visualizations

Like many music programs, iTunes can produce stunning visualizations to accompany your music. You can display visualizations at any of three sizes within the iTunes window (which can provide visual distraction while you work or play) or display them full screen to make your computer the life of the party.

Here's how to use visualizations:

- To start visualizations, press CTRL-T (Windows) or ⌘-T (Mac) or choose View | Show Visualizer.
- To stop visualizations, press CTRL-T (Windows) or ⌘-T (Mac) or choose View | Hide Visualizer.
- To change to another visualization mode on the Mac, choose View | Visualizer, and then choose Lathe, Jelly, or Stix from the submenu.
- To use the classic iTunes Visualizer, choose View | Visualizer | iTunes Classic Visualizer. (Choose View | Visualizer | iTunes Visualizer when you want to switch back.)
- To launch full-screen visualizations, press CTRL-F (Windows) or ⌘-F (Mac) or choose View | Full Screen.
- To stop full-screen visualizations, click your mouse button anywhere or press ESC or CTRL-T (Windows) or ⌘-T (Mac). Press CTRL-F (Windows) or ⌘-F (Mac) to switch back from full-screen visualizations to visualizations in a window.

11

Manage Your Music and Video Library with iTunes

HOW TO...

- Browse quickly through your library
- Search for songs and other items
- Create regular playlists and Smart Playlists
- Create powerful playlists with iTunes' Genius
- Enjoy podcasts
- Move your library from one folder to another
- Remove duplicate items from your library
- Use multiple libraries on the same computer
- Share your library with other iTunes users and access their shared library
- Build a media server for your household

This chapter shows you how to use iTunes to manage your library of music and video files. You'll learn how to browse quickly by using the column browser, how to search for songs and videos, and how to create playlists and Smart Playlists. You'll learn how to download podcasts and play them back, and find out how to mix up your music with the Genius feature and the iTunes DJ feature. After that, you'll meet iTunes' features for applying ratings and artwork to items, for consolidating your library so that it contains all your media files (or moving it to a different folder), and for removing any duplicate files that are wasting space.

Later in the chapter, you'll see how to export playlists so that you can share them with other people, import the playlists they share with you, and export your library to an XML file to store details of your playlists and ratings. You'll also learn how to build a media server for your household.

Browse Quickly by Using the Column Browser

iTunes provides the column browser (see Figure 11-1) to browse items quickly by artist, album, or genre. You can toggle the display of the column browser by choosing View | Column Browser | Show Column Browser or View | Column Browser | Hide Column Browser or by pressing CTRL-B (Windows) or ⌘-B (Mac).

In this section, we'll look at using the column browser with music, because that's what you'll probably find it most useful for. But it works the same way for other items.

 When you don't want to restrict the view by genre, select the All item at the top of the Genres column so that you see all genres at once. Similarly, select the All item at the top of the Artists column or the Albums column to see all the items in that column.

Use the Column Browser in Its Default Configuration

Once the column browser is displayed, you can use it to locate songs quickly:

- Click the genre in the Genres column to display only the artists in that genre.
- Click an artist in the Artists column to display the albums by that artist in the Albums column.
- Click an item in the Albums column to display that album in the lower pane.

FIGURE 11-1 iTunes' column browser lets you browse by genre, artist, and album.

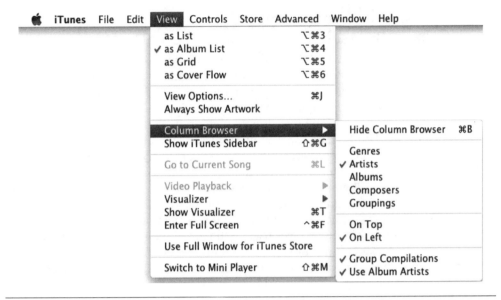

FIGURE 11-2   To customize the column browser, display the Column Browser submenu (shown here) or the context menu, and then choose the options you want.

Customize the Column Browser

To make the column browser work your way, you can customize it. Choose View | Column Browser to display the Column Browser submenu (see Figure 11-2), and then choose the items you want, as discussed next.

 You can also right-click (or CTRL-click on the Mac) any of the displayed column headings in the column browser to display the context menu, which contains the same options as the Column Browser submenu.

Choose Which Columns to Display

In the Genres, Artists, Albums, Composers, Groupings section of the submenu, click to put a check mark next to each column you want to see.

iTunes selects the Genres column, the Artists column, and the Albums column by default. So if, for example, you don't want to browse by genres, click to remove the Genres check mark.

 The Groupings column shows groups of songs that share the same data in their Grouping tag. For example, to create a grouping called Workout, enter **Workout** in the Grouping field in the Item Info dialog box for each song you want to include.

Choose Whether to Display the Column Browser at the Top or on the Left

Your next choice is whether to display the column browser at the top of the iTunes window—its default position—or on the left. Putting the column browser on the left lets you see a longer list in the column browser, but if you use multiple columns, the column browser takes up more of the iTunes window.

To move the column browser to the left of the iTunes window (see Figure 11-3), click the On Left item on the Column Browser submenu or the context menu. iTunes positions the column browser between the Source list and the list of songs. When you move the column browser to the left position, iTunes automatically displays only the Artists column. If you want to display other columns, right-click (or CTRL-click on the Mac) the Artists column heading, and then click to place a check mark next to the first column you want. Repeat the move if you want other columns too.

To put the column browser back at the top of the iTunes window, click the On Top item on the Column Browser submenu. The On Top item and the On Left item are mutually exclusive, like option buttons, even though they use check marks on the menu.

Choose Whether to Group Compilations and Use Album Artists

At the bottom of the Column Browser submenu are two more options you can turn on by clicking to place a check mark next to them: the Group Compilations option and the Use Album Artists option.

FIGURE 11-3 Displaying the column browser on the left of the iTunes window gives longer lists that can make for faster browsing.

Place a check mark next to the Group Compilations option if you want iTunes to group the songs in each compilation together.

A *compilation* is a group of songs that have the same album name (the compilation name) but different artists.

Place a check mark next to the Use Album Artists option if you want iTunes to use the Album Artist tag for sorting rather than the Artist tag. If the Album Artist tag is blank, iTunes uses the Artist tag instead.

The Album Artist tag is a tag you can fill in when the album's artist is different from the song's artist. For example, in a compilation of songs by different artists, the album's artist may be something like Soul Seekers, Soul Destroyers, or the amazingly prolific Various Artists. By filling in the Album Artist tag, you can make clear who's to blame for each song in the compilation.

Change the Display at the Bottom of the iTunes Window

The line of text at the bottom of the full iTunes window shows you how many songs or other items are in the current selection and how long they last. For example, when you're looking at the Music category in your library, you see the information for all the songs it contains. When you've selected a playlist, you see the details for the playlist's songs.

This readout has two formats for songs (5738 songs, 17.4 days, 22.98GB, and 5738 songs, 17:10:06:58 total time, 22.98GB) and three for items such as podcasts that contain episodes. To toggle between or cycle among the formats, click the item-and-time display.

Use Views to Skim Through Your Library

Browsing can be an effective way of finding the songs or other items you want, but you may make better progress—or have more fun browsing—if you change the view iTunes is using.

In Grid view and Cover Flow view, iTunes automatically hides the column browser. In List view and Album List view, you can hide the column browser by choosing View | Column Browser | Hide Column Browser.

iTunes provides four views: List view, Album List view, Grid view, and Cover Flow view. You can switch among views by clicking the View buttons (as shown in the next illustration) to the left of the Search box; by using the View | As List, View |

As Album List, View | As Grid, and View | As Cover Flow commands; or by pressing these keyboard shortcuts:

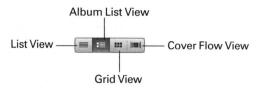

Windows	Mac	Switches to This View
CTRL-ALT-3	⌘-OPTION-3	List view
CTRL-ALT-4	⌘-OPTION-4	Album List view
CTRL-ALT-5	⌘-OPTION-5	Grid view
CTRL-ALT-6	⌘-OPTION-6	Cover Flow view

Sort Your Songs in List View

List view is the view in which iTunes normally starts. List view shows a simple list of the songs in the selected item—for example, your library or a playlist. Figure 11-4 shows List view.

To move to the first item in the current sort column that matches a certain letter or sequence of letters, click in the list, and then type the letter or sequence.

FIGURE 11-4   In List view, you can sort the songs quickly by any column heading.

For example, with the list sorted by the Album column, you might type **Tang** to jump to the first item by Tangerine Dream. You need to type your search term rapidly or iTunes interprets each letter separately.

To sort the songs in List view, click the heading of the column by which you want to sort. Click once for an ascending sort (alphabetical order and smaller numbers before larger numbers). Click again for a descending sort (reverse alphabetical order, larger numbers before smaller numbers). The column heading shows an upward-pointing arrow for an ascending sort and a downward-pointing arrow for a descending sort.

The exception is the Album column, which works a little differently:

- Click the column heading (but not the sort arrow) to cycle through the views: Album, Album By Artist, and Album By Year.
- Click the sort arrow to reverse the direction of the sort.

Browse Through Albums in Album List View

When you want to browse your library by albums rather than by artists or songs, try Album List view (see Figure 11-5). This view displays the album covers in the leftmost column, so you can identify the albums by their covers.

 Note   Album List view works best when you sort your music by albums or by artists. If you sort by song names, iTunes doesn't have enough space to display the album covers. (More on this in a moment.)

FIGURE 11-5   Use Album List view when you want to browse your album using the album covers.

Choose the Sort Order in Album List View

In Album List view, you can sort the albums in three ways by clicking the heading of the leftmost column and choosing the sort order:

- **Album By Title**   Sorts the albums in alphabetical order by their titles.
- **Album By Artist**   Sorts the albums in alphabetical order by the artist names. If the artist has multiple albums, those are sorted alphabetically under the artist.
- **Album By Artist/Year**   Sorts the albums in alphabetical order by the artist names. If the artist has multiple albums, those are sorted in ascending date order (earliest first) under the artist.

Choose the Artwork Size in Album List View

To change the artwork size, click the heading of the leftmost column, and then click the Small item, the Medium item, or the Large item, as needed. These items work like option buttons—you can select only one of them at a time.

Display the Artwork All the Time in Album List View

Normally, in Album List view, iTunes displays the album artwork only when there's enough space for it. For example, when you sort the songs by albums, and most albums contain several songs, there's space to display the artwork. But if you sort the songs by their names, there usually isn't enough space.

You can force iTunes to display the album artwork all the time by clicking the heading of the leftmost column, and then clicking the Always Show Artwork item, placing a check mark next to it.

Displaying the album artwork like this may give a well spread out list in iTunes, especially if you display the artwork at its Large size.

See Your Songs as Pictures on a Grid

In Grid view, iTunes displays the items as a grid of cover pictures or frames. For example, for songs, you see a grid of album covers (see Figure 11-6), allowing you to browse through your albums quickly by the pictures. You can click the tabs at the top of Grid view to switch among albums, artists, genres, and composers for songs, or among other items for movies, TV shows, and podcasts. You can drag the slider at the right side of the tab bar to resize the cover pictures.

To switch to Grid view, click the Grid View button to the left of the Search box. In Grid view, you can sort by clicking the column headings as described earlier in this chapter.

Flick Through Your CDs in Cover Flow View

If you've ever had a record collection, you'll remember the joy of browsing through the records by cover, finding the record you wanted by color and picture. (If you

FIGURE 11-6   Grid view lets you pick an album or other item quickly from its cover art. You can resize the pictures by dragging the slider in the upper-right corner.

haven't done this—finding a record by reading the tiny print on the spine of the album cover was far less fun.)

Cover Flow view is the iTunes equivalent of that experience—and it's pretty good. In Cover Flow view (see Figure 11-7), iTunes displays a carousel of covers. You can click a cover to move to it or scroll the scroll bar to move in larger jumps.

Tip   On Mac OS X Lion, move the mouse pointer over the covers and then flick your finger left or right on the Magic Mouse, Magic Trackpad, or a MacBook's trackpad to scroll quickly through the covers in Cover Flow view.

When you want to see the covers as large as possible, click the Full Screen button to the right of the horizontal scroll bar in the Cover Flow area to expand Cover Flow to take up the full screen.

FIGURE 11-7 In Cover Flow view, you can click the Full Screen button to view your album covers full screen.

Search for Particular Songs or Other Items

Sometimes you may need to search for particular songs. You can also turn up interesting collections of unrelated songs by searching on a word that appears somewhere in the artist name, song name, or album name.

To search all categories of information, type the search text in the Search box. iTunes searches automatically as you type, as shown in Figure 11-8. To constrain the search to artists, albums, composers, or songs, click the drop-down button and make the appropriate choice from the menu, as shown here.

To clear the Search box after searching, click the × button.

FIGURE 11-8 Click in the Search box and type a search term to quickly locate matching items in your iTunes library.

Use Playlists, Smart Playlists, and iTunes DJ

Typically, a CD presents its songs in the order the artist or the producer thought best, but often you'll want to rearrange the songs into a different order—or mix the songs from different CDs and files in a way that suits only you. To do so, you create playlists in iTunes, and iTunes automatically shares them with your iPod so that you can play them on it as well.

You'll probably want to start by creating playlists that contain songs. But playlists can also contain other items, such as TV shows, movies, or podcasts.

You can create playlists manually or use iTunes' Smart Playlist feature to create playlists automatically based on criteria you specify.

Create a Playlist Manually

To create a standard playlist, follow these steps:

1. Click the + button in the Source list, choose File | New Playlist, or press CTRL-N in Windows or ⌘-N on the Mac. iTunes adds a new playlist to the Source list, names it *untitled playlist* (or the next available name, such as *untitled playlist 2*), and displays an edit box around it.

2. Type the name for the playlist, and then press ENTER (Windows) or RETURN (Mac), or click elsewhere, to apply the name.
3. Click the Music item in the Source list to display your songs. If you want to work by artist and album, press CTRL-B (Windows) or ⌘-B (Mac), or choose View | Column Browser | Show Column Browser, to display the column browser.
4. Select the songs you want to add to the playlist and then drag them to the playlist's name. You can drag one song at a time, multiple songs, a whole artist, or a whole CD—whatever you find easiest. You can also drag an existing playlist to the new playlist.
5. Click the playlist's name in the Source list to display the playlist.
6. Drag the songs into the order in which you want them to play.

For you to be able to drag the songs around in the playlist, the playlist must be sorted by the track-number column. If any other column heading is selected, you won't be able to rearrange the order of the songs in the playlist.

You can also create a playlist by selecting the songs or other items you want to include and then pressing CTRL-SHIFT-N or ⌘-SHIFT-N (Mac) or choosing File | New Playlist From Selection. iTunes organizes the songs into a new playlist, with a provisional name (such as *untitled playlist* or the name of the artist culpable for the songs) and displays an edit box around the title so that you can change it immediately. Type the new name, and then press ENTER (Windows) or RETURN (Mac), or click elsewhere, to apply the name.

To delete a playlist, select it in the Source list and press DELETE (Windows) or BACKSPACE (Mac). Alternatively, right-click the playlist (or CTRL-click it on the Mac) and choose Delete from the shortcut menu. iTunes displays a confirmation dialog box:

Click the Delete button to delete the playlist. If you want to turn off the confirmation for playlists you delete from now on, select the Do Not Ask Me Again check box before clicking the Delete button.

iTunes also offers more complex ways of deleting playlists and their contents:

- If you choose not to turn off confirmation of deleting playlists, you can override confirmation by pressing CTRL-DELETE (Windows) or ⌘-DELETE (Mac) when deleting a playlist.
- On the Mac, to delete a playlist *and the songs it contains* from your library, select the playlist and press OPTION-DELETE. iTunes displays a confirmation dialog box for the deletion, as shown here. Click the Delete button. As before, you can select the Do

Not Ask Me Again check box to suppress this confirmation dialog box in the future, but because you're removing song files from your library, it's best not to do so.

- On the Mac, to delete a playlist and the songs it contains from your library *and* to temporarily suppress the confirmation dialog box while doing so, select the playlist and press ⌘-OPTION-DELETE. iTunes prompts you to decide whether to move the selected songs to the Trash or keep them in the iTunes Media folder, as shown here. Click the Keep Files button or the Move To Trash button as appropriate. If you click the Move To Trash button, iTunes deletes only those songs that are in your iTunes Media folder, not those that are in other folders.

Automatically Create Smart Playlists Based on Your Ratings and Preferences

Smart Playlist is a great feature that lets you instruct iTunes how to build a list of songs automatically for you.

You can tell Smart Playlist to build playlists by artist, composer, or genre; to select up to a specific number of songs at random, by artist, by most played, by last played, or by song name; and to automatically update a playlist as you add tracks to or remove tracks from your library. For example, if you tell Smart Playlist to make you a playlist of songs by Bon Iver, Smart Playlist can update the list with new Bon Iver tracks after you import them into your library or buy them from the iTunes Store.

By using Smart Playlist's advanced features, you can even specify multiple rules. For example, you might choose to include songs tagged with the genre Gothic Rock but exclude certain artists by name that you don't want to hear.

 Smart Playlist maintains playlists such as the My Top Rated playlist, the Recently Played playlist, and the Top 25 Most Played playlist, which iTunes creates by default.

Here's how to create a Smart Playlist:

1. Press CTRL-ALT-N (Windows) or ⌘-OPTION-N (Mac), or choose File | New Smart Playlist, to display the Smart Playlist dialog box (shown in Figure 11-9 with settings chosen).

Tip You can also start a new playlist by pressing a modifier key as you click the Add button. On Windows, SHIFT-click the Add button. On the Mac, OPTION-click the Add button. When you press the modifier key, the Add button's icon changes from its normal + sign to the gear icon that denotes a Smart item.

2. Make sure the Match The Following Rules check box is selected so that you can specify criteria. (The other option is to create a random Smart Playlist, which can sometimes be entertaining.) If you create multiple rules, this check box offers the choices Match All Of The Following Rules and Match Any Of The Following Rules. Choose the appropriate one.

3. Use the controls in the first line to specify the first rule:
   - The first drop-down list offers an extensive range of choices: Album, Album Artist, Album Artwork, Album Rating, Artist, Bit Rate, BPM, Category, Checked, Comments, Compilation, Composer, Date Added, Date Modified, Description, Disc Number, Genre, Grouping, Has Artwork, Kind, Last Played, Last Skipped, Media Kind, Name, Playlist, Plays, Purchased, Rating, Sample Rate, Season, Show, Size, Skips, Sort Album, Sort Album Artist, Sort Artist, Sort Composer, Sort Name, Sort Show, Time, Track Number, and Year.
   - The second drop-down list offers options suitable to the item you chose in the first drop-down list—for example, Contains, Does Not Contain, Is, Is Not, Starts With, or Ends With for a text field, or Is, Is Not, Is Greater Than, Is Less Than, or Is In The Range for the bitrate.

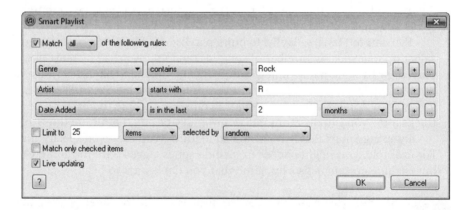

FIGURE 11-9 Smart Playlists are playlists that iTunes automatically populates with songs that match the criteria you specify.

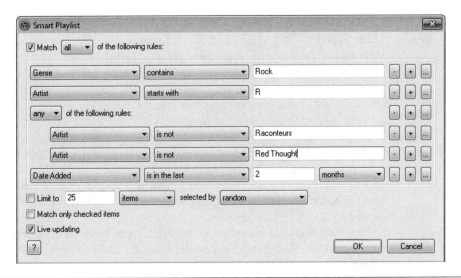

FIGURE 11-10   Click the ellipsis (...) button to the right of a rule to add a subrule below it. You can add subrules to subrules if you want.

4. To create multiple rules, click the + button at the end of the line. iTunes adds another line of rule controls, which you can then set as described in Step 3. To remove a rule, click the – button at the end of the line.

5. To create a subrule, click the ellipsis (...) button on the line of controls below which you want to add the subrule. On Windows, this button appears all the time; on the Mac, hold down OPTION to make it appear in place of the + button. Figure 11-10 shows the Smart Playlist dialog box with two subrules added below the Artist rule.

6. To limit the playlist to a maximum number of tracks, time, or disk space, select the Limit To check box and then specify the limit and how iTunes should select the songs. For example, you could specify Limit To 30 Songs Selected By Least Often Played or Limit To 8 Hours Selected By Random.

7. To make iTunes omit songs whose check boxes you've cleared, select the Match Only Checked Items check box.

8. Select the Live Updating check box if you want iTunes to update the playlist periodically according to your listening patterns. If you prefer not to update the playlist, clear this check box.

9. Click the OK button to close the Smart Playlist dialog box. iTunes creates the playlist, assigns a default name to it, and displays an edit box around the name so you can change it.

10. Type the new name for the playlist and then press ENTER (Windows) or RETURN (Mac).

Tip   A Smart Playlist limited by size can be a good way of selecting songs for an iPod whose capacity is substantially less than the size of your library. For example, you might create a Smart Playlist with the parameter Limit To 1700MB for loading on an iPod shuffle or with the parameter Limit To 12GB for an iPod nano.

How to... **Use the Playlist Item Effectively When Creating Smart Playlists**

The Playlist item in the first drop-down list in the Smart Playlist dialog box lets you specify a relationship between the Smart Playlist you're creating and an existing playlist (either Smart or regular).

For example, you might specify in a Smart Playlist the criterion "Playlist Is Not Recently Played" to prevent any songs that appear in your Recently Played playlist from appearing in the Smart Playlist. Similarly, you could create a Smart Playlist called, say, "Rock Types" that uses several rules to define all the types of music you consider "rock": Genre Contains Rock, Genre Is Alternative, Genre Contains Gothic, and so on.

You could then use the criterion Playlist Is Rock Types in a Smart Playlist to create a subset of your rock music—for example, 90s rock or rock by artists not named Bryan or Brian.

Mix Up Your Music with iTunes DJ

If you like having someone else choose music for you, you may well love iTunes' iTunes DJ feature. iTunes DJ (see Figure 11-11) automatically selects music for you based on four parameters that you specify.

FIGURE 11-11 iTunes DJ is like a giant Smart Playlist.

If the Source list doesn't include iTunes DJ, press CTRL-COMMA (Windows) to display the iTunes dialog box or ⌘-COMMA (Mac) to display the Preferences dialog box. On the General tab, select the iTunes DJ check box in the Show area, and then click the OK button to close the dialog box.

To use iTunes DJ, follow these steps:

1. Click the iTunes DJ item in the Source list.

 The first time you display the iTunes DJ item, you see an introductory screen. Click the Continue button to get started with iTunes DJ.

2. At the bottom of the pane, select the source for iTunes DJ in the Source drop-down list.
3. Click the Settings button to display the iTunes DJ Settings dialog box (see Figure 11-12).
4. In the Display area, choose how many recently played songs and how many upcoming songs to display. The display of recently played songs lets you see details of a song you didn't recognize—or start it playing again.
5. Select the Play Higher Rated Songs More Often check box if you want iTunes DJ to weight the selection toward songs you've given a higher rating.

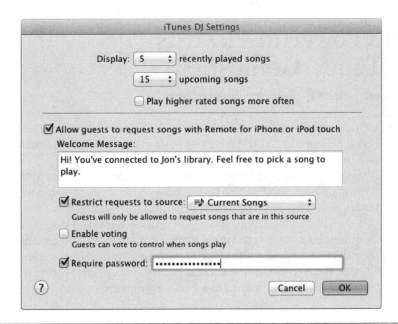

FIGURE 11-12 Use the iTunes DJ Settings dialog box to tell iTunes which songs you want and who may control them.

6. If you want to let guests control your library from an iPod touch, iPad, or iPhone, follow these steps:
   - Select the Allow Guests To Request Songs With Remote For iPhone Or iPod Touch check box.
   - Type a welcome message in the Welcome Message text box.
   - If you want to limit the selection of songs available to guests, select the Restrict Requests To Source check box, and then choose the source in the drop-down list. For example, you might choose a playlist that doesn't include any challenging or explicit songs.
   - Select the Enable Voting check box if you want guests to wrangle over which song plays when.
   - If you want to keep uninvited guests out, select the Require Password check box and type a password in the text box.
7. Click the OK button to close the iTunes DJ Settings dialog box.
8. Click the Play button to start the songs playing.
9. If you don't like the selection, click the Refresh button to display a new selection of songs.

Tip If you find that iTunes DJ dredges up many songs you don't like, you can use it as a means of finding songs for playlists. From the songs that iTunes DJ picks, select those you want to hear, and drag them to a playlist. Click the Refresh button to find more songs, add those you want to hear to the playlist, and repeat the process until you've got a long enough playlist. Then start that playlist playing.

Create Powerful Playlists with iTunes' Genius

iTunes' Genius is a feature with two facets:

- Genius can automatically create a Smart Playlist based on a single song you've chosen. Genius picks the songs from your iTunes library. iTunes calls such a playlist a Genius Mix.
- Genius can automatically recommend songs from the iTunes Store that are related to the song you've chosen. The relationship varies from the obvious to the surprisingly tenuous.

Genius's ability to create Smart Playlists is great, and I'd be surprised if you aren't tempted to test it. The disadvantage is sharing the contents of your iTunes library with Apple. But because of the second part of Genius—the recommendations from the iTunes Store—there's no way to use one feature without using the other as well.

Turn On Genius

Before you can create playlists with Genius, you need to turn Genius on and allow it to analyze the songs in your iTunes library so that it knows the material it has to work with.

 Using Genius involves transmitting the details of the songs in your iTunes library to Apple; without this, the feature can't work as it's designed to work. Apple uses your Apple ID to store the data, so you must create an Apple ID if you don't already have one. If you don't have an Apple ID, iTunes prompts you to create one when you try to launch Genius.

To get started with Genius, choose Store | Turn On Genius to display the Genius screen, which contains details on what Genius does, plus a Turn On Genius button.

Click the Turn On Genius button, and—if you haven't provided an Apple ID on this computer—either provide the details of your existing Apple ID or sign up for a new Apple ID. Genius then transmits the details of your songs to Apple. When it has finished, Genius creates a new playlist called Genius and displays an information screen telling you how to use Genius.

Create a Playlist with Genius

To create a playlist with Genius, simply click the song, and then click the Genius button in the lower-right corner of the iTunes window. You can also right-click the song (or CTRL-click on the Mac) and choose Start Genius from the context menu.

 When you're playing a song, you can quickly create a Genius playlist from it. Simply click the Genius icon on the right side of the display panel.

From the songs in your library, Genius creates a playlist with the song you picked as the first song, calls it Genius, and displays it. Figure 11-13 shows an example.

 If starting Genius produces a dialog box saying that "Genius is unavailable" for the song you chose, click the OK button, choose Store | Update Genius to update your Genius profile with the latest information, and then try again. If you strike out a second time, choose another song as your starting point.

From here, you can customize your Genius playlist as needed:

- **Start again**   If the songs don't appeal to you, click the Refresh button to make Genius crank out a new list.
- **Start from a song in the playlist**   To create a new playlist based on one of the songs, click the song, and then click the Genius button.
- **Edit the playlist**   You can delete songs from the playlist, or drag them up and down it to change the order, just as you can for any other playlist.

FIGURE 11-13 Genius quickly creates a custom playlist for you.

- **Lengthen or shorten the playlist** Choose a different number of songs from the Limit To drop-down list: 25 Songs, 50 Songs, 75 Songs, or 100 Songs. Genius uses 25 songs at first, but then uses whichever number you last used.
- **Save the playlist** Click the Save Playlist button to save the playlist under the name of its first song in the Genius category of the Source list. You can then change the name if you want.

Get Recommendations from Genius

Genius also displays in the iTunes Sidebar recommended songs from the iTunes Store based on what you're listening to. Click a Play button next to a song to play a snippet of it, or click the arrow button to display the song in the iTunes Store—or simply ignore the recommendations if you're not interested.

The iTunes Sidebar (see Figure 11-14) can be useful for finding related songs or bands, but it can also feel like in-your-face marketing. You can hide the iTunes Sidebar at any point by clicking the Show/Hide iTunes Sidebar button in the lower-right corner of the iTunes window, by choosing View | Hide iTunes Sidebar, or by pressing CTRL-SHIFT-G (Windows) or ⌘-SHIFT-G (Mac).

Show/Hide iTunes
Sidebar button

FIGURE 11-14   The iTunes Sidebar shows you songs related to the one you're listening to. You can easily turn it off if you don't like it.

Turn Off Genius

If you tire of Genius, you can turn it off by choosing Store | Turn Off Genius and clicking the Turn Off Genius button in the Are You Sure You Want To Turn Off Genius? dialog box (shown here).

Genius copies your current Genius playlist to a regular playlist. You can then rename it if necessary.

If you need to turn on Genius again, choose Store | Turn On Genius.

Enjoy Podcasts

A *podcast* is a downloadable show that you can play in iTunes or transfer to an iPod or iPhone. Some podcasts are downloadable versions of professional broadcast radio shows, while others are put together by enthusiasts.

Apple makes a wide selection of podcasts available through the iTunes Store, so getting started listening to podcasts or watching video podcasts is easy. You can also find many more podcasts on the Internet.

Explore Podcasts on the iTunes Store

To explore podcasts on the iTunes Store, click the Podcasts item in the Source list, and then click the Podcast Directory link in the bar at the bottom of the Podcasts screen. iTunes displays the Podcasts page of the iTunes Store (see Figure 11-15).

FIGURE 11-15 You can find a wide variety of podcasts on the Podcasts page of the iTunes Store.

From here, you can follow the links to the various podcasts. When you find a podcast that interests you, you can either click the Get Episode button to download a particular episode or click the Subscribe button to subscribe to the podcast. When you click the Subscribe button, iTunes displays a confirmation dialog box, as shown here. Select the Do Not Ask About Subscribing Again check box if you want to suppress confirmation in the future, and then click the Subscribe button to proceed with the subscription.

Configure Podcast Settings

Before you start working with podcasts, you should configure podcast preferences. These preferences cover how iTunes handles podcasts and which podcasts are synchronized with your iPod. To control how iTunes handles podcasts, follow these steps:

1. Click the Podcasts item in the Source list to display the Podcasts screen (shown in Figure 11-16 with several podcasts added).

FIGURE 11-16   Click the Settings button on the Podcasts screen to choose your podcast settings.

FIGURE 11-17 Choose podcast settings in the Podcast Settings dialog box.

Until you add one or more podcasts to iTunes, the Podcasts screen displays information about what podcasts are and links for getting them.

2. Click the Settings button to display the Podcast Settings dialog box (see Figure 11-17).
3. In the Check For New Episodes drop-down list, choose the appropriate frequency: Every Hour, Every Day, Every Week, or Manually. This setting applies to all the podcasts to which you subscribe.
4. In the Settings For drop-down list, pick the podcast for which you want to choose custom settings. To set default settings for all podcasts for which you don't specify custom settings, choose the Podcast Defaults item.
5. If you want to use iTunes' default settings for the podcast you've selected, select the Use Default Settings check box. If you've selected the Podcast Defaults item in the Settings For drop-down list, the Use Default Settings check box isn't available, because you're already working with the default settings.
6. In the When New Episodes Are Available drop-down list, choose what to do: Download All, Download The Most Recent One, or Do Nothing.
7. In the Episodes To Keep drop-down list, choose which episodes of the podcasts to keep: All Episodes, All Unplayed Episodes, Most Recent Episodes, or the last 2, 3, 4, 5, or 10 episodes.
8. Click the OK button to close the dialog box.

Once you've set up iTunes to handle podcasts, tell your iPod which podcasts you want to synchronize. Follow these steps:

1. Connect your iPod to your computer if it's not already connected.
2. Click the iPod's entry in the Source list to display its contents.

FIGURE 11-18   Use the Podcasts tab to tell iTunes which podcasts you want to put on your iPod.

3. Click the Podcasts tab to display that tab's contents (see Figure 11-18).
4. To synchronize podcasts at all, select the Sync Podcasts check box. iTunes enables the other controls on the Podcasts tab.
5. If you want to synchronize podcasts automatically, select the Automatically Include check box, and then use the two drop-down lists to specify which podcasts to include—for example, the 5 Most Recent Unplayed Episodes Of All Podcasts.
6. Use the controls in the Podcasts box and the Episodes box to specify which other episodes to synchronize. Click a podcast series in the Podcasts box, and then select the appropriate check boxes in the Episodes box.
7. In the Include Episodes From Playlists box, select the check box for any playlists that include episodes you want to synchronize.
8. Click the Apply button to apply your changes. iTunes synchronizes the podcasts with the iPod.

Add Podcasts from the Internet

If the range of podcasts available on the iTunes Store doesn't sate your appetite, you can find many other podcasts on the Internet. To add a podcast whose URL you know, choose Advanced | Subscribe To Podcast to display the Subscribe To Podcast dialog box (shown here), type or paste the URL of the podcast, and then click the OK button.

Listen to Podcasts

To listen to the podcasts that you've subscribed to, click the Podcasts item in the Source list to display your podcasts. You can choose different views by clicking the Podcasts tab, Categories tab, or Unplayed tab at the top of the Podcasts screens.

To play the latest episode of a podcast, hover the mouse pointer over it for a moment, and then click the Play Selected button or Play Podcast button that appears.

To play a particular episode, double-click the podcast that you want to open, and then double-click the episode.

You can then control the podcast by using the iTunes play controls as usual. From here, you can unsubscribe from a podcast by selecting it and clicking the Unsubscribe button. When you do so, iTunes adds a Subscribe button to the podcast, so that you can easily subscribe to it again if you choose.

To play a podcast on the iPod classic, choose the Podcasts item on the Music menu. Select the podcast you want to play, and then use the iPod's play controls as usual.

To play a podcast on the iPod nano, tap the Podcasts item on the home screen, tap the podcast's name, and then tap the episode you want to play. Once the podcast is playing, you can use the play controls as normal.

Apply Ratings to Items

iTunes' Rating feature lets you assign a rating of no stars to five stars to each item in your library. You can then sort the songs by rating or tell Smart Playlist to add only songs of a certain ranking or better to a playlist. (See "Automatically Create Smart Playlists Based on Your Ratings and Preferences," earlier in this chapter, for a discussion of Smart Playlist.)

You can apply a rating in three ways in iTunes:

- Select the song in iTunes, and then click in the Rating column to select the number of stars.
- Right-click a song or several selected songs (or CTRL-click on the Mac), choose Rating from the shortcut menu, and then select the appropriate number of stars from the submenu. This technique is useful when you've selected several songs and want to apply the same rating to them.
- Use the Rating box on the Options tab of the Item Information dialog box (press CTRL-I in Windows or ⌘-I on the Mac, or choose Get Info from the File menu or the shortcut menu) to specify the number of stars.

You can also rate a song on the iPod classic or the iPod nano:

- **iPod classic**   Press the Select button twice from the Now Playing screen while the song is playing, scroll left or right to select the appropriate number of stars, and then press the Select button again.
- **iPod nano**   Tap the Info button in the lower-right corner of the Now Playing screen, and then tap the star rating you want to assign.

iTunes picks up the rating the next time you synchronize the iPod with your computer.

Add Artwork to Items

iTunes lets you add artwork to songs and other items, and then display the artwork while the item is playing or is selected.

Most songs or other items you buy from the iTunes Store include artwork—for example, the cover of the single, EP, album, or CD that includes the song, or the cover of a video. And once you've created an account with the iTunes Store, you can have iTunes automatically add art to songs in your library that do not already have art.

Better yet, when you add songs to your library, or when you convert songs in your library to another format, iTunes adds art to the songs from online sources wherever possible.

Set iTunes to Automatically Add Art from the iTunes Store to Songs

To set iTunes to download art from the iTunes Store for songs that do not have art, follow these steps:

1. Click the iTunes Store item in the Source list to access the iTunes Store.

Tip   If you want to open a new window for displaying the iTunes Store, double-click the iTunes Store item in the Source list. Having a separate window open is handy because it leaves the main window open to the music you were playing.

2. If iTunes doesn't automatically sign you in, click the Sign In button, type your name and password in the Sign In dialog box, and then click the Sign In button.
3. Choose Advanced | Get Album Artwork. iTunes displays a confirmation dialog box, as shown here.

4. Select the Do Not Ask Me Again check box if you want to suppress this confirmation dialog box when you give the command in the future.
5. Click the Get Album Artwork button.

Set iTunes to Automatically Download Missing Album Artwork

To set iTunes to download missing album artwork automatically, follow these steps:

1. Create an account for the iTunes Store, and then sign in to it.
2. Display the iTunes dialog box or the Preferences dialog box:
   • In Windows, choose Edit | Preferences or press CTRL-COMMA or CTRL-Y to display the iTunes dialog box.
   • On the Mac, choose iTunes | Preferences or press ⌘-COMMA or ⌘-Y to display the Preferences dialog box.
3. Click the General tab to display its contents.
4. Select the Automatically Download Missing Album Artwork check box. iTunes displays a confirmation dialog box, as shown here.

5. Click the Automatically Get Artwork button to close the confirmation dialog box.
6. Click the OK button to close the iTunes dialog box or Preferences dialog box.

Add Artwork to Songs Manually

If iTunes can't find art for a song automatically, or if you want to add
art to a song that already has art, you can add the art manually. You
artwork pane in the iTunes window or the Artwork box in the Item Ir
box or the Multiple Item Information dialog box. The artwork pane i

You can apply any image you want to a song, provided that it is in a format that
QuickTime supports. (QuickTime's supported formats include JPG, GIF, TIFF, PNG,
BMP, and PhotoShop.) For example, you might download album art or other pictures
from an artist's website and then apply that art to the song files you ripped from the
artist's CDs. Or you might prefer to add images of your own to favorite songs or to
songs you've composed yourself.

Amazon.com (www.amazon.com) has cover images for millions of CDs and records.
For most music items, you can click the small picture on the item's main page to
display a larger version of the image.

Add Artwork to Songs by Using the Artwork Pane

To add an image by using the artwork pane, follow these steps:

1. Open iTunes, and then select the song or songs you want to affect.
2. If the artwork pane isn't displayed (below the Source list), display it by clicking
   the Show Or Hide Artwork button.
3. If the title bar of the artwork pane says Now Playing, click the title bar to change
   it to Selected Item.
4. Open a Windows Explorer window or a Finder window to the folder that
   contains the image you want to use for the artwork, or open a browser window
   to a URL that contains the image. For example, open an Internet Explorer
   window to Amazon.com, and then navigate to the image you want.
5. Arrange iTunes and the Windows Explorer window, Finder window, or browser
   window so that you can see them both.
6. Drag the image to the artwork pane and drop it there.
7. Add further images to the song or songs if you want while you have them selected.

Most CD cover images are relatively small in dimensions and are compressed, so
their file size is fairly small. Adding an image to a song increases its file size a
little, but not by a large amount. If you add a large image to a song, iTunes uses a
compressed version of the image rather than the full image.

Add Artwork to Songs by Using the Item Information Dialog Box or the Multiple Item Information Dialog Box

Follow these steps to add artwork by using the Item Information dialog box (for a
single song) or the Multiple Item Information dialog box:

1. Select the songs, right-click (or CTRL-click on the Mac), and choose Get Info from
   the shortcut menu to display the dialog box. (You can also choose File | Get Info
   or press CTRL-I in Windows or ⌘-I on the Mac to display the dialog box.)

2. Display the tab you need:
   - **Item Information dialog box**   Click the Artwork tab.
   - **Multiple Item Information dialog box**   Click the Info tab.
3. Open a Windows Explorer window or a Finder window to the folder that contains the picture you want to use for the artwork, or open a browser window to a URL that contains the picture.
4. Drag the image to the Artwork box in the Multiple Item Information dialog box or the open area on the Artwork tab of the Item Information dialog box.
5. If you're using the Item Information dialog box, add further images as needed. To change the order of the images, drag them about in the open area (see Figure 11-19). You may need to reduce the zoom by dragging the slider to get the pictures small enough to rearrange.

When you've added two or more pictures to the same song, the artwork pane displays a Previous button and a Next button for browsing from picture to picture.

You can display the current picture at full size by clicking it in the artwork pane. Hold the mouse over the artwork viewer window to display playback controls (see Figure 11-20). Click the Close button (the × button) to close the artwork viewer window.

To remove the artwork from a song, right-click (or CTRL-click on the Mac) the song and choose Get Info from the shortcut menu. Click the Artwork tab of the Item Information dialog box, click the picture, and then click the Delete button.

FIGURE 11-19   The Item Information dialog box lets you add multiple images to a song and rearrange them into the order you want.

FIGURE 11-20   Hold the mouse pointer over the artwork viewer window to display playback controls.

How to...   Copy a Picture from a Song to Other Songs

You can also paste a picture into the Artwork box or the Artwork tab. For example, if your library already contains one song that has a picture you want to apply to other songs, you can copy the picture from that song, and then paste it into the other songs. Follow these steps:

1. Display the artwork pane if it isn't already displayed. If the artwork pane is showing Now Playing, click its title bar to make it show Selected Item.
2. Click the song that contains the picture you want to use.
3. Right-click (or CTRL-click on the Mac) the picture in the artwork pane, and then choose Copy from the shortcut menu.
4. Select the songs to which you want to apply the picture.
5. Right-click (or CTRL-click on the Mac) in the selection, and then choose Get Info from the shortcut menu to display the Multiple Item Information dialog box.
6. Right-click in the Artwork box, and then choose Paste from the shortcut menu.
7. Click the OK button to close the dialog box.

Consolidate Your Music Library So You Can Always Access All Its Items

As you saw earlier in this book, you can set iTunes to copy to your iTunes Media folder the file for each song or other item that you add to your library from another folder. Alternatively, you can have iTunes add a reference to the file in its original folder.

Whether iTunes copies the file or simply adds the reference is controlled by the Copy Files To iTunes Media Folder When Adding To Library check box. You'll find this on the Advanced tab in the iTunes dialog box (Windows) or the Preferences dialog box (Mac).

Adding references rather than files keeps down the amount of space your media library takes up. But when your external drives, network drives, or removable media aren't available, the items stored on those drives or media won't be available. For example, when you grab your laptop and head over to a friend's house, you'll be able to play only the items on the laptop's own drive.

 You can also use the Consolidate command when you want to move your library to another folder.

To make sure you can play your media files wherever you want, you can *consolidate* your library, making iTunes copy all the files currently outside your library folder to the library folder.

Before you consolidate your library, it's vital that you understand the following about consolidation:

- Consolidation can take a long time, depending on the number of files to be copied and the speed of the network connection you're using. Don't consolidate your library just as the airport shuttle is about to arrive.
- The drive that holds your library must have enough space free to hold all your files. If lack of space was the reason you didn't copy the files to your media library in the first place, you probably don't want to consolidate your library.
- Files on removable media such as CDs, DVDs, or USB sticks won't be copied unless the medium is in the drive at the time.

To consolidate your library, follow these steps:

1. Choose File | Library | Organize Library. iTunes displays the dialog box shown here.
2. Select the Consolidate Files check box.
3. Click the OK button. iTunes displays the Copying Files dialog box as it copies the files to your library.

If consolidation goes wrong, see "iTunes Runs You Out of Hard-Disk Spa[c]
Windows" or "iTunes Runs You Out of Hard-Disk Space on the Mac" in Ch
for help.

Remove Duplicate Items from Your Library

Even if your library isn't huge, it's easy to get duplicate songs or videos in it, especially if you add folders of existing files as well as rip and encode your CDs and other audio sources. Duplicates waste disk space, particularly on your iPod, so iTunes offers a command to help you identify them so that you can remove them.

To remove duplicate items, follow these steps:

1. In the Source list, click the appropriate item in the Library category. For example, to look for duplicate songs, click the Music item. If you want to confine the duplicate-checking to a playlist, click that playlist in the Source list.
2. Choose File | Display Duplicates. iTunes displays a list of duplicate items. Figure 11-21 shows an example on Windows.

iTunes identifies duplicates by artist and name, not by album, length, or other often-useful details. Before deleting any duplicates, check that they're actually duplicates, not just different versions or mixes of the same item.

FIGURE 11-21   Use the File | Display Duplicates command to display a list of duplicate songs and videos in a playlist or in your library.

3. Decide which copy of each item you want to keep. To find out where an item is stored, right-click it (or CTRL-click it on the Mac) and choose Show In Windows Explorer (Windows) or Show In Finder (Mac) from the shortcut menu. You'll see a Windows Explorer window or a Finder window that shows the contents of the folder that includes the file.

Tip If your library contains various file formats, you may find it helpful to display the file type in iTunes so that you can see which item is which format. For example, when you have duplicate song files, you might want to delete the MP3 files rather than the AAC files. Right-click (or CTRL-click on the Mac) the heading of the column after which you want the Kind column to appear, and then select the Kind item from the shortcut menu.

4. To delete an item, select it and press DELETE (Windows) or BACKSPACE (Mac). Click the Remove button in the confirmation dialog box; select the Do Not Ask Me Again check box first if you want to turn off the confirmation.

5. If the file is stored in your library folder, iTunes prompts you to move it to the Recycle Bin (Windows) or to the Trash (Mac). Click the Keep File button if you want to keep the file or the Move To Recycle Bin button or Move To Trash button if you want to get rid of it.

To display all items again, click the Display All button at the bottom of the iTunes window.

Export and Import Playlists

If you create a great playlist, chances are that you'll want to share it with others. You can do so by exporting the playlist so that someone else can import it—provided that they have the items in their library. Follow these steps:

1. In the Source list, right-click (or CTRL-click on the Mac) the playlist, and then click Export on the context menu. iTunes displays the iTunes dialog box, which is a Save As dialog box with a different name.
2. Specify the filename for the list, and then choose the folder in which to store it.
3. Choose the format for the file. Windows lets you choose among Text Files, XML Files, M3U Files, and M3U8 Files; Mac OS X gives you these choices and Unicode Text as well. XML Files is the best choice for exporting a playlist to another copy of iTunes. When you're exporting a playlist for use with another program, use M3U Files or M3U8 Files instead.
4. Click the Save button to save the playlist.

You can then share the playlist with someone else—for example, by sending it via e-mail.

When you receive a playlist, you can import it by choosing File | Library | Import Playlist, selecting the file in the Import dialog box (change the Files Of Type setting in Windows if necessary), and then clicking the Open button. iTunes checks the playlist against your library and creates a playlist that contains as many of the items as you have available. If one or more items are unavailable, iTunes warns you, as shown here.

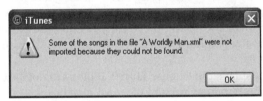

Export Your Library

You can export the details of your entire library and all your playlists as a backup in case your computer suffers data loss or damage. To export the library, choose File | Library | Export Library, specify the name and folder in the iTunes dialog box, and then click the Save button.

 When you export your library, you export only a list of what it contains and the information you've added—playlists, ratings, and so on. You don't export copies of your media files. A typical library export file is several megabytes in size.

As well as your playlists, your exported library contains details of your play count, ratings, equalizations, and other item-specific settings you've applied, such as start times and stop times.

Use Multiple Libraries on the Same Computer

Normally, you put all your songs, videos, and other items into a single iTunes library. This has several advantages, including simplicity and having all of your media items instantly accessible from iTunes.

But in some cases you may want to create different libraries for different categories of items. For example, you can have a family library containing songs that are safe for the kids, and an adult library that contains explicit material. Or you can have a library that contains only the songs on your laptop, plus a library that contains all those songs and those that appear on your removable drives or network drives.

You already have the standard library that iTunes has created for you, so your first step is to create a new library.

Create a New Library

To create a new library, follow these steps:

1. If iTunes is running, close it. For example, press ALT-F4 (Windows) or ⌘-Q (Mac).
2. Start iTunes using the special command for changing libraries:
   - **Windows**   Hold down SHIFT while you click the iTunes icon. For example, click the Start button, click All Programs, click the iTunes folder, and then SHIFT-click the iTunes icon. Keep holding down SHIFT until the Choose iTunes Library dialog box appears.
   - **Mac**   Hold down OPTION while you click the iTunes icon—for example, in the Dock. Keep holding down OPTION until the Choose iTunes Library dialog box appears.
3. iTunes displays the Choose iTunes Library dialog box. The next illustration shows the Windows version of this dialog box.

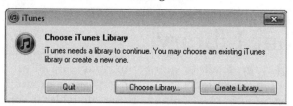

4. Click the Create Library button. iTunes displays the New iTunes Library dialog box. The next illustration shows the Windows version of this dialog box.

5. Type the name for the new library folder, choose the folder in which to store it, and then click the Save button. iTunes closes the New iTunes Library dialog box, creates the new library, and then opens itself, showing the contents of the new library.
6. Add songs and other items to the library using the techniques you learned in Chapter 10.

Switch to Another Library

When you start iTunes normally, the program loads the library you used last time. To switch from one library to another, follow these steps:

1. If iTunes is running, close it. For example, press ALT-F4 (Windows) or ⌘-Q (Mac).
2. Start iTunes using the special command for changing libraries:
   - **Windows**   Hold down SHIFT while you click the iTunes icon. For example, click the Start button, click All Programs, click the iTunes folder, and then SHIFT-click the iTunes icon. Again, keep holding down SHIFT until the Choose iTunes Library dialog box appears.
   - **Mac**   Hold down OPTION while you click the iTunes icon—for example, in the Dock. As before, keep holding down OPTION until the Choose iTunes Library dialog box appears.

3. iTunes displays the Choose iTunes Library dialog box.
4. Click the Choose Library button. iTunes displays the Open iTunes Library dialog box. The next illustration shows the Windows version of this dialog box.

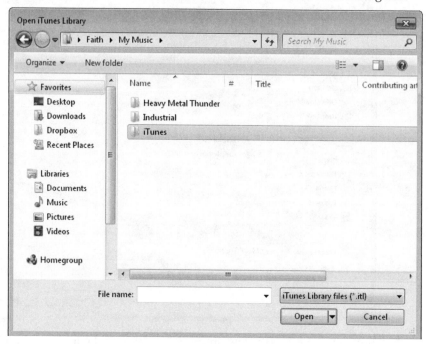

5. Open the folder in which you stored the library, select the iTunes Library.itl file, and then click the Open button.
6. iTunes opens, showing the contents of the library you selected.

Share Items and Access Shared Items

Listening to your own music collection is great, but it's often even better to be able to share your music with your friends or family—and to enjoy as much of their music as you can stand. In this section, we'll look at how to share your music in three ways:

- Share your own music with your other computers using iTunes' Home Sharing feature
- Share your music with other iTunes users on your network and play the music they're sharing
- Share your music with other users of your computer

You can also share other file types that iTunes supports—for example, videos.

Apple May Change the Details of Library Sharing

If you read through the license agreements for iTunes and the iTunes Store, you'll notice that Apple reserves the right to change the details of what you can and can't do with iTunes and the files you buy. This isn't unusual, but it's worth taking a moment to consider.

At this writing, Apple has made several changes. Some changes are no big deal. For example, Apple has reduced the number of times you can burn an individual playlist to CD from ten times to seven times. (You can create another playlist with the same songs and burn that seven times too, and then create another.)

More of a big deal are the changes Apple has made to sharing songs and other files on the network. When Apple first added sharing to iTunes, it could share songs not only on the computer's local network but also across the Internet. Apple quickly reduced this to the local network only, which seemed fair enough. iTunes could share music with five other computers at a time— enough to reach a good number of people, especially in a dorm situation with many people sharing music and listening to shared music.

Since then, Apple reduced the sharing from five computers at a time to five computers *per day* total. This still works fine for most homes, but on bigger networks, it's very restrictive. Once a computer has shared library items with its five computers for the day, you'll see one of the messages shown here if you try to connect.

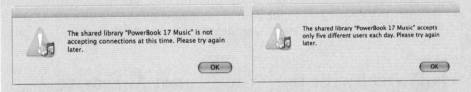

All the changes so far have been restrictive and have benefited the media providers (such as the record companies) rather than iTunes users. Further changes seem likely, so if iTunes doesn't behave as described here, check the latest license agreement on the Apple website.

Share Your Library with Your Other Computers

iTunes' Home Sharing feature makes it easy to share your library among your computers. You can use up to five computers.

Note   The big difference between Home Sharing and iTunes' library sharing is that Home Sharing enables you to copy songs from one computer to another. Regular sharing lets another computer play your shared songs but not copy the files to that computer.

To use Home Sharing, you set up each of the computers to use the same Apple ID. Using the same Apple ID is the mechanism for making sure that you're not violating copyright by giving copyrighted content to other people. If you don't have an Apple ID yet, you can create one from the Home Sharing screen.

To set up Home Sharing, follow these steps:

1. In the Source list, see if the Shared category is expanded, showing its contents. If not, expand it by holding the mouse pointer over the Shared heading and then clicking the word Show when it appears.
2. Click the Home Sharing item to display its contents.
3. Type your Apple ID in the Apple ID box.

 If you don't yet have an Apple ID, click the Need An Apple ID? link, and then follow through the process of signing up for one. Once you're armed with your Apple ID, go back to the Home Sharing screen.

4. Type your password in the Password box.
5. Click the Create Home Share button. iTunes checks in with the iTunes servers and sets up the account.

 If iTunes displays a dialog box saying that Home Sharing could not be activated because this computer is not authorized for the iTunes account associated with the Apple ID you provided, click the Authorize button.

6. When the Home Sharing screen displays the message that Home Sharing is now on, click the Done button. iTunes then removes the Home Sharing item from the Shared category in the Source list, and you have access to the libraries of the other computers on which you've set up Home Sharing.

How to... **Deal with the "You Cannot Authorize More Than 5 Computers" Message**

If iTunes displays the message "You cannot authorize more than 5 computers" (shown here) when you try to set up Home Sharing on one of your computers, you must deauthorize one of your currently authorized computers in order to use this one.

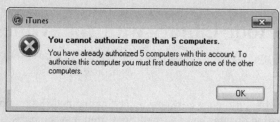

To deauthorize a computer, open iTunes on that computer, choose Store | Deauthorize This Computer, and then follow the instructions that appear.

If you no longer have access to a computer you've authorized, you can deauthorize all your computers, and then reauthorize those you want to use. You can perform the deauthorization only once per year.

To deauthorize all your computers, follow these steps:

1. In iTunes, double-click the iTunes Store item in the Source list to open a separate window showing the iTunes Store.
2. In the upper-right corner, click your account name, and then click Account on the drop-down list. (If the Sign In button appears instead of your account name, click the button and sign in.)
3. In the Sign In To View Account Information dialog box, type your password, and then click the Account Info button. The Account Information window appears.
4. In the Apple ID Summary box, click the Deauthorize All button. iTunes displays a confirmation dialog box, as shown here.

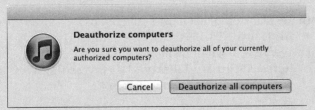

5. Click the Deauthorize All Computers button. iTunes gives the "kill" command and then displays the Deauthorization Complete dialog box (shown here).

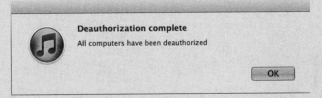

6. Click the OK button.

Now reauthorize each computer you want to use by opening iTunes on it and then giving the Store | Authorize This Computer command. After completing the authorization, iTunes displays the Computer Authorization Was Successful dialog box telling you how many of your five computers you've authorized, as shown here.

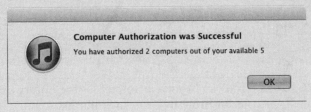

Copy Files Using Home Sharing

After setting up Home Sharing, you can quickly copy files from one installation of iTunes to another. To do so, follow these steps:

1. In the Source list, make sure the Shared category is expanded, showing its contents. If the Shared category is collapsed, expand it by holding the mouse pointer over the Shared heading and then clicking the word Show when it appears.
2. Click the Home Sharing library whose contents you want to see. The library's contents appear in the main part of the iTunes window, and you can browse them as usual (see Figure 11-22). For example, choose View | Column Browser | Show Column Browser to display the column browser so that you can browse by genres, artists, albums, or whichever other items you prefer.

 The Home Sharing libraries appear in the Shared category with a Home Sharing icon next to them. The Home Sharing icon shows a house containing a musical note.

3. In the Show drop-down list at the bottom, choose which items to display:
   - **All Items**   This is the default setting. Use it when you want to get an overview of what the library contains.
   - **Items Not In My Library**   Use this setting to display only the items you may want to copy to your library.

FIGURE 11-22   You can browse a Home Sharing library using the same techniques as for browsing your own library.

How to... **Make Home Sharing Automatically Import New Purchases from Your Other Computers**

You can set Home Sharing to automatically import your new purchases from the iTunes Store to your computer. So if you buy a song on your laptop computer, you can have iTunes automatically import it to your desktop computer as well.

To set Home Sharing to automatically import new purchases, follow these steps:

1. In the Source list, click a Home Sharing library to display its contents and the Home Sharing control bar.
2. Click the Settings button to display the Home Sharing Settings dialog box (shown here).
3. Select the Music check box, the Movies check box, the TV Shows check box, the Books check box, and the Apps check box, as needed.
4. Click the OK button to close the Home Sharing Settings dialog box.

4. Select the items you want to import to your library. If you've switched to the Items Not In My Library view, you may want to choose Edit | Select All (or press CTRL-A on Windows or ⌘-A on the Mac) to select everything.
5. Click the Import button. iTunes imports the files.

Share Your Library with Other Local iTunes Users

You can share either your entire library or selected playlists with other users on your network. You can share most items, including MP3 files, AAC files, Apple Lossless Encoding files, AIFF files, WAV files, and links to radio stations. You can't share Audible files or QuickTime sound files.

Note Technically, iTunes' sharing is limited to computers on the same TCP/IP subnet as your computer is on. (A *subnet* is a logical division of a network.) A home network typically uses a single subnet, so your computer can "see" all the other computers on the network. But if your computer connects to a medium-sized network, and you're unable to find a computer that you know is connected to the same network somewhere, it may be on a different subnet.

At this writing, you can share your library with up to five other computers per day, and your computer can be one of up to five computers accessing the shared library on another computer on any given day.

e shared library remains on the computer that's sharing it, and when a
)ating computer goes to play a song or other item, that item is streamed across
work. This means that the item isn't copied from the computer that's sharing it to
iputer that's playing it in a way that leaves a usable file on the playing computer.
When a computer goes offline or is shut down, library items it has been sharing
stop being available to other users. Participating computers can play the shared items
but can't do anything else with them; for example, they can't burn shared songs to CD
or DVD, download them to an iPod or iPhone, or copy them to their own libraries.

To share some or all of your library, follow these steps:

1. Display the iTunes dialog box or the Preferences dialog box:
   - In Windows, choose Edit | Preferences or press CTRL-COMMA or CTRL-Y to
     display the iTunes dialog box.
   - On the Mac, choose iTunes | Preferences or press ⌘-COMMA or ⌘-Y to display
     the Preferences dialog box.
2. Click the Sharing tab to display it. Figure 11-23 shows the Sharing tab of the
   iTunes dialog box with settings chosen.

FIGURE 11-23   On the Sharing tab of the iTunes dialog box or the Preferences
                dialog box, choose whether to share part or all of your library.

3. Select the Share My Library On My Local Network check box. (This check box is cleared by default.) By default, iTunes then selects the Share Entire Library option button. If you want to share only some playlists, select the Share Selected Playlists option button. Then, in the list box, select the check box for each playlist you want to share.
4. By default, your shared library items are available to any other user on the network. To restrict access to people with whom you share a password, select the Require Password check box, and then enter a strong (unguessable) password in the text box.

 If there are many computers on your network, use a password on your shared music to help avoid running up against the five-users-per-day limit. If your network has only a few computers, you may not need a password to avoid reaching this limit.

5. Select the Home Sharing Computers And Devices Update Play Counts check box if you want iTunes to update the play count for a song whenever any computer plays it, not just this computer.
6. Click the General tab to display its contents. In the Library Name text box near the top of the dialog box, set the name that other users trying to access your library will see. The default name is *username*'s Library, where *username* is your username—for example, Anna Connor's Library. You might choose to enter a more descriptive name, especially if your computer is part of a well-populated network (for example, in a dorm).
7. Click the OK button to apply your choices and close the dialog box.

 When you set iTunes to share your library, iTunes displays a message reminding you that "Sharing music is for personal use only"—in other words, remember not to violate copyright law. Select the Do Not Show This Message Again check box if you want to prevent this message from appearing again.

Disconnect Other Users from Your Shared Library

To disconnect other users from your shared library, follow these steps:

1. Display the iTunes dialog box or the Preferences dialog box:
   - In Windows, choose Edit | Preferences or press CTRL-COMMA or CTRL-Y to display the iTunes dialog box.
   - On the Mac, choose iTunes | Preferences or press ⌘-COMMA or ⌘-Y to display the Preferences dialog box.
2. Click the Sharing tab to display it.
3. Clear the Share My Library On My Local Network check box.

4. Click the OK button. If any other user is connected to your shared library, iTunes displays this dialog box to warn you:

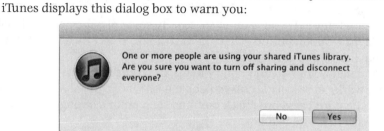

One or more people are using your shared iTunes library. Are you sure you want to turn off sharing and disconnect everyone?

No   Yes

5. Click the Yes button or the No button, as appropriate. If you click the Yes button, anyone playing an item from the library will be cut off abruptly without notice.

 Note   Home Sharing remains active even when you've turned off library sharing.

Access and Play Another Local iTunes User's Shared Library

iTunes automatically detects shared libraries when you launch the program while your computer is connected to a network. If iTunes finds shared libraries or playlists, it displays them in the Source list. Click a shared library to display its contents. Figure 11-24 shows an example of browsing the music shared by another computer.

FIGURE 11-24   Computers sharing libraries appear in the iTunes Source list, allowing you to quickly browse the songs and other items that are being shared.

If a shared library has a password, iTunes displays the Shared Library Password dialog box.

Type the password, and then click the OK button to access the library. Select the Remember Password check box before clicking the OK button if you want iTunes to save the password to speed up future access to the library.

 Double-click the entry for a shared library in the Source list to open a separate window that shows its contents.

When you've finished using a shared library, disconnect it by taking one of these actions:

- Click the Eject icon next to the library in the Source list.
- Click the library in the Source list, and then press CTRL-E (Windows) or ⌘-E (Mac).
- Click the library in the Source list, and then choose Controls | Disconnect *Library* from the shortcut menu (where *Library* is the name of the shared library).
- Right-click the library in the Source list (or CTRL-click on the Mac), and then choose Disconnect from the shortcut menu.

Share Your Music More Effectively with Other Local Users

As you saw in the previous section, iTunes makes it easy for you to share either your music library or specific playlists with other iTunes users on your local area network (LAN). You can share with up to five different computers per day, and of course your computer must be attached to the network and powered on for them to be able to access your music.

You may also want to share your music with other users of your computer. The security features built into Windows 7, Windows Vista, Windows XP, and Mac OS X mean that you have to do a little work to share it.

This section focuses on music files, but you can use the same approach for other media files—for example, video files.

Share Your Library with Other Users of Your PC

Windows automatically prevents other users from accessing your personal files, assigning each user a user account and keeping them out of other users' accounts. The result of this is that your iTunes library, which is stored by default in your Music\ iTunes\iTunes Media folder on Windows 7 or Windows Vista or the My Music\iTunes\ iTunes Media folder on Windows XP, is securely protected from other users of your computer. That's great if you want to keep your music to yourself, but not so great if you want to share it with your friends, family, or coworkers.

 Windows Media Player, the audio and video player that Microsoft includes with Windows at this writing, gets around this restriction by making the music and video files that any user adds to their music library available to all users. This is great if you want to share all your files but less appealing if you want to keep some of them private.

The easiest way to give other users access to your library is to move it to the Public Music folder (on Windows 7 or Windows Vista) or the Shared Music folder (on Windows XP). This is a folder created automatically when Windows is installed, and which Windows automatically shares with other users of your computer but not with other computers on the network.

Here's where to find this folder:

- **Windows 7 or Windows Vista** The Public Music folder is located in the Public folder.
- **Windows XP** The Shared Music folder is located in the \Documents and Settings\All Users\Documents\My Music folder.

Alternatively, you can put the library in another shared folder. This example uses the Public Music folder on Windows 7 and Windows Vista and the Shared Music folder on Windows XP. If you're using another folder, substitute it where appropriate.

Moving your library to the Public Music folder or the Shared Music folder involves two steps: moving the files, and then telling iTunes where you've moved them to.

To move your library files to the Public Music folder or the Shared Music folder, follow these steps:

1. Close iTunes if it's running. (For example, press ALT-F4 or choose File | Exit.)
2. Open your library folder:
   - **Windows 7 or Windows Vista** Choose Start | Music to open a Windows Explorer window showing your Music folder.
   - **Windows XP** Choose Start | My Music to open a Windows Explorer window showing your My Music folder.
3. Double-click the iTunes folder to open it. You'll see an iTunes Music Library.xml file, an iTunes Library.itl file, and an iTunes Media folder. The first two files must stay in your library folder. If you remove them, iTunes won't be able to find your library, and it will create these files again from scratch.

4. Right-click the iTunes Media folder, and then choose Cut from the shortcut menu to cut it to the Clipboard.
5. Open the Public Music folder or the Shared Music folder:
   - **Windows 7** In the left column of the Music window, expand the Libraries item, and then expand the Music library. Click the Public Music folder that appears under Music.
   - **Windows Vista** In the Music folder, double-click the shortcut to the Sample Music folder. The Sample Music folder is in the Public Music folder. In the Address bar, click the Public Music item to display the folder's contents.
   - **Windows XP** In the Other Places task pane, click the Shared Music link to display the Shared Music folder. (If the Shared Music folder doesn't appear in the Other Places task pane, click the My Computer link, click the Shared Documents link, and then double-click the Shared Music folder.)
6. Right-click an open space in the Public Music folder or the Shared Music folder, and then choose Paste from the shortcut menu to paste the iTunes Media folder into the folder.
7. Close the Windows Explorer window. (For example, press ALT-F4 or choose File | Close.)

Next, you need to tell iTunes where the song files and other media files are. Follow these steps:

1. Start iTunes. (For example, double-click the iTunes icon on your desktop.)
2. Press CTRL-COMMA or choose Edit | Preferences to display the iTunes dialog box.
3. Click the Advanced tab to display its contents.
4. Click the Change button to display the Browse For Folder dialog box.
5. Navigate to the Public Music folder or the Shared Music folder, and then click the OK button to close the Browse For Folder dialog box.
6. Click the OK button to close the iTunes dialog box.

After you've done this, iTunes knows where the files are, and you can play them back as usual. When you rip further song files from CD or import files, iTunes stores them in the Public Music folder or Shared Music folder.

You're all set. The other users of your PC can do either of two things:

- Move their library to the Public Music folder or Shared Music folder, using the techniques described here, so that all files are stored centrally. Instead of moving the library folder itself, move the folders it contains. Users can then add songs they import to the shared library, and all users can access them.
- Keep their library separate, but add the contents of the shared library folder to it. Here's how:
  1. Choose File | Add Folder To Library to display the Browse For Folder dialog box.
  2. Navigate to the Public Music folder or Shared Music folder.
  3. Select the iTunes Media folder.
  4. Click the Open button. iTunes adds all the latest songs to your library.

Whichever approach the other users of your PC choose, the songs that they add to the shared library don't appear automatically in your library. To add all the latest tracks, use the Add Folder To Library command, as described in the previous list.

Share Your Library with Other Users of Your Mac

Mac OS X's security system prevents other users from accessing your Home folder or its contents—which by default includes your library. So if you want to share your library with other users of your Mac, you need to change permissions to allow others to access your Home folder (or parts of it) or move your library to a folder they can access.

The easiest way to give other users access to your songs and other items is to put your library in the Users/Shared folder and put an alias to it in its default location. To do so, follow these steps:

1. Use the Finder to move the iTunes Media folder from your ~/Music/iTunes folder to the /Users/Shared folder.
2. Press ⌘-COMMA (or ⌘-Y) or choose iTunes | Preferences to display the Preferences dialog box.
3. Click the Advanced button to display the Advanced tab.
4. Click the Change button, and then use the resulting Change iTunes Media Folder Location dialog box to navigate to and select the /Users/Shared/iTunes Media folder.
5. Click the Choose button to close the Change Media Folder Location dialog box and enter the new path in the iTunes Media Folder Location text box on the Advanced tab.
6. Make sure the Keep iTunes Media Folder Organized check box is selected.
7. Click the OK button to close the Preferences dialog box.

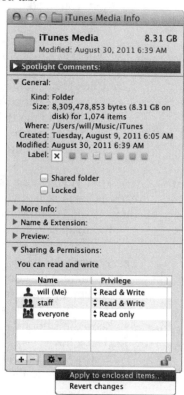

If you want other users to be able to put song files in the shared library (for example, if they import songs from CD), you need to give them Write permission for it. To do so, follow these steps:

1. Open a Finder window to the /Users/Shared folder.
2. CTRL-click or right-click the iTunes Media folder, and then choose Get Info from the shortcut menu to display the iTunes Media Info window, shown here.

3. In the Sharing & Permissions area, click the gray disclosure triangle to expand the area if it is collapsed.
4. Click the lock icon in the lower-right corner, type your password in the authentication dialog box that opens, and then click the OK button. The lock opens.

 If you are not an Administrator of your Mac, you will need to provide an administrator's username and password in the authentication dialog box to unlock the lock in the iTunes Media Info window.

5. Open the Everyone pop-up menu, and then click the Read & Write item instead of the Read Only item.
6. Click the Action button (the gear button) at the bottom of the Info window, and then click Apply To Enclosed Items on the pop-up menu. Mac OS X displays this dialog box:

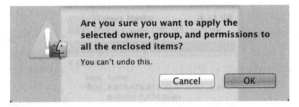

7. Click the OK button.
8. Click the Close button (the red button that displays a × when you hold the mouse pointer over it) to close the Info window for the library folder.

After you move your library to the /Users/Shared folder, the other users of your Mac can do one of two things:

- Move their library to the /Users/Shared folder, using the technique described here, so that all files are stored centrally. Users can then add songs they import to the shared library, and all users can access them.
- Keep their library separate, but add the contents of the shared library folder to it. Here's how:
  1. Press ⌘-o or choose File | Add To Library to display the Add To Library dialog box.
  2. Navigate to the /Users/Shared/iTunes Media folder.
  3. Click the Choose button. iTunes adds all the latest songs to the library.

Whichever approach the other users of your Mac choose, the songs that they add to the shared library don't appear automatically in your library. To add all the latest tracks, use the Add To Library dialog box, as described in the previous list.

Build a Media Server for Your Household

If you find that trying to play songs stored in libraries that keep disappearing from the network is too tedious, another option is to build a media server for your household. You can either build a server from scratch on a new computer or change the role of one of your existing computers—even a pensioned-off computer that's too old to run Mac OS X or Windows at a decent speed.

Whether you buy (or build) a new computer or repurpose an existing computer will color your choices for your server. Here are notes on the key components for the server:

- **Operating system** The server can run Windows or Mac OS X if you have a copy that you can spare; if not, you might consider using a less expensive (or even free) operating system, such as one of the many distributions of Linux.
- **Processor** The server can run on a modest processor—even an antiquated one by today's standards, such as a 1GHz or faster processor for a Windows or Linux server or a G4 or G5 processor for a Mac server.
- **RAM** The server needs only enough RAM to run the operating system unless you'll need to run applications on it. For example, 256MB of RAM is adequate for a server running Windows XP or an older version of Mac OS X. Windows 7 or Windows Vista requires 1GB—preferably more.
- **Disk space** The server must have enough disk space to store all the songs and other files you want to have available. A desktop computer is likely to be a better bet than a notebook computer, because you can add internal drives to it. Alternatively, you might use one or more external USB or FireWire drives to provide plenty of space.
- **Network connection** The server must be connected to your network, either via network cable or via wireless. A wireless connection is adequate for serving a few computers, but in most cases, a wired connection (Fast Ethernet or Gigabit Ethernet) is a much better choice.
- **Monitor** If the server will simply be running somewhere convenient (rather than being used for other computing tasks, such as running applications), all you need is an old monitor capable of displaying the bootup and login screens for the operating system. After that, you can turn the monitor off until you need to restart or configure the server.
- **Keyboard and mouse** Like the monitor, the keyboard and mouse can be basic devices, because you'll need to use them only for booting and configuring the server.
- **CD-ROM drive** Your server needs a CD-ROM drive only if you'll use it for ripping. If you'll rip on the clients, the server can get by without one.
- **Sound card** Your server needs a sound card only if you'll use it for playing music or other media files.
- **Reliability** Modest your server may be, but it must be reliable—otherwise the music won't be available when you want to play it. Make sure also that the server has plenty of cooling, and configure its power settings so that it doesn't go to sleep.

- **Location**   If you choose to leave your server running all the time, locate it somewhere safe from being switched off accidentally. Because the running server will probably make some noise, you may be tempted to hide it away in a closet. If you do, make sure there's enough ventilation so that it doesn't overheat.

To set up the server, follow these general steps. The specifics will depend on which operating system you're using for the server.

1. Create a folder that will contain the songs.
2. Share that folder on the network so that all the users you want to be able to play music are allowed to access it.
3. On each of the client computers, move the library into the shared folder.

PART III

Learn Advanced Techniques and Tricks

12

Use Multiple iPods, Multiple Computers, or Both

HOW TO...

- Move your iPod classic or iPod nano from Windows to the Mac or from the Mac to Windows
- Change the computer to which your iPod is linked
- Synchronize several iPods with the same computer
- Load your iPod from two or more computers

This chapter starts by walking you through the processes of moving your iPod classic or iPod nano from a Mac to a PC, and vice versa. Then it shows you how to change the computer to which your iPod is linked—a useful skill when you upgrade your computer.

The chapter explains the nuances of synchronizing several iPods with the same computer, and it walks you through loading your iPod from two or more computers at the same time.

Move Your iPod from the Mac to Windows—and Back

Ideally, you'd be able to plug your iPod into any computer—PC or Mac—and simply load media files onto it or copy them from it. But there are three complications:

- Apple has designed the iPod to synchronize only with a single computer at a time. So when you connect your iPod to another computer, you need to decide whether to switch the iPod's synchronization to that computer.

- For copyright reasons, iTunes doesn't let you copy music and video files from the iPod to a computer. (Chapter 14 shows you ways to work around this limitation—for example, to recover your iTunes library after your computer crashes.)
- The iPod classic and iPod nano use a different file system when used with Macs than when used with Windows. (See the sidebar "Which File System Does Your iPod Use?" for details.) As a result, you may have to "restore" your iPod's software when moving it between a PC and a Mac.

Restoring the iPod's software reformats the iPod. Reformatting erases all the iPod's contents—every file you've stored on it. If your iPod contains valuable files, back them up to your PC or Mac before reformatting your iPod.

Did You Know?

Which File System Does Your iPod Use?

The iPod classic ships with its hard disk formatted using the Mac OS Extended file system. When you connect a new iPod classic to a Windows PC, iTunes on the PC detects that the iPod needs to be reformatted, and it reformats the iPod using the FAT32 file system without notifying you. If your iPod contains files, iTunes warns you before reformatting it. We'll discuss this topic further later in this chapter.

The iPod nano ships with its memory formatted using the FAT32 file system. The first time you connect the iPod nano to a Mac, iTunes automatically—without consulting you—reformats the iPod nano with the Mac OS Extended file system. As it does so, iTunes displays the iPod: Optimizing Your iPod For Mac OS X dialog box shown here.

iPod
Optimizing your iPod for MacOS X...

iTunes automatically reformats the iPod nano only if you haven't synchronized it with another computer. If the iPod nano has been synchronized with a Windows PC, iTunes asks you to decide whether to reformat the iPod nano. This is because, once you've synchronized the iPod nano with a Windows PC, it normally contains files that you may not want to lose through reformatting.

The Mac OS Extended file system works better for the Mac than FAT32 does, but Windows can't read the Mac OS Extended file system; so the iPod classic and iPod nano use FAT32 for Windows instead. FAT32 works with Mac OS X as well as with Windows, so once you've formatted your iPod for Windows, you don't necessarily need to reformat it if you need to use it with a Mac again.

The iPod shuffle uses the FAT32 file system for both Windows and the Mac, so there's no need to convert your iPod shuffle from one format to another.

Move Your iPod classic or iPod nano from the Mac to Windows

If you've used your iPod classic or iPod nano only with a Mac, and you move it to Windows, you must reformat the hard disk or flash memory. This permanently removes all the contents of your iPod. Follow the procedure described in the upcoming section "Move a Mac-Formatted iPod classic or iPod nano to Windows."

If you've used your iPod classic or iPod nano with Windows, and then moved it to the Mac without reformatting it, and you then move it back to Windows, you won't need to reformat the iPod. Follow the procedure described in "Move a FAT32-Formatted iPod from the Mac Back to Windows."

If you have an iPod shuffle, it is formatted with FAT32, so use the procedure described in "Move a FAT32-Formatted iPod from the Mac Back to Windows," even if you've been using your iPod only with a Mac.

Move a Mac-Formatted iPod classic or iPod nano to Windows

To move your iPod from the Mac to Windows, follow these steps:

1. Make sure the PC has iTunes installed—preferably the latest version:
   - If the PC doesn't have iTunes installed, download the latest version from www.apple.com/itunes/download/ and install it.
   - If the PC does have iTunes installed, choose Help | Check For Updates to see if a newer version of iTunes is available.
2. If nobody has used iTunes on that computer, run iTunes, and close the iTunes Tutorials window. When the main iTunes window comes up, choose File | Exit to close iTunes.
3. Connect your iPod to the PC.
4. If Windows displays a Microsoft Windows dialog box telling you that you need to format the disk before you can use it, as shown here, click the Cancel button. You don't want to have Windows format the iPod as a removable drive—you want to have iTunes format it as an iPod.

5. Launch iTunes if it doesn't launch automatically. For example, choose Start | All Programs | iTunes | iTunes.

6. When iTunes displays the dialog box shown here, telling you that it has detected a Macintosh-formatted iPod and that you must restore the iPod before you can use it on Windows, click the OK button.

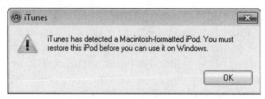

7. When iTunes displays the Summary screen for the iPod (see Figure 12-1), click the Restore button to format the iPod using the FAT32 file system and to reinstall the iPod firmware on it. iTunes displays a confirmation dialog box, as shown here, to make sure you know that all items and data will be erased.

8. Click the OK button to close the dialog box.

FIGURE 12-1 Click the Restore button on the Summary screen for the iPod to start restoring it to Windows format.

9. Click the Restore button, and then allow the restore process to continue. iTunes downloads the latest version of the iPod Software if necessary, and then installs the software. During the process, iTunes displays for ten

seconds the informational message box shown here. Either click the OK button to dismiss the message box, or allow the countdown to complete, after which iTunes closes the message box automatically.

10. iTunes displays the Set Up Your iPod screen (see Figure 12-2). Type the name you want to give the iPod, decide whether to sync songs, videos, and photos with the iPod automatically (and if so, choose the source or folder for the photos), and then click the Done button. The first time you set up an iPod, you can also choose whether to register it.

11. If you choose to sync songs and videos to the iPod automatically, and the iPod doesn't have enough space to contain them all, iTunes lets you know of the problem, as shown here. Click the Yes button if you want iTunes to create a playlist for your iPod. Click the No button if you want to choose songs for your iPod yourself.

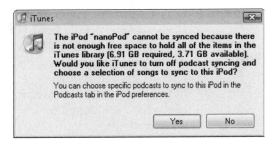

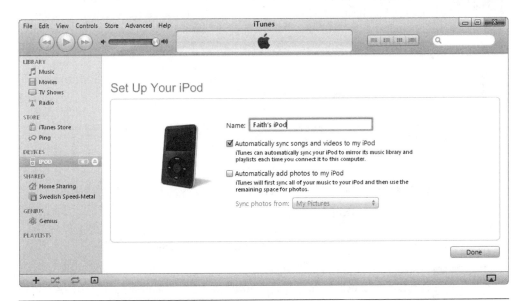

FIGURE 12-2   On the Set Up Your iPod screen, specify the name for the iPod, and choose whether to sync songs, videos, and photos with it.

12. When the restore operation (and synchronization, if you chose that option) has completed, the iPod appears in the Devices list with the name you gave it and its full set of control screens.

Move a FAT32-Formatted iPod from the Mac Back to Windows

If your iPod is formatted with FAT32, you can move it freely between Windows and the Mac. The iPod will be formatted with FAT32 in any of these three cases:

- It is an iPod shuffle. The iPod shuffle uses only the FAT32 file system.
- It is an iPod nano whose first computer connection was to a Windows PC.
- It is an iPod classic or an iPod nano that you have formatted with FAT32 by connecting it to a Windows PC.

To move a FAT32-formatted iPod from the Mac back to Windows, follow these steps:

1. Connect the iPod to the PC. iTunes detects the iPod and displays the dialog box shown here, warning you that the iPod is linked to another library and asking if you want to change the link and replace all its contents.

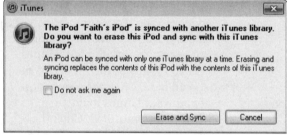

 If your iPod contains items you've purchased from the iTunes Store, the iTunes dialog box includes a Transfer Purchases button. See the section "Change the Computer to Which Your iPod Is Linked," later in this chapter, for coverage of this button.

2. Click the Erase And Sync button to associate the iPod with the Windows library and overwrite the Mac library.

Wait while iTunes associates the iPod with the Windows library and then syncs the songs, videos, and other items with the iPod.

Move Your iPod from Windows to the Mac

To move your iPod from Windows to the Mac, follow these steps:

1. For best results, update iTunes to the latest version available.

 The easiest way to check that iTunes is up to date is to choose Apple | Software Update to check for updates. If Software Update identifies any iTunes updates, or other updates that your Mac requires, install them before moving the iPod to your Mac.

2. Connect the iPod to the Mac. When iTunes detects the iPod, it displays a dialog box such as that shown here, pointing out that the iPod is linked to a different library and asking if you want to replace that library.

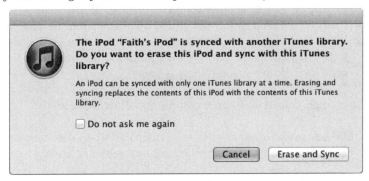

> **The iPod "Faith's iPod" is synced with another iTunes library. Do you want to erase this iPod and sync with this iTunes library?**
>
> An iPod can be synced with only one iTunes library at a time. Erasing and syncing replaces the contents of this iPod with the contents of this iTunes library.
>
> ☐ Do not ask me again
>
> [Cancel]   [Erase and Sync]

3. Click the Erase And Sync button. iTunes replaces the library on the iPod with the library on the Mac. This may take some time if the library is extensive. You can stop the sync at any point by clicking the × button at the right end of the iTunes information display.

Note If the iPod is synced with another photo library, iTunes prompts you to decide whether to replace the photos on the iPod with those on your Mac. Click the Yes button or the No button as appropriate.

At this point, you've set up the iPod to work with your Mac, but you've left it using the FAT32 file system. FAT32 works fine with Mac OS X but is marginally less efficient than the Mac OS Extended file system, so you won't be able to fit quite as many files on the iPod with FAT32 as with Mac OS Extended.

If you intend to use your iPod with the Mac for the long term, and if your iPod doesn't contain any valuable files that you want to keep, you may choose to convert it to Mac OS X Extended to pack on as many items as possible. To do so, restore the iPod by following the process described in the section "Restore the iPod on Mac OS X" in Chapter 15.

Note You must reformat the iPod with the Mac OS Extended file system if you want to update the iPod to the latest version of the iPod software using the Mac.

Change the Computer to Which Your iPod Is Linked

Apple has designed the iPods so that they can synchronize with only one computer at a time. This computer is known as the *home* computer—home to your iPod, not necessarily in your home. But you can use two or more Macs, or two or more

Windows PCs, to load files onto the same iPod. See the section "Load Your iPod from Two or More Computers at Once," later in this chapter, for details.

 Linking an iPod to another computer replaces all the songs, playlists, and other items on the iPod with those on the other computer. Be sure you want to change the link before you proceed. You can restore your previous library by linking again to the first computer, but, even with USB 2.0 file-transfer speeds, you'll waste a good deal of time if your library is large.

To change your iPod's home computer, follow these steps:

1. Make sure the other computer contains an up-to-date version of iTunes. If necessary, set up iTunes and install any relevant updates.

 If you're moving an iPod formatted with the Mac OS Extended file system to Windows, you'll need to restore it as described in "Move Your iPod from the Mac to Windows—and Back," earlier in this chapter.

2. Connect your iPod to the other PC or Mac. iTunes displays the following dialog box warning you that the iPod is synced to another iTunes library and asking if you want to change the sync to the current computer's iTunes library.

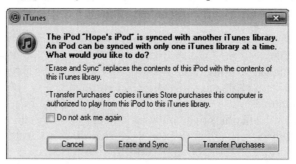

3. If you're sure you want to replace all the items on your iPod, click the Erase And Sync button. Click the Transfer Purchases button if you want to transfer items you've purchased from the iTunes Store from the iPod to your iTunes library.

4. If you don't transfer any purchased items, iTunes prompts you to copy them from your iPod to the iTunes library, as shown here. Click the Transfer button if you want to copy the items; if you don't, you'll lose them.

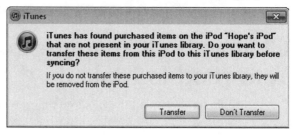

Because changing the iPod to a different home computer replaces the entire iTunes library, the initial synchronization may take a long time, depending on how big the library is and whether it's stored on a local drive or a network drive.

How to...

Deal with Purchased Items Your Computer Isn't Authorized to Play

If you try to transfer purchased items but your computer isn't authorized to play them, iTunes displays a dialog box such as the one shown here.

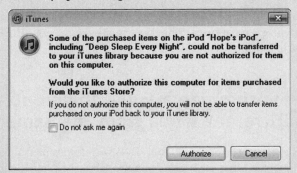

If you want to authorize the computer to play the items, click the Authorize button. In the Authorize This Computer dialog box (shown here), enter your Apple ID and password, and then click the Authorize button.

Once you've authorized the computer, click the Sync button on the Summary tab of the device's control screens to start the erase and sync operation again. This time, you'll be able to transfer your purchases to the computer.

If you prefer not to authorize the computer at this point, click the Cancel button in the first dialog box. When you're ready to authorize the computer, choose Store | Authorize This Computer.

Synchronize Several iPods with the Same Computer

As you've seen earlier in this book, usually a computer and an iPod have a mutually faithful relationship—but, as discussed in the previous section, the iPod can decide to leave its home computer and set up home with another computer. It can even switch from Windows to the Mac or vice versa.

For most people, such fidelity (or serial fidelity) works fine. But if you have several iPods and one computer, you can sync all the iPods from that computer. Keep the following points in mind:

- Even if your computer has plenty of USB ports, it's best not to plug in more than one iPod at once. That way, neither you nor iTunes becomes confused, and synchronization can take place at full speed.

How to...

Synchronize a Full—Different—Library onto Different iPods from the Same Computer

Synchronizing two or more iPods with the same computer works well enough provided that each user is happy using the same library or the same playlists (perhaps a different selection from the set of playlists). But if you want to synchronize the full library for each iPod, yet have a different library on each, you need to take a different approach.

In most cases, the easiest solution is to have a separate user account for each separate user who uses an iPod with the computer. Having separate user accounts is best in any case for keeping files and mail separate.

Place the media files that users will share in a folder that each user can access. In iTunes, make sure that the Copy Files To iTunes Media Folder When Adding To Library check box on the Advanced tab of the iTunes dialog box (in Windows) or the Preferences dialog box (on the Mac) is cleared so iTunes doesn't copy all the files into the media library.

If you have enough free space on your hard disk, you can set up your own libraries under your own user account and store all your media files in them. But unless your hard disk is truly gigantic, sharing most of the files from a central location is almost always preferable.

Another possibility is to start iTunes using a different library from within the same user account. To start iTunes using a different library:

- **Windows** Hold down SHIFT as you click the iTunes icon to start iTunes.
- **Mac** Hold down OPTION as you click the iTunes icon to start iTunes.

See the section "Use Multiple Libraries on the Same Computer" in Chapter 11 for more details on using multiple libraries.

- Each iPod has a unique ID number that it communicates to your computer on connection, so your computer knows which device is connected to it. You can even give two or more devices the same name if you find such ambiguity amusing rather than confusing.
- You can configure different updating for each iPod by choosing options on the iPod screens when the device is connected.

When you use the same user account on Windows or the Mac to synchronize multiple iPods, Apple recommends that you use the same synchronization settings for each. But this isn't an absolute requirement—which is just as well, because the iPods have such different capacities and capabilities. If you find yourself having problems synchronizing different iPods using different synchronization settings, consider creating a separate user account for synchronizing a particular iPod.

Load Your iPod from Two or More Computers at Once

As you read earlier in this chapter, you can synchronize your iPod with only one computer at a time—the device's home computer. You can change the home computer from one computer to another, and even from one platform (Mac or PC) to the other, but you can't actively synchronize your iPod with more than one computer at once.

But you *can* load songs, videos, or other items onto your iPod from computers other than the home computer. If your iPod is formatted using the FAT32 file system, you can use a mixture of Macs and PCs to load files onto the iPod. If your iPod is formatted using the Mac OS Extended file system, you can use only Macs.

All the computers you use must have iTunes installed and configured, and you must configure your iPod for manual updating on each computer involved—on the home computer as well as on each other computer. Otherwise, synchronizing the iPod with the home computer after loading tracks from other computers will remove those tracks because they're not in the home computer's library.

Configure Your iPod for Manual Updating

The first step in loading your iPod from two or more computers is to configure it for manual updating. You'll need to do this on your iPod's home computer first, and then on each of the other computers you plan to use.

To configure your iPod for manual updating, follow these steps:

1. Connect your iPod to your Mac or PC. Allow synchronization to take place. (If you need to override synchronization, see the sidebar "Temporarily Override Automatic Synchronization.")
2. Click the iPod's entry in the Source list to display the iPod screens.

3. Select the Manually Manage Music check box or the Manually Manage Music And Videos check box. iTunes displays a dialog box warning you that you'll need to eject the iPod manually before disconnecting it, as shown here.

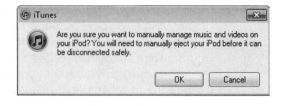

4. Click the OK button to return to the iPod screens. iTunes selects the Enable Disk Use check box (if it wasn't already selected) and makes it unavailable so that you can't clear it manually.
5. Click the Apply button to apply the changes.

Load Files onto Your iPod Manually

After you've configured your iPod for manual updating, you can load files onto it manually by following these general steps:

1. Connect the iPod to the computer that contains the files you want to load. The iPod appears in the Source list in iTunes.
2. Drag files from your iTunes library, or from a Windows Explorer window or a Finder window, and then drop them on the iPod or on one of its playlists.
3. After loading all the files you want from this computer, eject the iPod by clicking the Eject button next to its name in the Source list.

If you don't eject the iPod after configuring it for manual updating, you may lose data or corrupt the iPod's contents when you disconnect it.

You can then disconnect the iPod from this computer, move it to the next computer, and then add more files by using the same technique.

From this point on, to add further files to your iPod from your home computer, you must add them manually. Don't synchronize the iPod with your home computer, because synchronization will delete from the iPod all the files that do not appear in your library.

How to... Temporarily Override Automatic Synchronization

If your iPod is configured for automatic synchronization, you can override this setting by holding down keys when you connect the iPod:

- **Windows** Hold down CTRL-SHIFT.
- **Mac** Hold down ⌘-OPTION.

Release the keys when the iPod appears in the Source list in iTunes.

13

Use Your iPod for File Backup, Storage, and Transfer

HOW TO...

- Decide whether or not to use an iPod as an external drive
- Enable disk mode on an iPod using Windows
- Enable disk mode on an iPod using a Mac
- Transfer files to and from an iPod
- Back up an iPod so you don't lose your music or data

Apple sells the iPods primarily as portable media players—and they're the best ones around. But to a computer, the iPod is essentially an external USB drive with sophisticated audio and (in the iPod classic) video features. This chapter shows you how to use an iPod as an external drive for backup and portable storage.

 One external-drive feature this chapter *doesn't* show you is how to transfer files from an iPod's library onto your computer. Chapter 14 covers this subject.

Decide Whether to Use Your iPod as an External Drive

If all you want from your iPod is huge amounts of music and video to go, you may never want to use your iPod as an external drive. Here's why you should think about it again:

- *An iPod provides a great combination of portability and high capacity.* You can get smaller portable-storage devices (for example, USB keys, CompactFlash drives, SmartMedia cards, and Memory Sticks), but they're an extra expense and an extra device to carry with you. An iPod classic lets you carry around serious amounts of data, but even an iPod nano has enough space to carry several gigabytes of your most important files along with your songs and videos. On an iPod shuffle, you'll feel the pinch a bit more—but you can still take your essential files with you.

- *You can take all your documents with you.* For example, you could take home that large PowerPoint presentation you need to get ready for tomorrow. You can even put several gigabytes of video files on an iPod if you need to take them with you (for example, to a studio for editing) or transfer them to another computer.
- *You can use an iPod for backup.* If you keep your vital documents down to a size you can easily fit on an iPod (and still have plenty of room left for songs, videos, and other files), you can quickly back up the documents and take the backup with you wherever you go.
- *You can use an iPod for security.* By keeping your documents on an iPod rather than on your computer, and by keeping the iPod with you, you can prevent other people from accessing your documents.

The disadvantages to using an iPod as an external drive are straightforward:

- Whatever space you use on the iPod for storing other files isn't available for music and video.
- If you lose or break the iPod, any files stored only on it will be gone forever.

Enable Disk Mode on the iPod

Before you can use an iPod as an external drive, you must enable disk mode. In disk mode, your computer uses an iPod as an external disk drive. You can copy to the iPod any files and folders that will fit on it.

 You can copy song files, video files, and playlists to an iPod in disk mode, but you won't be able to play them on the iPod. This is because when you copy the files, their information isn't added to the iPod's database the way it's added by iTunes. So the iPod's interface doesn't know the files are there, and you can't play them.

From the computer's point of view, an external disk connected via USB works in largely the same way as any other disk. Here are the differences:

- The disk is external.
- The disk may draw power across the USB connection (as iPods do) rather than being powered itself (as high-capacity and high-performance external disks tend to be).
- If the iPod uses a USB connection, the USB controller and the USB cable or connection must supply enough power to feed the iPod. All USB connections supply power, but some don't supply enough for an iPod. (Other devices, such as USB keyboards and mice, require much less power than an iPod.) Apple refers to USB ports as "high-powered" (giving enough power for an iPod) and "low-powered" (not giving enough power).

Using an iPod classic as an external disk with a connection that can't supply power may run down the battery quickly. Part of the problem is that the iPod can't use its caching capabilities when you use it as an external disk. (Caching works only for playlists and albums, when the iPod knows which files are needed next and thus can read them into the cache.) If the iPod isn't receiving power, check the battery status periodically to make sure the iPod doesn't suddenly run out of power.

Enable Disk Mode on an iPod Using Windows

To use an iPod as an external disk on a PC, enable disk mode. Follow these steps:

1. Connect the iPod to your PC as usual.
2. Launch iTunes if it doesn't launch automatically.
3. In the Source list, click the iPod's icon to display the iPod screens.
4. For an iPod classic or an iPod nano, click the Summary tab if it isn't already displayed (see Figure 13-1). For an iPod shuffle, click the Settings tab if it isn't already displayed.

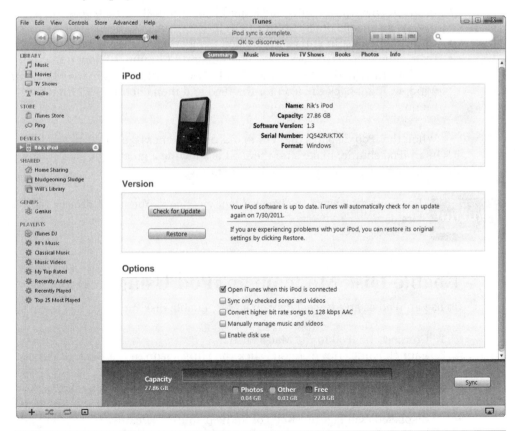

FIGURE 13-1 Select the Enable Disk Use check box on the Summary tab to enable disk mode on an iPod in Windows. For an iPod shuffle, this setting is on the Settings tab.

5. Select the Enable Disk Use check box. iTunes displays the following warning dialog box, telling you that using disk mode requires you to manually unmount the iPod before each disconnect, even when you're automatically updating music.

6. Select the Do Not Warn Me Again check box if you want to suppress this warning in the future, and then click the OK button. iTunes returns you to the Summary tab or Settings tab.
7. Click the Apply button to apply the changes.

Once you've enabled disk mode, the iPod appears to Windows Explorer as a removable drive. Windows Explorer automatically assigns a drive letter to the drive, so you can access it as you would any other drive connected to your computer.

To eject the iPod, take any of the following actions:

- In the Source list in iTunes, click the Eject icon next to the iPod's name. (This is the easiest means of ejection.)
- In the Source list in iTunes, right-click the icon for the iPod and then choose Eject.
- In Windows 7 or Windows Vista, choose Start | Computer to open the Computer window. In Windows XP, choose Start | My Computer to open the My Computer window. Right-click the icon for the iPod and then choose Eject from the shortcut menu.

When the iPod displays the "OK to disconnect" message, you can safely disconnect it. On an iPod shuffle, make sure the iPod is showing a green light or a steady orange light rather than a flashing orange light before you disconnect it.

 Don't just disconnect the iPod without ejecting it. You might damage files or lose data.

Enable Disk Mode on an iPod Using a Mac

To use an iPod as an external disk on a Mac, enable disk mode. Follow these steps:

1. Connect the iPod to the Mac as usual.
2. Launch iTunes (for example, click the iTunes icon in the Dock) if iTunes doesn't launch automatically.
3. In the Source list, click the iPod's entry to display the iPod's screens.
4. For an iPod classic or an iPod nano, click the Summary tab if it isn't already displayed (see Figure 13-2). For an iPod shuffle, click the Settings tab if it isn't already displayed.

FIGURE 13-2   Select the Enable Disk Use check box on the Summary tab to enable disk mode on an iPod on the Mac. For an iPod shuffle, this setting is on the Settings tab.

5. Select the Enable Disk Use check box. iTunes displays the following warning dialog box, telling you that using disk mode requires you to unmount the iPod manually before each disconnect, even when synchronizing songs (instead of being able to have iTunes unmount the iPod automatically).

How to... **Force Disk Mode on an iPod classic**

If your USB port is underpowered, you may need to force an iPod classic to enter disk mode. To force disk mode, follow these steps:

1. Connect the iPod via USB as usual.
2. Toggle the Hold switch on and off, and then hold down the Select button and the Menu button for about five seconds to reboot the iPod.
3. When the iPod displays the Apple logo, hold down the Select button and Play button briefly. The iPod sends the computer an electronic prod that forces the computer to recognize it.

6. Select the Do Not Warn Me Again check box if you want to suppress this warning in the future, and then click the OK button. iTunes returns you to the Summary tab or Settings tab.
7. Click the Apply button to apply the changes.

Once you've enabled disk mode, you'll need to eject the iPod manually after each connection. To eject the iPod, take any of the following actions:

- In the Source list in iTunes, click the Eject icon next to the iPod's name. (This is the easiest means of ejection.)
- In the Source list in iTunes, CTRL-click or right-click the icon for the iPod and then choose Eject from the shortcut menu.
- Click the icon for the iPod on the desktop and then issue an Eject command from the File menu or the shortcut menu. (Alternatively, press ⌘-E.)
- Drag the desktop icon for the iPod to the Trash.

When an iPod displays the "OK to disconnect" message, you can safely disconnect it. On an iPod shuffle, make sure the iPod is showing a green light rather than an orange light before you disconnect it.

 Don't just disconnect the iPod without ejecting it. You might damage files or lose data. Even if all the files remain intact, Mac OS X gives you a severe warning message.

Transfer Files to and from the iPod

When the iPod is in disk mode, you can transfer files to it by using the Finder (on the Mac), Windows Explorer (in Windows), or another file-management application of your choice. (You can transfer files by using the command prompt in Windows or the Terminal in Mac OS X, if you so choose.) Figure 13-3 shows Mac OS X transferring some files to an iPod classic. Figure 13-4 shows how the iPod appears in Windows Explorer.

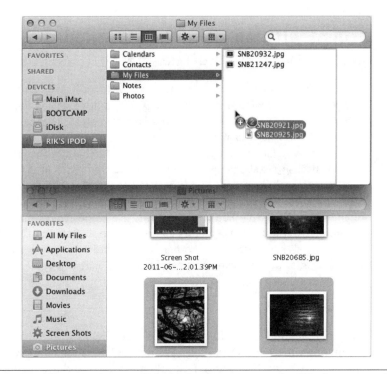

FIGURE 13-3 After turning on disk mode, you can use the Finder to transfer files to the iPod on Mac OS X.

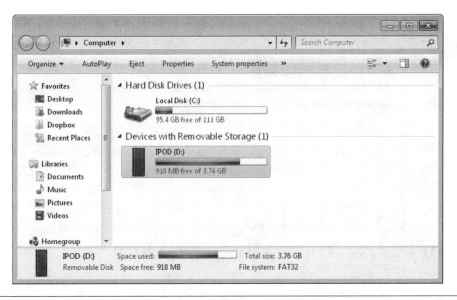

FIGURE 13-4 After you turn on disk mode, the iPod appears as a drive in Windows Explorer. You can transfer files to it by using copy and paste or drag and drop, just like any other drive.

How to... **Deal with an iPod That Windows Says Isn't Formatted**

If the iPod appears in the Computer window (on Windows 7 or Windows Vista) or My Computer window (on Windows XP) as a drive named Removable Drive, and Windows Explorer claims the disk isn't formatted, chances are you've connected a Mac-formatted iPod to your PC.

Windows Explorer can't read the HFS Plus disk format that Mac-formatted iPods use, so the iPod appears to be unformatted. (HFS Plus is one of the disk formats Mac OS X can use and is also called the Mac OS Extended format.)

If you've connected the wrong iPod by mistake, disconnect it. But if you need to use the iPod with Windows, use iTunes to restore the iPod, reformatting it so that Windows can recognize it. Reformatting the iPod removes all content from it, so before you restore it, connect it to a Mac and make sure that you have backups of any files that you value. The next section discusses backing up your files.

You can create and delete folders on the iPod as you would any other drive. But be sure you don't mess with the iPod's system folders, such as the Calendars folder, the Contacts folder, the Notes folder, the Photos folder, and the iPod_Control folder. The iPod_Control folder is a hidden folder, so it does not appear unless you have set Windows or Mac OS X to display hidden files.

As mentioned earlier, don't transfer music or video files to an iPod by using file-management software if you want to be able to play the files on the iPod. Unless you transfer the files by using iTunes or another application designed to access the iPod's database, the details about the files won't be added to the iPod. You won't be able to play those files on the iPod because their data hasn't been added to its database of contents.

The exception to transferring files from an iPod is transferring files that you've put on the iPod by using iTunes or another application that can access the iPod's database. Chapter 14 shows you how to do this.

Back Up an iPod So You Don't Lose Your Music or Data

If you synchronize your complete library with an iPod, and perhaps load your contacts, calendar information, and photos on the iPod as well, you shouldn't need to worry about backing up the iPod. That's because your computer contains all the data that's on the iPod. (Effectively, the iPod is a backup of part of your computer's hard disk.)

So if you lose the iPod, or it stops functioning, you won't lose any data you have on your computer.

If your computer's hard disk stops working, you may need to recover your library, contacts, calendar data, and photos from the iPod onto another computer or a new hard disk. You can transfer contacts, calendars, and full-resolution photos by enabling disk mode and using the Finder (Mac) or Windows Explorer (PC) to access the contents of the Contacts folder, the Calendars folder, and the Photos/Full Resolution folder. For instructions on recovering song and video files from an iPod, see Chapter 14.

So normally an iPod will be the vulnerable member of the tag team. But if you store files directly on an iPod, you should back them up to your computer to make sure you don't lose them if the iPod vanishes or its hard disk gives up the ghost.

To back up files, either use a file-management utility (for example, the Finder or Windows Explorer) to simply copy the files or folders to your computer, or use custom backup software to create a more formal backup. For example:

- **Windows 7**   Backup and Restore (Start | All Programs | Maintenance | Backup And Restore)
- **Windows Vista**   Backup and Restore Center (Start | All Programs | Maintenance | Backup And Restore Center)
- **Windows XP**   Backup Utility (Start | All Programs | Accessories | System Tools | Backup)

 If Backup Utility doesn't appear on the System Tools submenu in Windows XP, you may need to install it from your Windows XP CD or from the installation folder on your PC's hard disk. You'll find the files in the i386\MSFT\VALUEADD\NTBACKUP folder.

- **Mac OS X**   Time Machine (in System Preferences)

14

Recover Your Songs and Videos from Your iPod

HOW TO...

- Know why your iPod hides its song files and video files from you
- Understand how and where your iPod stores song files and video files
- Recover your songs and videos from your iPod in Windows
- Recover your songs and videos from your iPod on the Mac

As you saw in Chapter 3, you can copy all or part of your library onto your iPod almost effortlessly by choosing suitable synchronization settings and then synchronizing the device. Normally, any songs and videos on your iPod are also in your library, so you don't need to transfer the songs and videos from the iPod to your computer. But if you have a computer disaster, or if your computer is stolen, you may need to recover the songs and videos from your iPod to your new or repaired computer.

This chapter shows you how to recover songs and videos from your iPod on both Windows and the Mac. The chapter starts by explaining why your iPod hides the song and video files. It then covers where the files are stored on your iPod, how you can reveal them in Windows Explorer or the Finder, and why you need specialized tools to copy them from the iPod. The chapter ends by showing you the best recovery utilities for Windows and the Mac.

Why Your iPod Hides Its Song and Video Files from You

For copyright reasons, the iPod's basic configuration prevents you from copying music and video files from the iPod's library to your computer. This restriction prevents you from loading files onto the iPod on one computer via iTunes and then downloading them onto another computer, which would most likely violate copyright by making unauthorized copies of other people's copyrighted material.

But if you turn on disk mode (as discussed in the previous chapter), you can use your iPod as a portable drive. In disk mode, you can copy music and video files onto your iPod from one computer, connect the iPod to another computer, and copy or move the files from the iPod to that computer. The only limitation is that the files you copy this way aren't added to the iPod's music and video database, so you can't play them on the iPod.

In the standard scenarios that Apple envisions you using your iPod, you shouldn't need to copy songs and videos from your iPod to your computer, because your computer will already contain all the songs and videos that the iPod contains. But there may come a time when you need to get the song files and video files out of the iPod's library for legitimate reasons. For example, if you drop your MacBook, or your PC's hard disk dies of natural causes, you may need to copy the music files and video files from your iPod to a replacement computer or disk. Otherwise, you may risk losing your entire music and video collection.

To avoid losing data, you should back up all your valuable data, including any songs and videos that you can't easily recover by other means (such as ripping your CDs again), especially the songs and videos you've bought from the iTunes Store or other online stores. But the amount of data—and, in particular, the size of many people's libraries—makes backup difficult, requiring either an external hard drive or multiple DVDs.

To help you avoid this dreadful possibility, iPod enthusiasts have developed some great utilities for transferring files from the iPod's hidden music and video storage to a computer.

Where—and How—Your iPod Stores Song and Video Files

When you turn on disk mode, you can access the contents of the iPod's hard drive or flash memory by using Windows Explorer (in Windows) or the Finder (on the Mac). Until you create other folders there, though, you'll find only a few folders: Calendar, Contacts, Notes, Photos, and Recordings on the iPod classic, and Photos and Recordings on the iPod nano. (The Photos folder appears only after you've synchronized photos.) There's no trace of your song files and video files.

If you enable disk mode on an iPod shuffle, you'll find no folders at all, because the iPod shuffle can't hold contacts, calendars, or notes.

You can't see the song files and video files because the folders in which they are stored are formatted to be hidden in Windows and to be invisible on the Mac. Even if you make these folders visible, it doesn't help you much, because your iPod

How to... **Make Visible the iPod's Hidden or Invisible Folders**

If you want to make visible the iPod's hidden or invisible folders, follow these instructions:

- **Windows 7**   Choose Start | Computer, choose Organize | Folder And Search Options, and then click the View tab. Select the Show Hidden Files, Folders, And Drives option button, and then click the OK button.
- **Windows Vista**   Choose Start | Computer, choose Organize | Folder And Search Options, and then click the View tab. Select the Show Hidden Files And Folders option button, and then click the OK button.
- **Windows XP**   Choose Start | My Computer, choose Tools | Folder Options, and then click the View tab. Select the Show Hidden Files And Folders option button, and then click the OK button.
- **Mac OS X**   Download and install TinkerTool from www.bresink.de/osx/TinkerTool.html. Run TinkerTool, select the Show Hidden And System Files check box on the Finder tab, and then click the Relaunch Finder button. Quit TinkerTool.

Once you've made the folders visible, open a Windows Explorer window or a Finder window, and double-click the iPod. Double-click the iPod_Control folder to see its contents.

automatically assigns each song or video a short and cryptic filename. You can copy these files back to your computer, but doing so would take a while, especially because the iPod also stores the files in automatically named folders in apparently random order. The folders are named F00, F01, F02, and so on.

Windows Utilities for Transferring Song and Video Files from an iPod to Your PC

At this writing, there are several Windows utilities for transferring song and video files from an iPod to your PC. This section discusses two specialist utilities, iPod Access for Windows and iGadget.

iPod Access for Windows

iPod Access for Windows from Findley Designs (www.ipodaccess.com) lets you transfer files from an iPod to your PC. iPod Access for Windows (see Figure 14-1) costs $19.99,

FIGURE 14-1 iPod Access for Windows can recover files from an iPod to a PC.

but you can download a limited evaluation version to see if the application works for you. You can also use iPod Access to play back songs directly from an iPod.

 Tip Findley Designs also makes iPod Access Photo, a tool that lets you recover photos from an iPod.

iGadget

iGadget from iPodSoft (www.ipodsoft.com) lets you transfer files from an iPod to a PC. iGadget (see Figure 14-2) costs $19.99 and also lets you transfer to an iPod weather forecast, driving directions, gas prices, Outlook data, and other text.

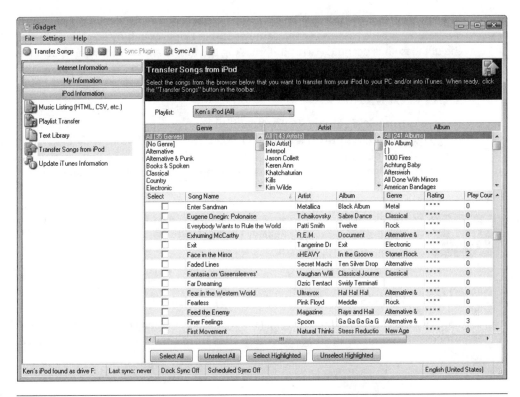

FIGURE 14-2   iGadget lets you recover songs and videos from an iPod to a PC.

Mac OS X Utilities for Transferring Song and Video Files from an iPod to Your Mac

iPod enthusiasts have created an impressive array of utilities for transferring song and video files from an iPod to a Mac. This section discusses some of the leading utilities for doing so.

If you don't like the look (or performance) of these utilities, search sites such as iLounge (www.ilounge.com), CNET Download.com (http://download.cnet.com), MacUpdate (www.macupdate.com), and Apple's Mac OS X Downloads page (www .apple.com/downloads/) for alternatives.

Different utilities work in different ways. The most basic utilities simply assemble a list of the filenames in the iPod's media folders, which leaves you with cryptic filenames. The best utilities read the database the iPod maintains of the files it holds, whereas other utilities plow painstakingly through each file on the iPod and extract information from its ID3 tags. Reading the iPod's database gives much faster results than assembling what's essentially the same database from scratch by scouring the tags. But if the database has become corrupted, reading the tags is a good recovery technique.

PodWorks

PodWorks from Sci-Fi Hi-Fi ($8; www.scifihifi.com/podworks) is a utility for transferring song and video files from an iPod to your Mac. Figure 14-3 shows PodWorks in action with an iPod. You can download an evaluation version that limits you to 30 days, copying 250 songs, and copying one song at a time—enough limitations to persuade you to buy the full version.

 PodWorks has an extra trick: you can install PodWorks on your iPod so that you can use it on a computer you haven't used before.

iPod Access

iPod Access from Findley Designs (www.findleydesigns.com) also simplifies the process of transferring song and video files from an iPod to a Mac. iPod Access

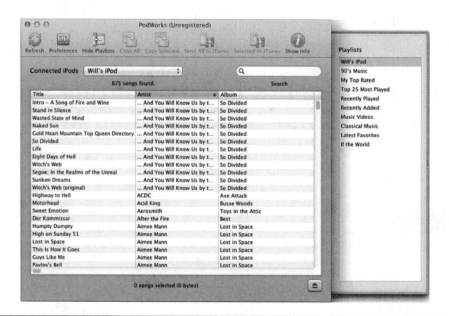

FIGURE 14-3 PodWorks can quickly recover songs and other media files from an iPod.

FIGURE 14-4 iPod Access can recover songs and other media files from an iPod or simply play them back.

(see Figure 14-4) costs $19.99, but you can download a limited evaluation version to see if the application works for you. You can also use iPod Access to play back media files directly from the iPod.

iRip

iRip from The Little App Factory PTY Ltd. ($19.95; www.thelittleappfactory.com) integrates with iTunes and enables you to play back songs and other media files from either your library or an iPod. iRip (see Figure 14-5) comes in a trial version that you can use ten times before it cripples itself. iRip's SmartSync feature enables you to automatically copy to your library songs and videos that you've loaded onto an iPod using a different computer.

FIGURE 14-5 iRip is a utility that can recover files from an iPod even if the device's database has been corrupted.

15

Troubleshoot Your iPod and iTunes

HOW TO...

- Understand what's in the iPod
- Avoid things that may harm your iPod
- Keep your iPod's operating system up to date
- Carry, clean, and look after your iPod—and avoid voiding the warranty
- Troubleshoot the iPod classic, iPod nano, and iPod shuffle
- Troubleshoot iTunes problems on Windows
- Troubleshoot iTunes problems on the Mac
- Recover from iTunes running you out of disk space on Windows or the Mac

Apple designs and builds the iPods to be as reliable as possible—after all, Apple would like to sell at least one iPod to everyone in the world who has a computer, and it would much prefer to be thwarted in this aim by economics or competition than by negative feedback. But even so, iPods go wrong sometimes. Other times, iTunes has problems, either in communicating with the iPod or in other ways.

This chapter shows you how to deal with problems with the iPod and iTunes. The chapter focuses on the models that are current at this writing—the iPod classic, the sixth-generation iPod nano, and the fourth-generation iPod shuffle—but also provides general information about troubleshooting that will help you with older iPod models too.

Know What's in the iPod

The iPod classic is based around a hard drive that takes up the bulk of the space inside the case. The hard drive is similar to those used in the smaller portable PCs—ultraportables, "laptots," netbooks, and so on.

The iPod nano and iPod shuffle use flash memory chips rather than a hard disk, which makes them more or less immune to shock.

Some of the remaining space is occupied by a rechargeable battery that provides between 10 and 30 hours of playback. The length of time the battery provides depends on the model of iPod and on how you use it. Like all rechargeable batteries, the iPod's battery gradually loses its capacity—but if your music collection grows, or if you find the iPod's nonmusic capabilities useful, you'll probably want to upgrade to a higher-capacity model in a couple of years anyway.

The iPod isn't user-upgradeable—in fact, it's designed to be opened only by trained technicians. If you're not such a technician, don't try to open the iPod if the iPod is still under warranty, because opening it voids the warranty. Open the iPod only if it's out of warranty and there's a problem you can fix, such as replacing the battery.

The iPod classic includes a 32MB memory chip that's used for running the iPod's operating system and for caching music from the hard drive. The cache reads up to 20 minutes of data ahead from the hard drive for two purposes:

- Once the cache has read the data, the iPod plays back the music from the cache rather than from the hard disk. This lets the hard disk *spin down* (stop running) until it's needed again. Because hard disks consume relatively large amounts of power, the caching spares the battery on the iPod and prolongs battery life.

After the hard disk has spun down, it takes a second or so to spin up again—so when you suddenly change the music during a playlist, there's a small delay while the iPod spins the disk up and then accesses the song you've demanded. If you listen closely (put the iPod to your ear), you can hear the disk spin up (there's a "whee" sound) and search (you'll hear the heads clicking).

- The hard disk can skip if you jiggle or shake the iPod hard enough. Modern hard drives can handle G loads that would finish off elite fighter pilots, so take this on trust rather than trying it out. If the iPod were playing back audio directly from the hard disk, such skipping would interrupt audio playback, much like bumping the needle on a turntable (or bumping a CD player, if you've tried that). But because the memory chip is solid state and has no moving parts, it's immune to skipping.

The length of time for which the caching provides audio depends on the compression ratio you're using and whether you're playing a playlist (or album) or individual songs. If you're playing a list of songs, the iPod can cache as many of the upcoming songs as it has available memory. But when you switch to another song beyond those cached, or to another playlist, the iPod has to start caching once again. This caching involves spinning the hard disk up again and reading from it, which consumes battery power.

The iPod classic caches video as well, but because video files are much larger than audio files, playing them makes the hard disk work more than does playing songs.

Avoid Things That May Harm Your iPod

This section discusses four items that are likely to make your iPod unhappy: unexpected disconnections, fire and water (discussed together), and punishment. None of these should come as a surprise, and you should be able to avoid all of them most of the time.

Avoid Disconnecting Your iPod at the Wrong Time

When you synchronize your iPod, always wait until synchronization is complete before disconnecting the player. The easiest way to be sure synchronization is complete is to watch the readout in iTunes. Alternatively:

- **iPod classic or iPod nano**   Make sure your iPod is showing the "OK to disconnect" message.
- **iPod shuffle**   Make sure the green light or amber light stays on steadily.

 If you have turned on disk mode for your iPod, you must eject the iPod manually after each sync. The easiest way to eject it is to click the Eject button that appears next to it in the Source list in iTunes.

Disconnecting at the wrong time may interrupt data transfer and corrupt files. In the worst case, you may need to restore your iPod, losing any data on the iPod that wasn't already on your computer (for example, data files you have copied to your iPod in disk mode from another computer).

If you disconnect your iPod from your Mac at the wrong time, your Mac displays the Device Removal dialog box, shown in Figure 15-1, telling you that you should have ejected it properly and that data may have been lost or damaged.

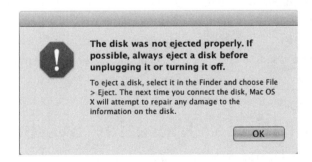

FIGURE 15-1   Mac OS X objects when you disconnect your iPod at the wrong time.

At this writing, iTunes for Windows tends either not to object or even not to notice if you disconnect an iPod when it's telling you not to. If you find that the device's entry is showing up in the Source list in iTunes for Windows long after the iPod has bolted, shut the stable door by clicking the Eject button to the right of the device's entry in the Source list.

After an unexpected disconnection, the iPod simply figures out there's a problem and dusts itself down. The iPod classic or iPod nano then displays its main screen; the iPod shuffle stops showing an orange light.

Avoid Fire and Water

The iPods have a wider range of operating temperatures than most humans, so if you keep the iPod in your pocket, it will generally be at least as comfortable as you are.

Where an iPod may run into trouble is if you leave it running in a confined space, such as the glove box of a car parked in the sun, that might reach searing temperatures. If you live somewhere sunny, take the iPod with you when you get out of the car.

 If the iPod gets much too hot or much too cold, don't use it. Give it time to return to a more normal temperature before trying to find out if it still works.

Further, the iPods aren't waterproof, so don't expect to use them for swimming or in the bath unless you get a fully waterproof case (see Chapter 5).

Avoid Physically Abusing Your iPod

Apple has built the iPods to be tough, so they will survive an impressive amount of rough handling. If you're interested in finding out how tough a particular model is without funding the experiment yourself, check out sites such as these:

- Ars Technica (http://arstechnica.com) performs real-world tests to destruction, such as dropping devices.
- Will It Blend (www.willitblend.com) tests devices in a blender, which is entertaining if less practical.

 Use a case to protect the iPod. Chapter 5 outlines some of the many options available.

Keep Your iPod's Operating System Up to Date

To get the best performance from your iPod, it's a good idea to keep its operating system (or *firmware*) up to date. To do so, follow the instructions in this section to update the iPod on Windows or Mac OS X.

Update Your iPod on Windows

iTunes is set to check automatically for updates, and it displays a message box such as that shown here if it finds an update. Click the Download And Install button to download the update and install it immediately.

If you don't want iTunes to check for updates automatically, clear the Check For New Software Updates Automatically check box on the General tab of the iTunes dialog box.

Alternatively, you can check for updates manually. Follow these steps:

1. Connect your iPod to your computer. The computer starts iTunes (if it's not running) or activates it (if it is running).
2. In iTunes, click the iPod's entry in the Source list to display the iPod screens.
3. Click the Summary tab if it's not automatically displayed. (For an iPod shuffle, click the Settings tab.)
4. Click the Check For Update button.

When the update is complete, the iPod appears in the Source list in iTunes.

Update Your iPod on Mac OS X

You can get iPod updates on Mac OS X in three ways:

- **iTunes**   iTunes checks periodically for updates. When it finds an update, iTunes displays a dialog box prompting you to download and install it. Click the Download And Install button to download the update and install it immediately.

If you don't want iTunes to check for updates automatically, clear the Check For New Software Updates Automatically check box on the General tab of the Preferences dialog box for iTunes.

- **Software Update**   Choose Apple | Software Update to check for updates to Mac OS X and all Apple software. Mac OS X presents all updates to you in the Software Update dialog box. Click the Install button, and then enter your administrative password in the authentication dialog box. Mac OS X downloads the updates and installs them.

Alternatively, you can check for updates manually. Follow these steps:

1. Connect your iPod to your computer. The computer starts iTunes (if it's not running) or activates it (if it is running).
2. In iTunes, click the iPod's entry in the Source list to display the iPod screens.
3. Click the Summary tab if it's not automatically displayed. (For an iPod shuffle, click the Settings tab.)
4. Click the Check For Update button.

When the update is complete, the iPod appears in the Source list in iTunes.

Carry and Store Your iPod Safely

Carrying and storing your iPod safely is largely a matter of common sense:

- Use a case to protect your iPod from scratches, dings, and falls. A wide variety of cases are available, from svelte-and-stretchy little numbers designed to hug your body during vigorous exercise, to armored cases apparently intended to survive *Die Hard* movies, to waterproof cases good enough to take sailing, swimming, or even diving. See Chapter 5 for details.
- If your iPod spends time on your desk or another surface open to children, animals, or moving objects, use a dock or stand to keep it in place. A dock or stand should also make your iPod easier to control with one hand. For example, if you patch the iPod in to your stereo, use a dock or stand to keep it upright so you can push its buttons with one hand. See Chapter 5 for more information on docks and stands.

 How to... ## Clean Your iPod

To keep your iPod looking its best, you'll probably need to clean it from time to time. Before doing so, unplug it to reduce the chance of short disagreements with the basic principles of electricity. Treat the Dock Connector port and headphone port with due care; neither is waterproof.

Various people recommend different cleaning products for cleaning iPods. You'll find assorted recommendations on the Web—but unless you're sure the people know what they're talking about, proceed with great care. In particular, avoid any abrasive cleaner that may mar an iPod's faceplate or its polished back and sides.

Unless you've dipped your iPod in anything very unpleasant, you'll do best to start with Apple's recommendation: Simply dampen a soft, lint-free cloth (such as an eyeglass or camera-lens cloth) and wipe the iPod gently with it.

But if you've scratched the iPod, you may need to resort to heavier-duty cleaners. PodShop iDrops seems to have a good reputation; you can get it from Amazon.com and other online retailers, or directly from PodShop (http://podshop.com).

Understand Your Warranty and Know Which Actions Void It

Like most electronics goods, your iPod almost certainly came with a warranty. Unlike with most other electronics goods, your chances of needing to use that warranty are relatively high. This is because you're likely to use your iPod extensively and carry it with you. After all, that's what it's designed for.

Even if you don't sit on your iPod, rain or other water doesn't creep into it, and gravity doesn't dash it sharply against something unforgiving (such as the sidewalk), the iPod may suffer from other problems—anything from critters or debris jamming the Dock Connector port, to its flash memory becoming faulty or its hard drive getting corrupted, or its operating system getting scrambled. Perhaps most likely of all is that the battery will lose its potency, either gradually or dramatically. If any of these misfortunes befalls your iPod, you'll probably want to get it repaired under warranty—provided you haven't voided the warranty by treating the iPod in a way that breaches its terms.

All the iPods come with a one-year warranty. To find details of whether your iPod is under warranty, enter your iPod's serial number and your country into Apple's Online Service Agent (https://selfsolve.apple.com).

Most of the warranty is pretty straightforward, but the following points are worth noting:

- You have to make your claim within the warranty period, so if the iPod fails a day short of a year after you bought it, you'll need to make your claim instantly. Do you know where your receipt is?
- If the iPod is currently under warranty, you can buy an AppleCare package for it to extend its warranty to two years. Most extended warranties on electrical products are a waste of money, because the extended warranties largely duplicate your existing rights as a consumer to be sold a product that's functional and of merchantable quality. But given the attrition rate among hard-used iPods, AppleCare may be a good idea.
- Apple can choose whether to repair the iPod using either new or refurbished parts, exchange it for another device that's at least functionally equivalent but may be either new or rebuilt (and may contain used parts), or refund you the purchase price. Unless you have valuable data on the iPod, the refund is a great option, because you'll be able to get a new iPod—perhaps even a higher-capacity one.
- Apple takes no responsibility for getting back any data on the iPod. This isn't surprising because Apple may need to reformat the memory or hard drive or replace the player altogether. But this means that you must back up the iPod if it contains data you value that you don't have copies of elsewhere.

You can void your warranty more or less effortlessly in any of the following easily avoidable ways:

- Damage the iPod deliberately.
- Open the iPod or have someone other than Apple open it for you. The iPods are designed to be opened only by trained technicians. The only reason to open an iPod is to replace its battery or replace a component—and you shouldn't do that yourself unless the iPod is out of warranty (and out of AppleCare, if you bought AppleCare for it). If you're tempted to replace a battery, make sure you know what it involves: Replacing the battery in some iPods requires a delicate touch with a soldering iron. You can find detailed instructions online, especially in YouTube videos.
- Modify the iPod. Modifications such as installing a higher-capacity drive in an iPod classic would necessarily involve opening it anyway, but external modifications can void your warranty, too. For example, if you choose to trepan your iPod so as to screw a holder directly onto it, you would void your warranty. (You'd also stand a great chance of drilling into something sensitive inside the case.)

Troubleshoot Your iPod

When something goes wrong with your iPod, take three deep breaths before you do anything. Then take another three deep breaths if you need them. Then try to work out what's wrong.

Remember that a calm and rational approach will always get you further than blind panic. This is easy to say (and if you're reading this when your iPod is running smoothly, easy to nod your head at). But if you've just dropped your iPod onto a hard surface from a great enough height for gravity to give it some acceleration, left it on the roof of your car so it fell off and landed in the perfect position for you to reverse over it, or gotten caught in an unexpectedly heavy rainfall, you'll probably be desperate to find out if the iPod is alive or dead.

So take those three deep breaths. You may well *not* have ruined the iPod forever—but if you take some heavy-duty troubleshooting actions without making sure they're necessary, you may lose some data that wasn't already lost or do some damage you'll have trouble repairing.

Things can go wrong with any of the following:

- The iPod's hardware—anything from the Dock Connector port or headphone port to the battery, the hard disk, or the flash memory
- The iPod's software
- The cable you're using to connect your iPod to your computer
- Your computer's USB port or USB controller
- iTunes or the other software you're using to control the iPod

Given all these possibilities, be prepared to spend some time troubleshooting any problem.

This section discusses several maneuvers you may need to use to troubleshoot the iPod: resetting the iPod, draining its battery, restoring its operating system on either Windows or Mac OS X, and running a disk scan.

Reset Your iPod

If your iPod freezes so it doesn't respond to the controls, you can reset it. As you'd imagine, each iPod has a different method.

Reset the iPod classic

To reset the iPod classic, follow these steps:

1. Connect it to a power source—either a computer that's not sleeping or the Apple USB Power Adapter plugged into an electrical socket. (The Apple USB Power Adapter, or a generic equivalent, is a great weapon to have in your troubleshooting arsenal. You can buy it from the Apple Store.)
2. Reset the iPod: Move the Hold switch to the On position, and then move it back to the Off position. Hold down the Menu button and the Select button for about six seconds, until the iPod displays the Apple logo.
3. After you release the buttons, give the iPod a few seconds to finish booting.

If the iPod freezes when you don't have a power source available, try resetting it by using the preceding technique without the power source. Sometimes it works; other times it doesn't. But you've nothing to lose by trying.

Reset the iPod nano

To reset the iPod nano, press and hold the Sleep/Wake button and the Volume Down button until the iPod's screen goes dark. Release the buttons, and wait while the iPod restarts. When the home screen reappears, you're back in business.

Reset an iPod shuffle

To reset a fourth-generation iPod shuffle, move the switch to the Off position, wait ten seconds, and then move it back to the On position.

Drain the iPod's Battery

If you can't reset the iPod, its battery might have gotten into such a low state that it needs draining. This supposedly seldom happens—but the planets might have decided that you're due a bad day.

To drain the battery, disconnect the iPod from its power source and leave it for 24 hours. Then try plugging the iPod into a power source—either a USB socket on a computer or the Apple USB Power Adapter (if you have one). After the iPod has received power for a few seconds, reset the iPod, as described in the previous sections.

If draining the battery and recharging it revives the iPod, update the iPod's software with the latest version to try to prevent the problem from occurring again. See the section "Keep Your iPod's Operating System Up to Date," earlier in this chapter, for details on how to update the operating system.

Restore Your iPod

If your iPod is having severe difficulties, you may need to restore it. Restoring the iPod replaces its operating system with a new copy of the operating system that has Apple's factory settings.

 Restoring the iPod deletes all the data on the iPod's hard disk or flash memory—the operating system and all your songs, photos, videos, contacts, calendar information, and notes—and returns the iPod to its original factory settings. So restoring the iPod is usually a last resort when troubleshooting. Unless the iPod is so messed up that you cannot access its contents, back up all the data you care about that's stored on the iPod before restoring it.

Restore the iPod on Windows

To restore the iPod on Windows, follow these steps:

1. Connect your iPod to your PC via USB as usual. Allow iTunes to synchronize with the iPod if it's set to do so.
2. In iTunes, click the iPod's entry in the Source list to display the iPod screens.
3. Click the Summary tab if it's not already displayed. For an iPod shuffle, click the Settings tab.
4. Click the Restore button. iTunes warns you that you will lose all the media and other data currently stored on the iPod, as shown here.

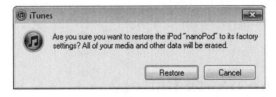

5. Click the Restore button. iTunes displays an iPod Software Update dialog box showing the changes in the latest version of the software.

6. Click the Next button. The iPod Software Update dialog box displays the license agreement.

7. Read the license agreement, and then click the Agree button if you're okay with it. iTunes downloads the latest version of the software, formats the iPod's hard disk or flash storage, and then restores the iPod's operating system.

8. iTunes displays a message box on a ten-second countdown telling you (as shown here) that the iPod is restarting and that it will appear in the iTunes Source list after that. Either click the OK button to dismiss this message box, or wait for the timer to close it automatically.

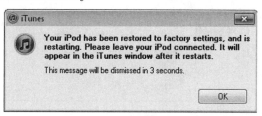

9. When iTunes notices the iPod after it restarts, iTunes displays the Set Up Your iPod screen. Type the name you want to give your iPod; choose whether to sync songs, videos, and photos with it; and then click the Done button.

After you disconnect the iPod, set the language it uses.

Restore the iPod on Mac OS X

To restore the iPod on Mac OS X, follow these steps:

1. Connect your iPod to your computer as usual. If the iPod is set to synchronize automatically with iTunes, allow it to do so.

2. In iTunes, click the iPod's entry in the Source list.

3. Click the Summary tab if it's not already displayed. For an iPod shuffle, click the Settings tab.

4. Click the Restore button to start the restore process. iTunes warns you that you will lose all the media and other data currently stored on the iPod, as shown next.

5. Click the Restore button if you want to proceed. Mac OS X displays the authentication dialog box to check that you have administrative rights.

6. Type your password in the Password text box, and then click the OK button. iTunes formats the iPod's hard disk or flash storage, and then restores the iPod's operating system.

7. iTunes displays a message box on a ten-second countdown telling you (as shown here) that the iPod is restarting and that it will appear in the iTunes Source list after that. Either click the OK button to dismiss this message box, or wait for the timer to close it automatically.

8. When iTunes notices the iPod after it restarts, iTunes displays the Set Up Your iPod screen. Type the name you want to give your iPod; choose whether to sync songs, videos, and photos with it; and then click the Done button.

After you disconnect the iPod, set the language it uses.

How to... **Recover from a Disk Insertion Error on the Mac**

If something goes wrong while you're restoring the iPod, Mac OS X may display a Disk Insertion error message box such as the one shown here.

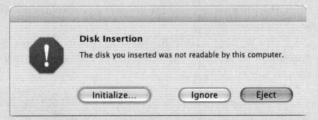

The large red exclamation icon makes the problem seem severe, but click the Ignore button rather than the Initialize button. (Clicking the Initialize button launches Disk Utility, the tool used for partitioning, repairing, and initializing regular hard disks, as opposed to the iPod.) Then try the Restore operation again. Usually, you'll be able to make it work after an attempt or two.

Troubleshoot Specific Problems with the iPod classic, iPod nano, and iPod shuffle

This section discusses how to troubleshoot specific problems with the iPods, starting with the more common problems and moving gradually toward the esoteric end of the spectrum.

The iPod classic Won't Respond to Button Presses

If the iPod classic won't respond to button presses, follow as many of these steps, in order, as are necessary to revive it:

1. Check that the Hold switch on the iPod isn't on. If you're using a remote control that has a Hold switch, check that too.
2. Check that the battery is charged. When the battery is too low to run the iPod (for example, for playing back music), the iPod displays a low-battery symbol—a battery icon with an exclamation point—for a few seconds when you press a button. (You may miss this icon if you're using a remote or you're pressing the iPod's buttons without looking at the screen.) Connect the iPod to a power source (either a computer that's not asleep or the Apple USB Power Adapter, if you have one), give it a few minutes to recharge a little, disconnect it again, and then try turning it on.
3. Reset the iPod by holding down the Select button and the Menu button for about six seconds, until the Apple logo appears.
4. Enter diagnostic mode and run the KeyTest test like this:
   - Reset the iPod again. Hold down the Select button and the Menu button for about six seconds, until the Apple logo appears.
   - As the iPod restarts, hold down the Previous button and the Select button for a few seconds until the iPod displays the initial diagnostics screen.
   - Open the IO category, then the Wheel subcategory, and then run the KeyTest test.
   - When prompted, press each of the buttons in turn. See if the iPod registers the presses.

Your Computer Doesn't React When You Plug In the iPod

If your computer (Mac or PC) doesn't react when you plug in the iPod, any of several things might have gone wrong. Try the actions described in the following subsections.

Unplug Any Other Devices in the USB Chain   If there's another device plugged into your computer's USB controller, try unplugging it. The problem may be that the controller can't supply power to another unpowered device as well as to the iPod.

   If the connection uses a hub, disconnect the hub and try a direct connection.

Check That the Cable Is Working   Make sure that the cable is firmly connected to the iPod (or its dock) and to the USB port on your computer. If you normally use a dock or connecting stand for the iPod, try the connection without it in case the dock or stand is causing the problem.

If you're not sure the cable is working, and you have an Apple USB Power Adapter, you can run a partial check by plugging the cable into the iPod and the Apple USB Power Adapter, and then plugging the Apple USB Power Adapter into an electrical socket. If the iPod starts charging, you'll know that at least the power-carrying wires on the cable are working. It's likely that the data-carrying wires are working as well.

Check That the USB Port on the Computer Is Working   In most cases, the easiest way to check is by plugging in another device that you know is working. For example, you might plug in a USB scanner or external CD-ROM drive.

The iPod Says "Do Not Disconnect" for Ages When Connected to Your Computer

When you connect your iPod to your PC or Mac, the iPod displays the "Do not disconnect" message while it synchronizes with iTunes. When synchronization is complete, the iPod should display the charging indicator for as long as it's taking on power via the USB cable.

But sometimes it doesn't. If the iPod displays the "Do not disconnect" message for long after synchronization should have finished, first try to remember if you've enabled disk mode on the iPod. If so, you always need to eject the iPod manually, so this message doesn't mean that there's a problem. You can eject the iPod in one of these ways:

- Click the Eject button next to the iPod's entry in the Source list in iTunes.
- Right-click (or CTRL-click on the Mac) the iPod in the Source list, and then choose Eject from the shortcut menu.
- Right-click the iPod's drive icon in a Computer window (Windows 7 or Windows Vista) or My Computer window (Windows XP), or CTRL-click the iPod's icon on your Mac desktop, and then choose Eject from the shortcut menu.
- On the Mac, from the Finder, drag the iPod to the Trash, or select it and press ⌘-E.

The iPod should then display the "OK to disconnect" message.

If you haven't enabled disk mode, and the iPod is an iPod classic, the iPod's hard drive may have gotten stuck spinning. If you pick up the iPod to scrutinize it further, you'll notice it's much hotter than usual if the drive has been spinning for a while. Try unmounting it anyway using one of the methods described in the preceding list. The iPod should then display the "OK to disconnect" message, and you can disconnect it safely.

If that doesn't work, you may need to reset the iPod (see "Reset Your iPod," earlier in this chapter). After the iPod reboots, you should be able to eject it by taking one of the actions listed previously.

If you experience this problem frequently, try updating the iPod to the latest software version available. If there's no newer software version, or if an update doesn't help, use an AC adapter to recharge the iPod rather than recharging it from your computer.

Your iPod Displays Only the Apple Logo When You Turn It On

If, when you turn on the iPod, it displays the Apple logo as usual but goes no further, there's most likely a problem with the iPod software. Try resetting the iPod first to see if that clears the problem. (See "Reset Your iPod," earlier in this chapter.)

If resetting doesn't work, usually you'll need to restore the iPod as described in "Restore Your iPod," earlier in this chapter. Restoring the iPod loses all data stored on it, so try several resets first.

Songs in Your Library Aren't Transferred to Your iPod

If songs you've added to your library aren't transferred to your iPod even though you've synchronized successfully since adding the songs, there are two possibilities:

- First, check that you haven't configured your iPod for partial synchronization or manual synchronization. For example, if you've chosen to synchronize only selected playlists, the iPod won't synchronize new music files not included on those playlists.
- Second, check that the songs' tags include the artist's name and song name. Without these two items of information, iTunes won't transfer the songs to the iPod, because the iPod's interface won't be able to display the songs to you. You can force iTunes to transfer song files that lack artist and song name tags by adding the song files to a playlist, but in the long run, you'll benefit from tagging all your song files correctly.

Troubleshoot iTunes on Windows

This section shows you how to troubleshoot the problems you're most likely to encounter when running iTunes on Windows.

iTunes Won't Start on Windows

If iTunes displays the Cannot Open iTunes dialog box saying that you can't open iTunes because another user currently has it open, it means that Windows is using Fast User Switching and that someone else is logged on under another account and has iTunes open. The following illustration shows the Cannot Open iTunes dialog box on Windows 7, but this dialog box also appears on Windows Vista and Windows XP.

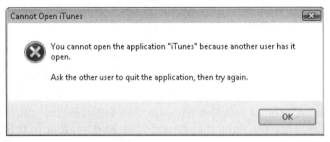

Click the OK button to dismiss the dialog box. If you know the other user's password, or if you know they have no password, switch to their account, close iTunes, and then switch back to your own account.

If you don't know the other user's password and you have a Standard user account (Windows 7 or Windows Vista) or a Limited user account (Windows XP), you'll need to get them to log on and close iTunes for you.

If you have an Administrator account, you can use Windows Task Manager to close iTunes. Follow these steps:

1. Right-click the taskbar, and then choose Task Manager from the shortcut menu to open Task Manager.
2. Click the Processes tab to display its contents. At first, as shown on the left in Figure 15-2, Task Manager shows only the processes running for your user session of Windows, not for other users' sessions.
3. Display processes for all users:
   - **Windows 7 or Windows Vista**   Click the Show Processes From All Users button. You may then need to go through User Account Control for the Windows Task Manager feature. Task Manager replaces the Show Processes From All Users button with the Show Processes From All Users check box (which it selects), and then adds the other users' processes to the list.
   - **Windows XP**   Select the Show Processes From All Users check box.
4. Select the iTunes.exe process in the Image Name column, as shown on the right in Figure 15-2. (If the list isn't sorted by the Image Name column, click the Image Name header to sort it that way.)
5. Click the End Process button. Task Manager displays the dialog box shown next, confirming that you want to end the process.
6. Click the End Process button. Task Manager closes the instance of iTunes in the other user's session.
7. Click the Close button (the × button) to close Task Manager.

You can now start iTunes as normal.

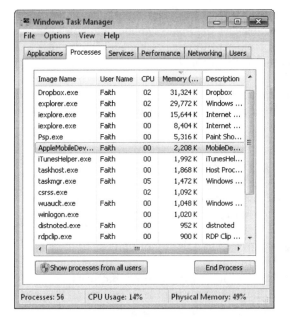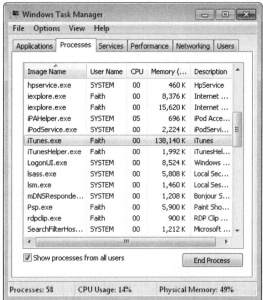

FIGURE 15-2   If someone else is running iTunes on a Windows PC that uses Fast User Switching, you may need to use Task Manager to close iTunes before you can use it.

iTunes Doesn't Recognize the iPod

If the iPod doesn't appear in the Source list in iTunes, take as many of the following steps as necessary to make it appear there:

1. Check that the iPod is okay. If you find it's displaying an exclamation point or the Sad iPod symbol, you'll know iTunes isn't guilty this time.
2. Check that the iPod knows it's connected to your PC. The iPod should be displaying the "Do not disconnect" message. If it's not, fix the connection so that it does display this message.
3. Reset the iPod as discussed earlier in this chapter, and then see if it appears in the Source list. Here's a recap of how to reset the iPod:
   - **iPod classic**   Toggle the Hold switch on the iPod, and then restart the iPod by holding down the Play button and the Menu button together for several seconds.
   - **iPod nano**   Press and hold the Sleep/Wake button and the Volume Down button until the iPod's screen goes dark, and then release the buttons.
   - **iPod shuffle**   Move the switch to the Off position, wait ten seconds, and then move it back to the On position.

If resetting an iPod classic doesn't make it appear in iTunes, repeat the process for restarting it. This time, when the iPod displays the Apple symbol, hold down the Select button and the Play button for a moment to force disk mode. Forcing disk mode sends a request to the computer to mount the iPod as a drive.

4. Restart iTunes, and see if it notices the iPod this time.
5. If restarting iTunes doesn't make it recognize the iPod, restart Windows, and then restart iTunes.

iTunes Won't Play Some AAC Files

iTunes and AAC go together like pizza and beer, but you may find that iTunes can't play some AAC files. This can happen for either of two reasons:

- You're trying to play a protected AAC file in a shared library or playlist, and your computer isn't authorized to play the file. In this case, iTunes skips the protected file.
- The AAC file was created by an application other than iTunes that uses a different AAC standard. The AAC file then isn't compatible with iTunes. To play the file, use the application that created the file, or another application that can play the file, to convert the file to another format that iTunes supports—for example, MP3 or WAV.

"The iPod Is Linked to Another iTunes Library" Message

If, when you connect your iPod to your computer, iTunes displays a message such as "The iPod 'iPod_name' is linked to another iTunes library," chances are that you've plugged the wrong iPod into your computer. The message box also offers to change this device's allegiance from its current computer to this PC. Click the No button and check which iPod this is before synchronizing it.

 For details about moving the iPod from one computer to another, see "Change the Computer to Which Your iPod Is Linked," in Chapter 12.

iTunes Runs You Out of Hard-Disk Space on Windows

As you saw earlier in the book, when you add files to your library, you can choose how to add them:

- Copy the files to your library folder.
- Leave the files in their current folders and add to your library references saying where the files are.

Adding all the files to your library means you have all the files available in one place. This can be good, especially if your computer is a laptop and you want to be able to access your music and videos when it's not connected to your external drives or network drives. But if you have a large library, it may not all fit on your laptop's hard disk. In this case, adding references enables you to add the files to your library without taking up extra space.

If your files are stored on your hard drive in folders other than your library folder, you have three choices:

- You can issue the File | Library | Organize Library command, and then select the Consolidate Files check box, to make iTunes copy the files to your library folder, doubling the amount of space they take up. In almost all cases, this is the worst possible choice to make. (Rarely, you might want redundant copies of your files in your library so you can experiment with them.)
- You can have iTunes store references to the files rather than copies of them. If you also have files in your library folder, this is the easiest solution. To do this, clear the Copy Files To iTunes Media Folder When Adding To Library check box on the Advanced tab in the iTunes dialog box in Windows.
- You can move your library to the folder that contains your files. This is the easiest solution if your library is empty.

If you choose to consolidate your library, and there's not enough space on your hard disk, you'll see the following message box. "IBM_PRELOAD" is the name of the hard disk on the computer.

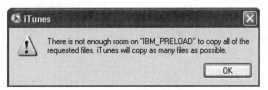

Clearly, this *isn't* okay, but iTunes doesn't let you cancel the operation. Don't let iTunes pack your hard disk as full of files as it can, because that may make Windows crash. Quit iTunes by pressing ALT-F4 or choosing File | Exit. If iTunes doesn't respond, right-click the taskbar and choose Task Manager to display Windows Task Manager. On the Applications tab, select the iTunes entry, and then click the End Task button. If Windows double-checks that you want to end the task, confirm the decision.

Once you've done this, you may need to remove the files you've just copied to your library from the folder. You can do this by using the Date Created information about the files and folders, because Windows treats the copy made by the consolidation as a new file.

To find the files and folders, search for them. The process differs on Windows 7, Windows Vista, and Windows XP, so follow the instructions in the next sections for the OS you're using.

Search for the New Files and Folders on Windows 7

To search for the new files and folders on Windows 7, follow these steps:

1. Choose Start | Computer to open a Computer window.
2. Click in the Search box in the upper-right corner of the window to place the insertion point there.
3. Type **datecreated:** (including the colon) to start a search filter based on the Created attribute of the folders. Windows opens the Select A Date Or Date Range panel.
4. In the Select A Date Or Date Range Panel, double-click today's date. Windows returns a list of the folders created today (see Figure 15-3).
5. Select the folders created by the consolidation, and then press SHIFT-DELETE to delete them without adding them to the Recycle Bin (because you're out of space).

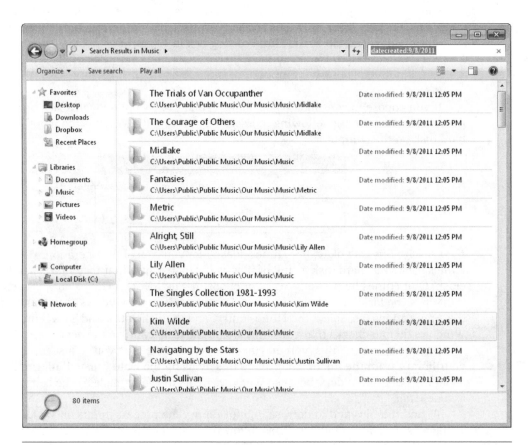

FIGURE 15-3   Use the datecreated: search term to search for items created today.

Search for the New Files and Folders on Windows Vista

To search for the new files and folders on Windows Vista, follow these steps:

1. Choose Start | Search to display a Search Results window.
2. Click the Advanced Search link at the right end of the toolbar to display the Advanced Search options.
3. In the Location drop-down list, click the Choose Search Location item to display the Choose Search Locations dialog box.
4. In the Change Selected Locations box, navigate to the folder that contains your iTunes Media folder. For example, if your iTunes Media folder is in its default location, follow these steps:
   a. Click the triangle next to your username to expand its contents.

> If you're not sure where your iTunes Media folder is, switch to iTunes, press CTRL-COMMA, and look at the iTunes Media Folder Location box on the Advanced tab in the iTunes dialog box.

   b. Click the triangle next to the Music folder to expand its contents.
   c. Click the triangle next to the iTunes folder to expand its contents.
   d. Click the iTunes Media folder to select its check box. Windows adds the folder to the Summary Of Selected Locations list box.
5. Click the OK button to close the Choose Search Locations dialog box and enter the folder you chose in the Location drop-down list in the Search Results window.
6. On the line below the Location drop-down list, set up the condition Date Created (in the first drop-down list), Is (in the second drop-down list), and today's date (in the third drop-down list).
7. Click the Search button. Windows searches and returns a list of the files and folders created.
8. If the Search Results window is using any view other than Details view, choose Views | Details to switch to Details view.
9. Display the Date Created column by taking the following steps:
   a. Right-click an existing column heading, and then choose More from the shortcut menu to display the Choose Details dialog box.
   b. Select the Date Created check box.
   c. Click the OK button to close the Choose Details dialog box.
10. Click the Date Created column heading twice to make Windows Explorer sort the files by reverse date. This way, the files created most recently appear at the top of the list.
11. Check the Date Created column to identify the files created during the consolidation, and then delete them without putting them in the Recycle Bin. (For example, select the files and press SHIFT-DELETE.)
12. Click the Close button (the × button) to close the Search Results window.

After deleting the files (or as many of them as possible), you'll need to remove the references from iTunes and add them again from their preconsolidating location before iTunes can play them. When iTunes discovers that it can't find a file where it's supposed to be, it displays an exclamation point in the first column. Delete the entries with exclamation points and then add them to your library again.

Search for the New Files and Folders on Windows XP

To search for the new files and folders on Windows XP, follow these steps:

1. Choose Start | Search to display a Search Results window.
2. On the What Do You Want To Search For? screen, click the Pictures, Music, Or Video link. (If Search Companion displays the Search By Any Or All Of The Criteria Below screen instead of the What Do You Want To Search For? screen, click the Other Search Options link to display the What Do You Want To Search For? screen. Then click the Pictures, Music, or Video link.)
3. On the resulting screen, select the Music check box and the Video check box in the Search For All Files Of A Certain Type, Or Search By Type And Name area.
4. Click the Use Advanced Search Options link to display the remainder of the Search Companion pane.
5. Display the Look In drop-down list, select the Browse item to display the Browse For Folder dialog box, select your iTunes Media folder, and then click the OK button.

 If you're not sure where your iTunes Media folder is, switch to iTunes, press CTRL-COMMA, and look at the iTunes Media Folder Location box on the General subtab of the Advanced tab in the iTunes dialog box.

6. Click the When Was It Modified? heading to display its controls and then select the Specify Dates option button. Select the Created Date item in the drop-down list and then specify today's date in the From drop-down list and the To drop-down list. (The easiest way to specify the date is to open the From drop-down list and select the Today item. Windows XP then enters it in the To text box as well.)
7. Click the Search button to start the search for files created in the specified time frame.
8. If the Search Results window is using any view other than Details view, choose View | Details to switch to Details view.
9. Click the Date Created column heading twice to make Windows Explorer sort the files by reverse date. This way, the files created most recently appear at the top of the list.

10. Check the Date Created column to identify the files created during the consolidation and then delete them without putting them in the Recycle Bin. (For example, select the files and press SHIFT-DELETE.)

After deleting the files (or as many of them as possible), you'll need to remove the references from iTunes and add them again from their preconsolidating location before iTunes can play them. When iTunes discovers that it can't find a file where it's supposed to be, it displays an exclamation point in the first column. Delete the entries with exclamation points and then add them to your library again.

"iTunes Has Detected That It Is Not the Default Player" Message on Startup

When you start iTunes, you may see the message box shown next, telling you that "iTunes has detected that it is not the default player for audio files" and inviting you to go to the Default Programs control panel to fix the problem.

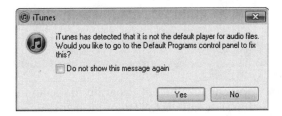

This message box doesn't indicate a problem as most people understand the word, but having it appear each time you start iTunes grows old fast, so you'll probably either want to suppress the message box or deal with the problem.

What's happened is that some other audio player has grabbed the associations for one or more of the audio file types that iTunes can play. For example, Windows Media Player may have taken the association for the MP3 file type. In this case, if you double-click an MP3 file in a Windows Explorer window, the file will play in Windows Media Player rather than in iTunes.

If you've set up your file associations deliberately to use different programs, simply select the Do Not Show This Message Again check box, and then click the No button. iTunes will drop the matter and not bug you again.

If you want to reassign the file associations to iTunes, click the Yes button. iTunes opens the Set Program Associations window (see Figure 15-4), which shows you the available associations and the programs to which they are assigned.

Select the check box for each file type you want to associate with iTunes, and then click the Save button.

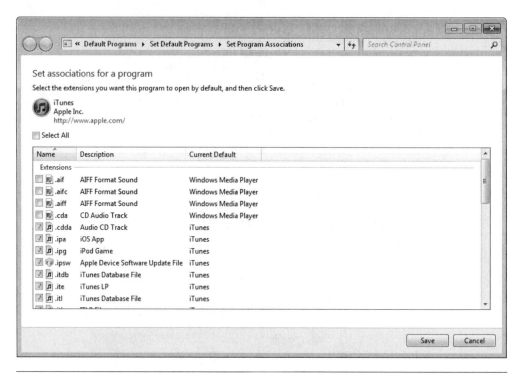

FIGURE 15-4 You can use the Set Program Associations window to reassign audio file associations to iTunes after other programs have grabbed them.

Troubleshoot iTunes on the Mac

This section shows you how to troubleshoot a handful of problems that you may run into when running iTunes on the Mac.

"The iPod Is Linked to Another iTunes Library" Message

If, when you connect your iPod to your computer, iTunes displays a message such as "The iPod 'iPod_name' is linked to another iTunes library," chances are that you've plugged the wrong iPod into your computer. The message box also offers to change this device's allegiance from its current computer to this Mac. Click the No button and check which iPod this is before synchronizing it.

For details about moving an iPod from one computer to another, see the section "Change the Computer to Which Your iPod Is Linked" in Chapter 12.

Eject a "Lost" CD

Sometimes Mac OS X seems to lose track of a CD (or DVD) after attempting to eject it. It's as if the eject mechanism fails to get a grip on the CD and push it out, but the commands get executed anyway, so that Mac OS X believes it has ejected the CD even though the CD is still in the drive.

When this happens, you probably won't be able to eject the disc by issuing another Eject command from iTunes, but it's worth trying that first. If that doesn't work, use Disk Utility to eject the disc. Follow these steps:

1. Press ⌘-SHIFT-U or choose Go | Utilities from the Finder menu to display the Utilities folder.
2. Double-click the Disk Utility item to run it.
3. Select the icon for the CD drive or the CD itself in the list box.
4. Click the Eject button.
5. Press ⌘-Q or choose Disk Utility | Quit Disk Utility to quit Disk Utility.

If that doesn't work, you may need to force your Mac to recognize the drive. If it's a hot-pluggable external drive (for example, FireWire or USB), try unplugging the drive, waiting a minute, and then plugging it back in. If the drive is an internal drive, you may need to restart your Mac to force it to recognize the drive.

 See also the sidebar "Eject Stuck Audio Discs from a Mac" in Chapter 7 for instructions on ejecting an optical disc using the Mac's Open Firmware mode.

"You Do Not Have Enough Access Privileges" When Importing Songs

The following error occurs when you've moved the iTunes Media folder to a shared location and the user doesn't have Write permission to it.

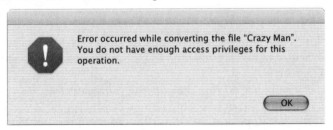

To fix this problem, an administrator needs to assign Write permission for the iTunes Media folder to whoever received this error.

iTunes Runs You Out of Hard-Disk Space on the Mac

As you saw earlier in the book, when you add files to your library, iTunes can copy the files to your library folder. Adding all the files to your library means you have all the files available in one place. This can be good when (for example) you want your MacBook's hard disk to contain copies of all the song and video files stored on network drives so you can enjoy them when your computer isn't connected to the network. But it can take more disk space than your Mac's hard disk has free.

If your files are stored on your hard drive in folders other than your library folder, you have three choices:

- You can choose File | Library | Organize Library, select the Consolidate Files check box, and then click the OK button to cause iTunes to copy the files to your library. This doubles the amount of space the files take up and is usually the worst choice. (Rarely, you might want redundant copies of your files in your library so you can experiment with them.)
- You can have iTunes store references to the files rather than copies of them. If you also have files in your library folder, this is the easiest solution. To do this, clear the Copy Files To iTunes Media Folder When Adding To Library check box on the Advanced tab in the Preferences dialog box.
- You can move your library to the folder that contains your files. This is the easiest solution if your library is empty.

If you choose to consolidate your library, and your Mac doesn't have enough disk space, iTunes displays this message box to alert you to the problem.

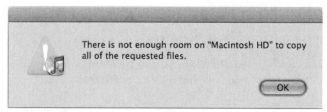

Click the OK button to dismiss this message box—iTunes gives you no other choice. Worse, when you click the OK button, iTunes goes ahead and tries to copy all the files anyway.

This is a bad idea, so stop the copying process as soon as you can. To do so, quit iTunes by pressing ⌘-Q or choosing iTunes | Quit iTunes. If you can't quit iTunes gently, force quit it: OPTION-click the iTunes icon in the Dock, and then choose Force Quit from the shortcut menu. (Failing that, press ⌘-OPTION-ESC to display the Force Quit dialog box, click the entry for iTunes, and then click the Force Quit button.)

Once you've done this, remove the files you've just copied to your library from the folder. Unfortunately, Mac OS X maintains the Date Created information from the original files on the copies made by the consolidation, so you can't search for the files by date created on the Mac the way you can on Windows.

Your best bet is to search by date created to identify the folders that iTunes has just created in your library folder so that you can delete them and their contents. This approach will get all of the consolidated songs and videos that iTunes put into new folders, but it will miss any songs and videos that were consolidated into folders that already existed in your library.

For example, if the song file I Love That Girl.m4a is already stored in your library with correct tags, your library will contain a John Hiatt/Dirty Jeans & Mudslide Hymns folder. If you then consolidate your library so that other songs from that album are copied, the files will go straight into the existing folder, and your search will miss it. The date-modified attribute of the Dirty Jeans & Mudslide Hymns folder will change to the date of the consolidation, but you'll need to drill down into each modified folder to find the song files that were added.

To search for the new folders, follow these steps:

1. Open a Finder window to the folder that contains your iTunes Media folder. For example, in Column view, click the Finder icon on the Dock, click the Music item in the Sidebar, click the iTunes folder, and then click the iTunes Media folder.

 If you're not sure which folder the iTunes Media folder is in, look on the Advanced tab in iTunes' Preferences dialog box.

2. Press ⌘-F or choose File | Find to display the Search bar, and then click the iTunes Media button on it to tell Mac OS X to search in that folder.
3. In the top search line, set up this condition: Kind: Folders.
4. In the second search line, set up this condition: Created Date Is Today. Mac OS X searches for folders created today and displays a list of them.
5. Sort the folders by date created, identify those created during the consolidation by the time on the date, and then delete them.
6. Verify that the Trash contains no other files you care about, and then empty the Trash to get rid of the surplus files.

After deleting the files (or as many of them as possible), you'll need to remove the references from iTunes and add them again from their preconsolidating location before iTunes can play them. When iTunes discovers that it can't find a file where it's supposed to be, it displays an exclamation point in the first column. Delete the files with exclamation points and then add them to your library again.

Index

ML   8/12